The Social Construction of Literacy

Literacy – the ability to produce and interpret written text – has long been viewed as the basis of all school achievement; a measure of success that defines both an 'educated' person, and an educable one. In this volume, a team of leading experts raise questions central to the acquisition of literacy. Why do children with similar classroom experiences show different levels of educational achievement? And why do these differences in literacy, and ultimately employability, persist? By looking critically at the western view of a 'literate' person, the authors present a new perspective on literacy acquisition, viewing it as a socially constructed skill, whereby children must acquire discourse strategies that are socially 'approved'. This extensively revised second edition contains an updated introduction and bibliography, and each chapter has been rewritten to account for the most recent research. Groundbreaking and revealing, this volume will continue to have far-reaching implications for educational theory and practice.

JENNY COOK-GUMPERZ is Professor in the Gervirtz Graduate School of Education, University of California, Santa Barbara. She has previously published *The Social Construction of Literacy* (Cambridge University Press, 1986), *Children's Worlds and Children's Languages* (1986), and *Social Control and Socialization: A Study of Class Differences in the Language of Maternal Control* (1973).

Studies in Interactional Sociolinguistics

1 *Discourse Strategies* John J. Gumperz
2 *Language and Social Identity* edited by John J. Gumperz
3 *The Social Construction of Literacy* edited by Jenny Cook-Gumperz
4 *Politeness: Some Universals in Language Usage* Penelope Brown and Stephen C. Levinson
5 *Discourse Markers* Deborah Schiffrin
6 *Talking Voices: Repetition, Dialogue, and Imagery in Conversational Discourse* Deborah Tannen
7 *Conducting Interaction: Patterns of Behaviour in Focused Encounters* Adam Kendon
8 *Talk at Work: Interaction in Institutional Settings* edited by Paul Drew and John Heritage
9 *Grammar in Interaction: Adverbial Clauses in American English Conversations* Cecilia E. Ford
10 *Crosstalk and Culture in Sino-American Communication* Linda W. L. Young
11 *AIDS Counselling: Institutional Interaction and Clinical Practice* Anssi Peräkylä
12 *Prosody in Conversation; Interactional Studies* edited by Elizabeth Couper-Kuhlen and Margret Selting
13 *Interaction and Grammar* Elinor Ochs, Emanuel A. Schegloff and Sandra A. Thompson
14 *Credibility in Court: Communicative Practices in the Camorra Trials* Marco Jacquemet
15 *Interaction and the Development of Mind* A. J. Wootton
16 *The News Interview: Journalists and Public Figures on the Air* Steven Clayman and John Heritage
17 *Gender and Politeness* Sara Mills
18 *Laughter in Interaction* Philip Glenn
19 *Matters of Opinion: Talking about Public Issues* Greg Myers

20 *Communication in Medical Care: Interaction between Primary Care Physicians and Patients* edited by John Heritage and Douglas Maynard
21 *In Other Words: Variation in Reference and Narrative* Deborah Schiffrin
22 *Language in Late Modernity: Interaction in an Urban School* Ben Rampton
23 *Discourse and Identity* edited by Anna De Fina, Deborah Schiffrin and Michael Bamberg
24 *Reporting Talk: Reported Speech in Interaction* edited by Elizabeth Holt and Rebecca Clift

The Social Construction of Literacy

Second edition

Edited by
JENNY COOK-GUMPERZ
University of California, Santa Barbara

KH

CAMBRIDGE UNIVERSITY PRESS
Cambridge, New York, Melbourne, Madrid, Cape Town, Singapore, São Paulo

CAMBRIDGE UNIVERSITY PRESS
The Edinburgh Building, Cambridge CB2 2RU, UK
Published in the United States of America by Cambridge University Press, New York

www.cambridge.org

Information on this title: www.cambridge.org/9780521525671

Second edition, first published 2006

Printed in the United Kingdom at the University Press, Cambridge

A catalogue record for this book is available from the British Library

ISBN-13 978-0-521-81963-3 hardback
ISBN-10 0-521-81963-6 hardback
ISBN-13 978-0-521-52567-1 paperback
ISBN-10 0-521-52567-5 paperback

11/3/06

Contents

Figures

Tables

Contributors

DOUGLAS R. CAMPBELL School of Education, Michigan State University, East Lansing, MI

JAMES COLLINS School of Education, University at Albany, State University of New York

JENNY COOK-GUMPERZ Professor, Gervirtz Graduate School of Education, University of California, Santa Barbara

DONNA EDER Professor of Sociology, Indiana University

JOHN J. GUMPERZ Professor Emeritus, University of California, Berkeley

SARAH MICHAELS Associate Professor, Department of Education, Clark University, Worcester MA

SANDRA MURPHY Professor, School of Education, University of California, Davis

MARY CATHERINE O'CONNOR Director, Program in Applied Linguistics, and Associate Professor of Education, School of Education, Boston University

HERBERT D. SIMONS Associate Professor, Graduate School of Education, University of California, Berkeley

GORDON WELLS Professor, Department of Education, University of California, Santa Cruz

Preface

First published in an earlier edition twenty years ago, this book was part of a new wave of studies exploring literacy from anthropological and social historical perspectives that began to appear from the late 1970s, beginning with the publication of Goody's *Domestication of the Savage Mind* (1977). The volume differs from others in that it focuses on literacy as a sociolinguistic process, in which language and language use in all their ramifications are central to the study of literacy. Most usually described as the production and interpretation of written text, literacy in this volume is seen as interactively and therefore socially constructed through verbal exchanges that take place over time in many communicative settings. It is literacy in this broader sense that defines not just an educated person, but also and more importantly, an educable one.

Like others in the Interactional Sociolinguistics series, this volume seeks to provide insights into the workings of institutional processes in contemporary urban societies through case studies of verbal encounters that typify individuals' experiences in these institutions. The assumption is that many issues that have long been at the center of public debate such as equal access to educational opportunity arise at least in part as a result of inferences and judgments made in the course of everyday interactive experience. By studying the often unstated beliefs and preconceptions on which such judgments are based along with the verbal exchanges in which interactants participate, we can gain an understanding of how evaluations and educational outcomes are socially constructed. In this way the process of schooling, a key constituent of social reproduction, can be opened up to micro-analytic scrutiny through in-depth analysis of verbal communication in specific educational settings.

The immediate context for the book was a two-year investigation of classroom interaction in an ethnically diverse Northern California school system (Cook-Gumperz et al. 1981), funded by the US National Institute of Education (NIE) under the 'Teaching as a Linguistic Process' program which sought to apply ethnographic and linguistic perspectives on language use to educational problems of learning and school achievement. Although classroom interaction studies have a long history most existing research has tended to concentrate either solely on macro-societal issues or on psychometric assessments of test performance and teacher–student relations. It is only during the last decades that the potential of in-depth analysis of the context-bound ways in which information is conveyed, and understandings are negotiated, has come to be realized. Earlier on such research was influenced by studies in the ethnography of communication where language use was treated as a social phenomenon and the grammatical characteristics of verbal behavior were analyzed in the context of cultural values and social attributes of participants in naturally occurring situations (Gumperz and Hymes, *Directions in Sociolinguistics* 1972/86; Cazden, John and Hymes *Functions of Language in the Classroom* 1972/85).

The historical impetus for the work reported in this volume were the studies conducted at the Language Behavior Research Laboratory in University of California, Berkeley. Beginning with a summer workshop, 'Language, Society and the Child', held shortly after the Laboratory was founded in 1968, researchers set out to explore perspectives on language socialization concentrating on cross-cultural and cross-class comparisons in context specific settings. Many of the participants in the work of the Laboratory and in the original conference have gone on to play important roles in developing new approaches to language acquisition, language use, and language in education.

From this newly emergent focus, the classroom came to be seen as an important setting for research on social issues in urban society. The volume owes an intellectual debt to this tradition. The chapters by Campbell, Collins, Michaels, O'Connor, Simons and Murphy, Gumperz and Cook-Gumperz continue this tradition in some part while taking the approach to language use further through detailed sociolinguistic analyses of key interactive situations. In selecting from the original NIE research materials for this volume it seemed necessary to add additional comparative perspectives to document the importance of findings which might otherwise be seen as specific to the particular socio-ecological setting of Berkeley, a city with an ethnically diverse population and a largely white upper middle class known for its commitment to social/cultural heterogeneity. To this end several additional studies were incorporated: one, from an urban setting in Britain (Wells), that looked at a traditional white middle and working class, a second from an American mid-Western suburb of exclusively middle-class families (Eder), and a third from a bilingual parochial school in the Philippines with a predominantly middle-class population (Campbell). Not only do these studies widen the range of settings explored but they also reflect additional contrasting traditions and ideologies of learning.

Finally, this book focuses on what is one of the most urgent problems of recent educational policy making: the need to achieve a higher level of literacy through public education. Behind the statistics of annual school test results and school-leaver employment lies an accumulation of knowledge about classroom-based interactional processes and on-site teacher evaluations. The use of interactional sociolinguistics to explore the way in which these moment-to-moment decisions are made and how they result in school-career patterns is a special focus of these studies. However, no work on literacy can ignore the essential vagueness and the often prescriptively charged meaning of the term 'literacy'. We hope that by setting these detailed interactional studies in a critical historical perspective this book can contribute to the creation of a non-prejudicial climate in which the inevitable social constraints that affect schooling and literacy acquisition can be reconsidered.

Acknowledgments

Research for this book was supported by grants from the National Institute of Education and the National Institute of Mental Health. We would like to thank all the members of the School–Home Ethnography project who assisted at various stages of the research: Helen Clifton, Sarah Michaels, Janice Shafer, Herb Simons and Lynn Worsley.

Thanks are also due to Judith Green, Shirley Brice Heath, Hugh (Bud) Mehan and Frederick Erickson for providing valuable comments at different stages of this work.

Special thanks go to Penny Carter of Cambridge University Press who helped see the intial project through to its completion. The editor and contributors to this volume would like to thank the series editors for their support. Special thanks go to Andrew Winnard, senior editor for Linguistics at Cambridge University Press for seeing this revised volume through to publication.

1

The social construction of literacy

Jenny Cook-Gumperz

Educational institutions, their promises and limitations were at the center of public debate for most of the twentieth century. Now in the twenty-first century schooling continues to be seen as an institutional force both for bringing about social change and for providing stability. When outcomes are not as expected or when desired transformations do not come about, then the problems are seen as directly attributable to educational failure. Over the past hundred years of universal schooling, literacy rates have served as a barometer of society such that illiteracy takes on symbolic significance, reflecting any disappointment not only with the workings of the educational system, but with the society itself. An assumption often expressed is that if educational institutions cannot manage the simple task of teaching basic decoding and encoding skills, they cannot prepare future generations to deal with more complex questions of technological change (Kozol 1985). However, literacy needs to be seen as providing not just technical skills but also a set of prescriptions about using knowledge. In this sense literacy is a socially constructed phenomenon, not simply the ability to read and write. As this book demonstrates, by performing the tasks that make up literacy, we exercise socially approved and approvable talents. Literacy as socially constructed is both a historically based ideology and a collection of context-bound communicative practices.

An historical view of literacy begins in early modernity when literacy became regarded as a virtue, and some elements of such moral virtue still seem to attach to its use. A literate person was not only a good person, rather someone capable of exercising good or reasonable judgment, for a literate person's taste and judgment depended upon access to a written tradition – a body of texts – reflecting centuries of collective experience. Even today it is denigrating to describe someone as being 'illiterate'. Such words suggest not a lack of specific skill, like failure to have musical ability, but a lack of proper judgment (this term is rarely, if ever, used to describe an inability to read). Thus, by any criterion literacy has much more than a simple descriptive meaning. To claim, as the US one penny stamp does: 'the ability to write, a root of democracy' (the ability to read, it should be noted, appeared on the four penny stamp) is to put forward a view of the sociopolitical value of literacy. Does such literacy represent a different phenomenon from that measured in standardized reading, writing and comprehension tests? Can literacy as a social virtue and as a root of democracy be evaluated in the same way as the functional literacy that underlies school and work placement tests? Some of the problems that arise in discussing any contemporary concern with literacy may well derive from the complex issues that surround attempts to define literacy itself.

Much of the literature of the past decade speaks of a multiplicity of literacies, and we have come to appreciate that literacy has many facets (Collins 1995; Gee 1996). From this perspective we see that earlier research took an exclusively Western-centric view, so failing to take into account the true diversity of the world's literate cultures (Collins and Blot 2003). By treating Western social development and uses of literacy as central to the history of literacy itself, it distorted the idea of what it meant to be literate. Much of this previous discussion saw the presence or absence of literacy as an individual attribute that either transforms a person's life chances or exists as a sign of social and personal failure.

However, looking at the issues from a global position we become aware that reading, writing and speaking in everyday life and in formal instructional situations require us to ask how literacy affects people's everyday uses of language; not how people are judged literate but how they use or negotiate literate resources. What is more, a non-Western dominant perspective makes it possible to recognize more clearly the ideological components at work in any commonly used conception of literacy, and to see how much of what we take to be an essential part of literacy is actually shaped by specific biases in the study of language. Is it the case as Sylvia

Scribner pointed out two decades ago, that an ideologically charged view reveals literacy as made up of a collection of metaphors describing the power of language as a sociopolitical phenomenon (1984)? Or as Street (1984; 1993) in a similar vein has commented, past research has juxtaposed what he called the autonomous view of literacy as a reified, decontextualized construct with the ideological view that conceives of literacy as a collection of socioculturally embedded activities.

From an ideological perspective we can recognize that literacy is both a set of practices for understanding the world around us, in which written and spoken language form a continuum, and a set of statements about the value or necessity of these activities. Emphasizing the textual dominance of contemporary life in which all kinds of daily bureaucratic transactions depend on written records and the ability to construct written arguments, shows the limits of the argument that contextual dependence could be considered to limit oral language use (Silverstein and Urban 1996). From a sociolinguistic view oral and the written literacy are different but supporting facets of language use. Literate and oral practice cannot be considered as opposites, rather it is our definitions of literacy that have had at their center conflict between oral and written disciplinary traditions, which are directly traceable to our own cultural history. As socially constructed, literacy is best regarded as part of an ideology of language, a sociocultural phenomenon where literacy and orality coexist within a broader communicative framework not as opposites, but as different ways of achieving the same communicative ends (Cook-Gumperz 2005).

This book attempts to address these questions not by looking at a global perspective per se, but by exploring in greater detail the social and linguistic practices that add up to literate activities within the institutionalized process of transmission. When we describe literacy as a socially constructed process we are not looking solely at the history of the literacy–schooling relationship, as Ian Hacking's criticism of this book as a fashionable exercise in studying children's reading and writing abilities suggested (Hacking 1999), rather at a complex of situated, context-embedded communicative practices. To this end the studies reported on here set out to develop a sociolinguistic perspective on literacy and on its acquisition within the context of contemporary schooling.

While no single volume can take into account all the complexity of factors that enter into the ways we define, evaluate or assess literacy, we claim that a sociolinguistic perspective will focus on the processes by which literacy is constructed in everyday life, through conversational exchanges and the negotiation of interactional meanings in many different contexts of schooling. It is through the processes of classroom exchanges, learning-group formation, through informal judgments and standardized tests and all the other evaluative apparatus of schooling that a *schooled literacy* is formed. Whatever historically formed value judgments about literacy may be implicit, when we use the terms 'functional literacy' or 'literate consciousness' in present-day contexts, the reference is always in large part to a school-taught and classroom-learnt collection of skills. These skills reflect a particular theory of pedagogy developed over the past sixty years, that is the period in which the expectation of universal literacy has begun to be fully realized in many nation states. Over this period educational institutions have come to play an ever larger role as the arbiters of personal, socioeconomic opportunity. In learning to be literate in contemporary schools children are involved in processes central to the social transmission of knowledge in society. This view highlights the inherent selectivity that pervades contemporary educational systems; from choices of career pathways to access to everyday learning opportunities in classrooms, and in turn to later career opportunities.

However, while acknowledging the overall macro-view of social reproduction, this book looks in detail at the actual processes of transmission within the communicative contexts of classrooms and at the selectivity that results when children are evaluated in what appear to be similar school settings. From the interactional sociolinguistic perspective we see that the selection–reproduction cycle arises as a function of detectable decisions that involve evaluations and judgments of children's performance in classrooms and how a series of sociolinguistic activities lead to what later become institutional assessments of their learning potential. The social perspective on literacy looks at literacy learning not only as the acquisition of cognitive skills but rather as a means for demonstrating knowledgeability. Literacy involves a complex of socio-cognitive processes that are part of the production and comprehension of texts and talk within interactional contexts that in turn influence how these literate products will be valued. Psychological and linguistic theories alone cannot account for the essential conditions for learning written or spoken language; the value placed on features of language use, such as coherent argumentation, narrative skill, and rhetorical style, are part of a cultural inheritance that comes from lives lived in the company of others that recognize and value these uses.

However questions remain: how and by what means do children and adults learn to be literate? In what settings does this learning take place? Is it not only in schools and through school-like instructional programs, but through a multiplicity of experiences outside of school, beyond school textbooks and school curricula that a meaningful sense of the uses of literacy becomes established? The problem that several decades of research on literacy in schools have wrestled with is also an evaluative one: how is literacy best acquired? The fact that this question is asked reflects the very social character of what is meant by being literate. This in turn affects what is viewed as learning itself.

The research in this volume that took place in the late 1970s and early 1980s was influenced by three controversies within the, then, newly emerging field of literacy research:

1. How is literacy acquired, what is the role of the nature/nurture debate in its acquisition; if social environment is an essential influence on language and literacy learning what role do home and school play?
2. Is access to learning opportunities a problem in home or school acquisition?
3. If literacy is a school-based skill dependent on decontextualized uses of language as part of conceptual, intellectual growth, can this take place outside of specialized learning institutions?

A major feature of the schooling–literacy controversy focused on a debate over whether literacy learning is exclusively school based; and whether it is based on school learning or on a set of activities taking place wherever written inscriptions are used. In response to this debate, the linguist Wayne O'Neill suggested literacy acquisition '*properly*' (his emphasis) takes place outside of formal institutions of learning, and that schools do not have the best methods for literacy practice because of the way they conceive of literacy:

> Schools render their S's able to read – some of them – and in the process destroy their 'proper literacy'. Before they go off to school children have engaged in five years of bringing coherent (unspoken) explanations to the world of experiences, linguistic, social, etc. that they face. They're doing pretty well at it, too. The school tries to tell them, and generally succeeds in telling them, that common sense explanations won't do ever. It's really much simpler, the school says, experience should be understood linearly not hierarchically; it's all there on the surface, not deeply and complexly organized. O' Neill 1970:262

By opposing a *schooled* to a *commonsense* literacy, O'Neill is drawing into contrast vernacular and bureaucratic definitions of knowledge in much the same way that recent debates have revived the question of whether there exists such a thing as a standard language (Bex and Watts 1999; Gumperz and Cook-Gumperz 2005). O'Neill argues that school curricula tend to concentrate on decontextualized language skills that will necessarily separate children's naturally developed (or innate) linguistic competencies from the tasks of verbal decoding and encoding that the school requires. There are two questions here. First, is O'Neill accepting the innateness of language acquisition (nature) and implicitly rejecting the role of the communicative environment (nurture) in children's development? His view juxtaposes the 'natural' development of language with the imposition of schooled instruction. Second, he is arguing against a particular definition of school-based learning and the construction of curricula that focus too narrowly on the genesis of literacy as a skill, thus making any out-of-school knowledge of little importance. His view of schools as having a narrowly decontextualized idea of literacy as a basis for their assessments takes decontextualization in one of two different senses. It can be taken to mean either the linguistic and cognitive processing necessary to acquire the ability to reason abstractly, that from the perspective of formal instruction is usually regarded as one of the goals of literate development; alternatively, he is suggesting that school-specific knowledge outlaws or devalues the commonsense ways of arguing as not making sense in the classroom. And it seems it is this latter meaning that O'Neill intends. These two are similar but obviously not synonymous.

The implication of O'Neill's argument is that we cannot adequately criticize what schools do by depending only on a narrow school-defined notion of literacy. However any attempt to consider the range or extent of literacy without looking at the wider communicative and linguistic contexts in which literacy is acquired in conjunction with the values society assigns to these literate skills, will simplify and distort the relationship of contexts of acquisition to literate practices. No matter how carefully technical the definition, any consideration of the uses of literacy must come back to a social judgment about its uses. It is in the nature of literacy to have this dual character, prescriptive and instrumental, and research on the topic must always take this into account.

Whether difficulties in literacy acquisition in school should be attributed primarily to home or to school learning experiences was one of the key questions raised in the decades preceding this volume (see Chapter 3): whether the home-language usage and learning contexts provided equal access to literacy for all children, or whether some were seen as having a more limited range of communicative experiences, that were judged insufficient in the school classroom (Heath 1983). This first became known as the 'language deficit thesis': the view that some kinds of home-language experiences were less useful as a preparation for literacy shaped much educational research through the 1960s, and later continued to be influential on literacy research as the home–school mismatch hypothesis. In either form the suggestion was that the language of literacy used at home and school was likely to be different for many children. The role of the school in the social-transmission process became critical, and one that raised essential questions of equity of access to literacy. As the historian of education Patricia Graham pointed out:

> To recognize the centrality of the schools in the educational process then is the first and vital step in achieving equity in education. The next is to gain agreement on what the most important tasks of the schools are. The role of the school in increasing equity in education will only be effective if it is able to articulate its purpose, to gain public agreement for it, and to demonstrate that it can fulfill it. This means that the central purpose of schooling must be identifiable, popular, definable, and fair. Literacy is such a goal. Literacy is primarily a cognitive enterprise. By literacy I mean the ability to read, communicate, compute, develop independent judgments and take actions resulting from them. Graham 1980: 127

Patricia Graham's case for studying literacy as a school-based skill suggests that if schools are to be seen to have identifiable, popular and fair goals for all students, then more needs to be understood about the cognitive process by which literacy is acquired. However such a view of literacy fails to see how literacy is not simply acquired in school, but also constructed through a process of tests and evaluations both standardized and informal that are a daily part of life in classrooms and schools. Schooling is not only knowing how to do things, but rather demonstrating this knowing in appropriate contexts. The success of the endeavor, however, can be affected by a number of factors outside as well as inside the classroom. Neither school personnel nor students meet in the classroom without some preconceptions about each other's performance. Classroom and teachers are part of schools, school systems and societal/political educational policy, and students' home-community experience will already have prepared them in some way for schooling. After more than a century of universal education, most have assumptions and expectations about the outcomes, goals and failures of the schooling process. We also need to consider how such assumptions reflect ideologies of learning and of pedagogy that have become established over the past two centuries. Traditionally many factors were seen as important. To quote Graham again:

> For a variety of reasons, school officials traditionally made tacit assumptions about the attitudes, habits and talents that children brought with them into the classroom. Generally teachers believed that children from prosperous families did better than those from poor unstable families. There were always some exceptions to the general rule but research findings and conventional wisdom supported these beliefs about school achievement measured in conventional ways through teacher made tests, standardized tests and course grades. The job of the teacher and of the school was to move the children into the curriculum that was also organized along these assumptions. 1980: 120

As Graham points out, although the principal aim of public education is to overcome the diversity of background experiences by means of an organized curriculum of instruction, this does not mean that implicit assumptions of socially distributed differences will not remain. Inside classrooms many other factors influence and shape the outcome of learning processes, but the one that is preeminent is spoken, and written language – the medium of all educational exchange. While other factors have been acknowledged as important for school success, language differences were until recently overlooked as incidental handicaps to the learning process. Children come to school as communicatively competent speakers and listeners but the way children are judged, not only in their speaking performance but also in matters of their attitude and motivation, are reflected back within the evaluative context of classrooms as differential language abilities.

The empirical studies collected in Chapters 4–11 of this volume seek to show how the social transmission process works in schooling, by focusing on key classroom activities as ordinary communicative encounters that in turn lead to assessments of achievement. They demonstrate that learning is not just a matter of cognitive processing in which individuals receive, store and use certain kinds of instructional messages organized into a body of school knowledge. Literacy learning takes place in a social environment through interactional exchanges in which what is to be learnt is to some extent a joint construction of teacher and student. It is the purpose of educational settings to make possible this mutual construction. When we look at *schooled literacy* we are concerned with the ways in which skills are developed throughout a student's school career. Whether we agree with the socially formulated definitions and tests of ability, whether the range of cognitive skills that make up school literacy seem too broad or too narrow, the first task of research is to explore in critical detail the workings of these practices; not to make judgments, but to uncover biases when they affect practices, and to deconstruct the many ways that an ideology of literacy enters into our evaluations of educational effectiveness.

Thirdly, one of the most enduring issues of literacy research is the issue of the development of literate consciousness as culturally determined cognitive processes for the production and comprehension of language as written inscription (Olsen 1994). In other words, is acquiring some literate ability the precondition for consistent and logical thought? And if so, does this acquisition require specialized institutional practices, or put simply, what makes the difference, schooling or literacy? A bold experimental attempt to untangle the two sides of this proposition was made by Sylvia Scribner and Michael Cole (1981). In a major research project conducted in Liberia they explored literacy acquisition and its socio-cognitive consequences in a cultural context that enabled the two to be separated. Building on Luria's pioneering work in the 1930s (published in English translation in 1976), Scribner and Cole began a comparative research project in West Africa to examine the social and cognitive consequences of literacy in a cultural context that was removed from the ideological pressures of Western urban schools and which provided a natural experimental situation with special literacy in a local vernacular script (the Vai script), reading knowledge of classical Koranic Arabic and some Western-style schooling. In *The Psychology of Literacy* they looked at the different ways that literacy can be acquired both inside and outside the school. Just six months of schooling they found was responsible for changes in the ability to handle complex and abstract verbal reasoning tasks with students literate in a local Vai vernacular language and script, yet not previously exposed to Western-style schooling experiences. Previously, the ability to reason abstractly had been seen as the main consequence of literacy alone. These findings suggested to them that Western-style schooling might be responsible for specific social and cognitive experiences that operate independently of the effects of literacy. They concluded that some of the cognitive changes and benefits in terms of reasoning that are usually attributed to literacy by itself, are more likely to be a consequence of the process of schooling. The learning of local language and scriptural texts did not have these same effects possibly because traditional literacy skills were learnt in contexts that differed from Western-style schooling. However, Scribner and Cole's findings raised as many issues as they appeared to solve about the character of literacy as collection of communicative practices. In the context of the literacy debates in the 1970s and 1980s their conclusions appeared to add to the already identified power of schooling as a reproductive force in society. It is with such research as a background that the contributors to this book began their own investigations of literacy as a socially defined phenomenon, constructed through a process of schooling. While, as chapter 2 argues, historically established conceptions of literacy that inform our sense of a 'literate consciousness' may be complex, part of our intellectual inheritance is a notion of *schooled literacy* as a sociopolitical force that promotes or rejects change.

In addressing these issues of the social construction of literacy this book takes the following form: Chapter 2 reviews the history of the relationship of literacy to schooling and examines how this shapes our present-day ideologies of literacy and learning. Chapter 3 discusses more recent history of educational issues in relation to language and cultural difference. It presents a discussion of the sociolinguistic/linguistic anthropological theories that guide the empirical studies that follow, and provides the theoretical basis essential to our understanding of the negotiated interactional character of classroom life.

Following these two more general review chapters, the empirical studies make an argument about schooling as an institutional context that frames sociolinguistic practice and determines what counts as acceptable literate knowledge. The chapters set up a social progression from the earliest entry from home into full-time school, through various defining classroom evaluative learning experiences to the final assessment testing that takes place on leaving that institution. Arguments made throughout all these chapters are based on different empirical data.

The first two empirical chapters explore the initial encounter with school learning. In chapter 4, Gordon Wells deals with an issue that has received a great deal of attention in recent years: the apparent discontinuity between the language experience of home and school. Summarizing findings from longitudinal research, he compares interactive profiles of two children with those of a classroom population to illustrate the nature of social-class difference in language usage. Lower-(working-)class children are perceived as less responsive to teachers' questions in classrooms than middle-class children, but at home they reveal themselves to be very apt communicators. It seems that the performance discrepancy that is often seen as the root of learning problems may not be a matter of competence as such but rather of a context-bound response to the school situation. Wells goes on to argue that the theory of learning that underlies our evaluation of school literacy, and shapes most curricula, rests on sentence-level grammar and therefore neglects discourse-based understanding.

Sarah Michaels takes further the exploration of the relation between the communicative skills that children bring with them and schools' uses of these. Her argument in Chapter 5 provides a response to Wells' comment: 'It is ironic to see just how restricted are the opportunities provided in many classrooms for children to exploit the linguistic resources that they show evidence of possessing in their interactions with adults at home.' Michaels' examination of a common classroom activity, variously called 'sharing time' or 'news time', shows how first-grade children begin to adapt home-based oral discourse to the demands of classroom expository prose. She suggests that teachers' instructional strategies can serve as a bridge into literacy. Frequently, teachers cooperate with children in the production of oral narratives, showing by example how this transition is made. Difficulties arise, however, when children of minority cultural background have problems in conforming to the teachers' performance expectations and when, in spite of good intent, teacher–student communication fails to establish a common basis and be communicatively effective in terms of the school-established norms. By means of a detailed analysis Michaels is able to identify specific contextualization cues (Gumperz 1982a) as a basis for these teacher and student interactional mismatches. In these exchanges we can see the beginnings of school-based communicative problems that will at a later stage continue to affect the translation of orally produced discourse into written prose. Because of the nature of children's school careers, such early learning failures are likely to be magnified in later school performance (Mehan, Hertweck, and Meihls 1983).

The next two chapters explore further constraints on teacher–student interaction and their effects on classroom-learning experiences. Chapter 6 by James Collins and Chapter 7 by Donna Eder deal with questions arising in the early stages of children's school careers. In chapter 6, Collins examines the language and interactional strategies of second-grade reading instruction. He focuses on the verbal strategies that teachers employ in responding to children's reading performance, and on how these influence the learning opportunities that children encounter in formal classroom settings. By means of comparative analyses of teaching practices in high and low reading groups, he shows that what is actually taught varies between the differently ranked groups. As a consequence children in high or low groups develop quite different perceptions of the reading task. A detailed discourse analysis shows that the instructional strategies interacting with the children's own processing produce unintended differential effects. Thus, the nature of the differential learning that children experience in ranked reading groups is more complex than a simple shift in teaching strategy could easily remedy. Furthermore, these processes of differential learning add to the cumulative handicap that children experience through the course of their school careers.

Eder further underlines the character and consequences of the differential learning identified by Collins. In chapter 7 she shows that while ranking of reading groups is initially undertaken to improve teaching effectiveness, once a classroom is divided, a form of *institutional inertia* is likely to set in which effectively freezes the original grouping. That is, in spite of the pedagogical goal of allowing children to develop at their own pace, it becomes difficult to move children into higher groups which often are, or soon become, overcrowded. These two chapters, one written from the linguistic-anthropologist's and the other from the sociologist's perspective, demonstrate how situated occasions of differential learning can build up in the course of schooling into school-career patterns. The ideological underpinning of US education is the ideal that in the 'best system' of education available talent will be allocated to the highest available rank possible. However in its actual workings this educational system has been metaphorically described as a 'game or tournament' in which at each developmental stage in schooling, a person who does less well is further and further handicapped by the cumulative record of earlier performances (Mehan et al. 1983; Rosenbaum 1976). This model stands in marked contrast to the ideal of schooling as an open-contest system in which each new grade transition provides new opportunities for the pupils as contestants. While such a model is developed specifically to refer to the United States of America it is applicable to all contemporary complex stratified educational systems, although the sociological explanations for the distributions vary (Bourdieu and Passeron 1977). Eder's findings show that those who get placed in lower groups at the outset of schooling build up a handicap that becomes ever more difficult to overcome. Thus, if cultural differences in children's interpretations and sociolinguistic variation in their responses (such as those identified by Wells, by Michaels, and by O'Connor in the final chapter) can affect the teacher's or other gatekeeper's decision-making, then this will in turn determine such classroom matters as group placement. Cumulatively, over time these decisions become established as institutional career patterns that will be increasingly hard to change as the student passes through the educational system.

Douglas Campbell's study of questioning and answering strategies in chapter 8 provides a situated, ethnographically detailed account of how teachers' and students' verbal interactions can create conditions for information transfer and promote learning. Bourdieu's comment (1977), though perhaps ironically intended, that teachers and students collude in overestimating the transfer of information (of what in the school context is regarded as knowledge) supports this. Campbell suggests that the process of schooling is more realistically treated as the acquisition of discourse strategies for presenting information that can count as valid knowledge when given in appropriate form rather than as the straightforward acquisition of information/knowledge per se. It is not wholly ironic to describe this way of learning as a matter of correct style as much as of content. Discourse form mediates the acquisition of cognitive skills in school.

The fact that Campbell's study was done in a bilingual classroom highlights the point that it is how discourse strategies are used that is important; language as code is not at issue. Appropriate discourse strategies must be learned in all technical fields before one can demonstrate what one has learnt. So for example what is considered mathematical literacy, usually considered a language-independent cognitive skill, is in actuality a demonstration of discourse-based reasoning at the level of classroom instruction.

Campbell's study has much in common with Eder's in its approach to the issue of school competence. Both depend on ethnographic observation as the basis of the analyses although the explorations of classroom instructional issues are differently focused. Campbell examining details of conversational interaction and Eder looking at objectives of teachers, both find important similarities in the problem context. Both studies examine monocultural classroom learning situations, where students and teachers are from the same language background. Thus, neither sociocultural nor linguistic differences can be said to influence the learning process in these classrooms. Even though Eder's classroom is in a suburban, middle-class school with no social class or dialectal variation there are ranked groups for reading instruction and group position appears to have an effect on reading performance. While in Campbell's classroom, although mathematical instruction is in a second language, this situation is so for both teacher and students who are culturally and linguistically homogeneous, all being middle-class Filipino. Yet, in both studies the interactional and discourse effects of the structure of the learning environment can clearly be seen to shape the actual schooling process of literacy acquisition. Each study in its own way underlines the importance of classroom interaction processes as intervening factors in the learning process. Together these two chapters demonstrate the explanatory power that analysis of classroom interaction can achieve if it is based on the notion of communicative practice.

We see developed throughout this book that when it comes to teaching literacy, it is necessary to understand that what on the surface may be considered a simple skill is in actuality acquired in multiple ways. In order to explore the complexities of these acquisition processes we need a theory of communication that has literacy at its core. Finally in Chapters 9, 10 and 11 literacy acquisition is explored from the wider perspective of the linguistic and cognitive problems that all students face in moving from speaking and conversational understanding to writing and text-based understanding, and how discourse strategies are shown to mediate this acquisition process. In chapter 9, Herbert Simons and Sandra Murphy consider the early stages of text-based literacy from a psycholinguistic perspective. Looking at the nature of the child's experience they take a wider view of what is involved in the decoding tasks that make up reading than has been common practice. While they accept – as do most reading specialists – the importance of learning to be analytic about the relationship of sounds to written symbols as a first step in reading, they point out that reading texts provide a much richer and more confusing semantic field than is often realized. Students, Simons and Murphy argue, must acquire more than what is usually referred to as 'metalinguistic awareness' in order to read. Those constructing reading texts for children have too often ignored the discourse constraints on sense-making that students take for granted in everyday communicative practices. Similarly, linguist Charles Fillmore argues (1982) in comparing real readers to the text makers' 'ideal reader', real readers must use their discourse experience to develop context-free strategies for reducing the number of confusing options a reading text presents. Simons and Murphy demonstrate that communicative awareness is related to performance on certain tasks that show the student's ability to deal with language as a thing in itself, i.e. a way of dealing with meanings that are relatively independent of the immediate context.

In Chapter 10, James Collins and Sarah Michaels further explore the nature of this discourse awareness, and look at the special linguistic–pragmatic problems that students face in transforming oral discourse into written text. They studied fourth graders in an ethnically mixed urban school who were asked to retell in speech and writing a visually presented story. Comparing the written and oral stories, they comment that while contemporary discourse theory sees speaking and writing as two nodes on a single stylistic continuum (Tannen 1982), the task for children appears more complicated. For children the linguistic–pragmatic differences between producing written expository prose as opposed to giving an oral presentation of the same story present major difficulties. A key difficulty is the need to achieve coherence in expository prose. Certain features of spoken language, such as prosodic markers signaling intersentence cohesion, have important discourse functions that cannot be transferred directly to the written page, but need to be lexicalized in a way that may recode the entire utterance/passage. Thus, young writers need to learn alternative ways of signaling relationships in written prose and to develop rather different strategies for writing than those they rely on for talking. This recoding task may be more difficult for those children whose spoken discourse conventions differ from what the school expects. Community-based differences in discourse style may lead to different assumptions about the construction of meaningful and coherent texts. This can in turn (as Michaels shows in chapter 5) affect teachers' instructional strategies that may themselves give rise to special, and frequently unrecognized writing problems in children. Once we can identify such pragmatic problems in children's discourse understanding, we can see more clearly what is involved in achieving literacy in school and why, for some, sociolinguistic problems make moving from speaking to writing more difficult than most school-based tests allow and reinforce differential access to learning.

Finally, in Chapter 11 Catherine O'Connor takes up the issue of how differential access to learning can bring about different, potentially inequitable outcomes by looking in detail at the SAT (Scholastic Aptitude Test), the examination for entry to US higher education. In a detailed examination of the discourse of testing she argues that the design of test questions provides a link between communicative practice and the institutional reality that testing reflects. While public policy on language in schooling rests to a large part on literacy assessments and on formal tests results, O'Connor shows the language of test questions and responses makes clear that the formal language of the tests reifies specific stylistic elements of a bureaucratically supported standard English. Although the grammar of the test is English grammar, understanding of what the questions intend or convey requires background knowledge and indirect inferences that are particular to certain culturally embedded discourse conventions. These test-specific discourse conventions, especially those concerned with the interpretation of verbal-analogy items, rely greatly on denotational meanings abstracted from the context in which they are used. The resulting assessments are likely to reproduce a gap between educational performance, vernacular discourse and the dominant linguistic conventions for written text. O'Connor explores an issue very close to the original Scribner and Cole work on the implications of reasoning ability, literacy and schooling but her findings are strikingly different. She concludes that schooling through all twelve grades does not seem to alter the ability to separate out specific test items and terminology from everyday context-bound uses of language. And that by implication the socially constructed nature of the tested reality is somewhat different from the generally accepted notion.

To sum up: all of the studies in this book from several different methodological perspectives, sociolinguistic, sociological, psycholinguistic, explore the same set of issues: how the language and communicative practices involved in the teaching and evaluating of literate practices in classrooms construct the phenomenon that is known as literacy. In other words literacy is not a single entity but a complex of communicative language practices and historically influenced attitudes to these practices that unite or divide a community. Inherent in our contemporary views of literacy and schooling is a confusion between prescriptive notions of literacy, as a statement about the values and uses of knowledge, and an analytic view of literacy, as socio-cognitive abilities which are promoted and assessed through schooling. This latter notion of literacy becomes transformed through the institutional process of schooling into standardized tests assumed to assess linguistic and cognitive abilities. Such tests continue to form the principal basis of selection procedures within bureaucratic educational systems. The culture of testing results in a spiral of reinforcement of decision-making in which individual students' competencies are categorized, and at the same time the results of tests are used as indicators of the effectiveness of their schooling. Scores on tests of literacy are also computed as group aggregates, and thus may serve as devices for drawing sociopolitical boundaries that determine future opportunities for critical social groups. In other words test scores convey much more social information than their function as measures or indicators of abilities may provide, for ultimately they serve as indicators of what can be taken as the knowledge base of society. It is in this way that test results may also become self-fulfilling prophecies as the writers of *Inequality by Design: Cracking the Bell Curve Myth* point out (Fischer et al. 1996).

However, for individual students the essential question remains: what must they do in order to demonstrate that they are knowledgeable? At the basis of our notion of schooling is the assumption that information is transformed through the written record into organized knowledge as it passes through the process of textual representation (Silverstein and Urban 1996). It should be emphasized, however, as the evidence from the history of literacy reminds us, that when we ask how knowledge is transmitted, we are making assumptions about what constitutes valid knowledge. Such valid knowledge is a creation of the society, its ideology of learning and its pedagogy. Nowhere is this better shown than in the history of literacy as an ideology (see chapter 2). The character of schooled literacy can only be revealed by exploring the explicit and implicit communicative practices that guide instructional activities in actual school settings. It is all of these processes that are implicated when we regard literacy as we do in this volume as socially constructed.

2

Literacy and schooling: an unchanging equation?

Jenny Cook-Gumperz

[When] we speak of a cultural revolution, we most certainly see the aspiration to extend the active process of learning, with the skills of literacy and other advanced communication, to all people rather than limited groups, as comparable in importance to the growth of democracy and the rise of scientific industry...

The long revolution, which is now at the centre of our history, is not for democracy as political system alone, nor for the equitable distribution of more products, nor for general access to the means of learning and communication. Such changes, difficult enough in themselves, derive meaning and direction, finally, from new conceptions of man and society which many have worked to describe and interpret.

(Williams 1961)

The literacy–schooling equation: does it depend on a single point of view?

Since the beginning of the twentieth century, it has been unquestioningly assumed that literacy is both the purpose and product of schooling (Cicourel and Mehan 1984), and that the possession of literacy will improve the quality of life for individuals, social groups, and even society as a whole. However, as this chapter will show, the terms of this equation cannot be taken for granted. Raymond Williams, above, presents in perhaps its most idealized terms, a view of literacy as the key element that transforms human consciousness through the achievements of schooling and other social changes. There is good reason for this eloquence, for the study from which the chapter's epigram is taken describes the culmination of a progression toward enfranchisement of the majority of working people in the social and cultural life of British society by the mid-twentieth century (the period when Williams began writing). Through these social changes, Williams suggests, a long revolution was begun in which the coming of mass literacy meant for the majority of individuals that they could better control and shape their common social destiny.

Williams is looking back over the past two hundred years of British history (which parallels that of most industrial capitalist societies) and from this standpoint he is able to assess some of the consequences of present-day literacy achievements. On the other hand, Niyi Akinnaso, an African anthropologist writing about world literacy, takes quite another perspective. He considers a1970s UNESCO report stating:

> Rather than an end in itself, literacy should be regarded as a way of preparing man for a social, civic, and economic role that goes beyond the limits of rudimentary literacy training, consisting merely in the teaching of reading and writing. The very process of learning to read and write should be made an opportunity for acquiring information that can immediately be used to improve living standards: reading and writing should not lead only to elementary general knowledge but to training for work, increased productivity, a greater participation in civil life and a better understanding of the surrounding world, and should ultimately open the way to basic human knowledge.

He then goes on to comment:

> the argument about the consequences of literacy. . .seems to run somewhat as follows: with the advent of writing and the spread of literacy came a new resource both of knowledge and technology that, over time, has systematically affected the nature of existing cognitive, linguistic and social structures and led to the gradual deployment into new channels of people's cognitive, linguistic and organizational potential. Akinnaso 1982: 167

He goes on to state that this argument is based on the erroneous assumption that societies lacking Western-style written literacy also lack the potential for complex cognitive and social organizational accomplishments.

Ten years later he further argues:

> [such] a simplistic view gives rise to a major misconception that education in non-literate societies either does not exist in terms of organized training or [it does not affect] the systematic transfer of knowledge . . . such notions about education in non-literate societies apparently derive, in part, from a narrow ethnocentric view of schooling that misconstrues the true nature of education. Akinnaso 1992: 69

Although Williams and Akinnaso are writing only about twenty years apart, their views of the effects of literacy on social thinking clearly differ, not only because of the passage of time, but essentially because of their differing sociogeographic viewpoints. Williams looking backwards, was describing literacy as the product of an odyssey toward social and cultural changes in the West, specific to the process of industrialization begun in the nineteenth century, most particularly in Britain; whereas Akinnaso is looking forward, from a post-colonial, developing-world perspective, at a different tradition, and at changes yet to come. While Williams, with a mixture of pride and concern, envisages an historical progression in which literacy through compulsory schooling brings about political enfranchisement and the possibilities of social change, Akinnaso, reflecting on the result of allowing literacy through Western-style schooling to dominate as the only pathway to social and economic change, argues that this results in the devaluing of non-Western traditions.

What we glimpse from these two contrasting points of view is that our conception of literacy is inseparable from the specific circumstances of the historical context, and the fact that prescriptive elements have remained a part of even the most sensitive definitions of this term.

Literacy, thus, is usually taken to refer not only to the ability to understand written and printed inscriptions but also to the socio-cognitive changes that result from being literate, and from having a literate population. Yet, at the same time, literacy connotes an assessment of the usefulness of this ability. We see that literacy cannot be judged apart from some understanding of the social circumstances and specific historical traditions which affect the way literacy is conceived of within each society. When we investigate how schooling is used to achieve literacy we are drawn even more into making judgments about the values and opportunities that it brings about. Such a value-laden situation makes research on literacy and schooling an area that requires more than a simple descriptive account. This chapter attempts to explore some of the changes and complexities these factors have brought about in our understanding of literacy and its equation with schooling.

Literacy: a search for definitions from rudimentary to functional

Literacy exists in many equations. It can be coupled either with what is usually regarded as its essential facilitating cause, schooling; or with the consequence of a long-term process, literacy and cognitive change; or with the broader effects of literacy for the society's economic development. Comparisons of literacy as a catalyst for social change are often made across rather extended timescales that can vary from recent historical times to the classical past; but discussions of the consequences of literacy are as likely to be set in the abstract ethnographic present as in any real-time period. It is necessary therefore, when considering the relationship of literacy to schooling, to be very specific about our comparisons. Furthermore, how we view the consequences or effects of literacy is related essentially to our definition or assessment of the activity itself.

Discussions of the value of literacy have ranged from looking at the spread of a rudimentary literacy, that is, basic decoding skills involved in reading and writing familiar materials, as historians do (Cipolla 1969), to the development of an increasingly specific concept of literacy as the assessment of skills involved in reading and writing new and novel materials. But the major debate focuses on the more recent questioning of the assumption that there is an inevitable entailment in the relationship between literacy rates and the socioeconomic development of a society. This view is based on the past few centuries of Western experience. Critical analysis has shown that comparisons of the effects and consequences of literacy are often made between essentially incomparable societies (Goody 1977). Furthermore such an unchanging quality to the literacy–schooling equation has been questioned by cognitive psychologists, anthropologists, and historians (Akinnaso 1982; Goody 1968; Resnick and Resnick 1977; Scribner and Cole 1981). All agree that previous views of literacy have not only taken the ultimate value of literacy and schooling for granted, but have also assumed that there is agreement about what constitutes 'full' literacy. Levine (1982), in an exploration of the concept, shows that no such agreement exists, even at the level of such general documents as the UNESCO literacy reports (UNESCO 1976). Definitions are constantly changing as can readily be seen if we contrast the historians' attempts to describe the limited literacy of the past while avoiding evaluative judgments (Furet and Ozouf 1983) with the recent bureaucratic attempts to set goals for a concept of minimal but full literacy. Changes in bureaucratic definitions respond to what are perceived as changing needs, particularly in developing societies. Attempts to estimate the effectiveness of literacy programs, or to make guidelines for programs, lead to judgments of the usefulness of literacy, and this in turn creates the bureaucratic demands for a sufficiently general, formal definition. In discussing the development of such a concept of functional literacy Levine (1982: 250–1) finds that:

> The original conjunction of the terms *functional* and *literacy* is hard to date with any certainty. The notion of a level of literacy more sophisticated than mere capacity to write one's name and to read a simple message, but less than 'full fluency,' appears to have gained currency in specialist circles during World War II. This intermediate level of attainment was assumed from the outset to be associated with employability and, in a loose and unclarified way, with the social integration and adjustment of its possessors . . . At first, UNESCO's literacy activities were placed in the context of 'functional education,' which aimed to 'help people develop what is best in their own culture' (UNESCO 1949: 16). The core content of fundamental education embraced the skills of thinking, speaking, listening, and calculating, as well as reading and writing. The need for these and associated skills was recognized to exist in both highly industrialized and developing societies (1949: 11, 29).

Initial attempts to reach a definition of 'literacy skills' included both a wider range of skills and some latent assumptions about the psychological abilities of literate people. The more specific the definitions and standards tried to be, the more difficult it was to make judgments about literate behavior. Moreover, administrators of these programs tend to see the range of skills considered necessary for functional literacy as an integral part of the repertoire of skills taught through schooling rather than through daily interaction in practical tasks (Goody 1983). Literacy campaigns, while trying to be sensitive to different cultural needs, also assumed that these skills were of central importance to all people's lives. Levine (1982: 251) goes on to discuss this problem of cultural relativity:

> In [a 1956] survey of literacy a person was considered functionally literate 'when he has acquired the knowledge and skills in reading and writing which enable him to engage in his culture or group'. This definition was intentionally relativistic, allowing for different thresholds of literacy in

various societies, while leaving unspecified what standard could apply to wholly preliterate cultures. This formulation did not associate functional literacy training with work or other specific social settings; it merely emphasized that the content of the training should reflect the needs and motivations of the group served, and aim for a self-sustaining standard – one which permits pupils to make independent use of what they have learned without further help from an instructor.

While functional literacy is the ability not only to read, write, and calculate 'in some manner', it is also seen as the ability to use these skills to generate new literate materials and new understanding. Even when assessments of functionality remain technical, literacy judgments are likely to shift from the factual level onto the evaluative, and likely to contain culturally taken-for-granted positions. The desire to achieve bureaucratic precision in a definition of literacy is part of a growing movement to give technical meaning to skills that have previously been considered to be inestimable parts of more general abilities. However the new 'functional literacy' contains social judgments about abilities that are specific to advanced technological societies. As literacy becomes ever more precisely yet expansively defined, the notion of illiteracy takes on a new specificity as the absence of all such 'functional' skills and so makes the negative association with limited ability even more likely. So that no matter how carefully technical the definition appears to be, it ultimately contains implicit evaluative and prescriptive elements.

Let us now return to our initial concern with the equation between literacy and schooling. During the past two centuries when literacy rates and values have changed and expanded in Western societies, schooling as a social movement has also developed. But the relationship between schools and their essential product, literacy, has been part of established knowledge only over the past century. Before considering the historical details of this relationship, we must first be aware that throughout their development schools have been concerned not only with the teaching of literacy skills, that is with decoding and encoding of written symbolic systems, but also with the uses of these skills; and these latter are primarily social. It is for this reason that school learning cannot be considered only as cognitive learning. If we contrast the present-day situation with the history of literacy and schooling, we find that prior to the development of a complex bureaucratic universal education system, the acquisition of literacy was more likely to be through informal interaction in localized groups. In looking at contemporary judgments on the effectiveness of schooling in providing for a universal functional literacy, two researchers in reading and cognitive development, Lauren and David Resnick, have pointed out that such criteria have only in the past decades been attainable. In comparing the historical development of a standardized notion of literacy with that existing in the United States of America they conclude that it is the present standard for literacy itself which 'influences our contemporary and negative views of schooling achievements'. They suggest that:

> This nation perceives itself as having an unacceptable literacy level because it is applying a criterion that requires, at a minimum, the reading of new material and the gleaning of new information from that material . . . This high literacy standard is a relatively recent one as applied to the population at large and much of our present difficulty in meeting the literacy standard we are setting for ourselves can be attributed to the relatively rapid expansion to a large population of educational criteria that were once applied to only a limited elite. Resnick and Resnick 1977

If it is the case that previous elite standards of literacy are now being applied at all levels then the forces which shape these standards of evaluation will become clearer as we look at historical developments. Such an inquiry will enable us to ask whether these standards and definitions are the only problem informing our contemporary concern with literacy, or whether, as was suggested earlier, the problems over literacy are a part of the wider issue about the goals of contemporary education.

Some historical evidence for changing views of literacy and schooling

Historians have recently pointed out that a reversal has taken place in views of literacy over the past century. There was a time when those with influence or power in Western society considered literacy as a dangerous possession for the majority population, the lower or the working classes. This reverses the present-day view that it is the continuing existence of illiteracy that is a social danger. The best way to examine the historical evidence for this reversal is to locate our discussion in a specific time and place; particularly to look back at our own historical development over the past century in which literacy and schooling have moved into a central position as a key socio-technical force in contemporary life.

Looking at such changes historically can have its dangers for when literacy is considered as a necessary catalyst for social change or development, implicit comparisons are often made based on a single social and historical standpoint (Goody 1977). Scholars taking a third-world or global perspective therefore are critical of many current writings on literacy (Akinnaso 1982; Scollon and Scollon 1982). Furthermore, cross-cultural comparisons of literacy development too often start from an exclusively Western standpoint (Finnegan 1981), and result in many contradictory views and hard-to-maintain dichotomies between forms of language, forms of historical development and the consequences of social change. Equally important is the fact that historical and cultural comparisons may distort the most essential aspect of literacy and society, that is, that irreversible changes occur once literacy has become established in society and that our own historical heritage in this regard is particular rather than general. With these provisions to guide us, it seems that a view of literacy development which focuses more specifically upon the English-speaking tradition over the past two centuries may be able to show how historical studies can show how contemporary concerns with standards of literacy and with socially perceived 'failures' can be seen for what they are, socially constructed notions of activities and benefits of literacy.

One of the main thrusts of recent historical studies in this area has been to document the many ways in which literacy has existed in Western society over the past five centuries (Graff 1981); even the literacy rates which in recent years have come to assume such great importance have only been recorded for just over a hundred years (Oxenham 1980). So it can be argued that the shift from the eighteenth century onwards has not been from total illiteracy to literacy, but from a hard-to-estimate multiplicity of literacies, a *pluralistic* idea about literacy as a composite of different skills related to reading and writing for many different purposes and sections of a society's population, to a notion of a single, standardized *schooled literacy.* What is the available historical evidence for this shift from a limited home-based learning to a school-based standard? We know that there were changes in literacy expectations in the period that has often been called 'the great transformation', that is, during the move from a primarily agrarian to a primarily industrial and urban economy (Lockridge 1981; Salaman 1981). Moreover, the time-span needed to work through this transformation cannot be underestimated: it took the whole of the nineteenth century for the modern industrial state to be developed in Britain and America, but the literacy rates did not accompany this change in a simple unilinear progression. For while the degree of literacy attained by and expected of ordinary people was increasing, a good percentage of these people were already minimally literate. Undoubtedly there was a progression over a century or so, from the rudimentary and already widespread ability to read a little and perhaps to sign one's name to the ability to read unfamiliar material and to learn new information. But the transformation was regionally varied. Thus, the literacy of a substantial proportion of the population can be seen as having preceded industrial development, rather than the reverse. How is it then that the popular view, that it was the coming of industrial society that led to literacy and schooling, came about? Furthermore, why do we usually assume that literacy is the purpose of schooling when there is so much historical evidence to the contrary?

The result of recent historians' work on popular culture describes through detailed studies of everyday affairs and day-to-day political activity the existence of an active literate culture during the eighteenth century, well before the coming of compulsory, universal schooling. Therefore the introduction of schooling must have had other purposes than the promotion of literacy. Recent studies of eighteenth- and early nineteenth-century Britain, Europe, and America have gone some way toward establishing the extent to which a *commonplace literacy* affected the lives of ordinary people before industrialization (Cipolla 1969; Graff 1979; Laqueur 1976a; Stone 1967). In eighteenth-century America, for example, personal letters, diaries, notes, and record-keeping, as well as books, were an essential part of ordinary people's daily lives (S. B. Heath 1981; Lockridge 1981). Even more significantly, literacy was not just a *small* part of daily life but had a major value for many people, not just for special classes or groups. Many kinds of books, tracts, and almanacs were in common use in urban and rural households. Laqueur, an historian of popular culture, asks:

> How and why did this literate culture come into being; for what reasons did ordinary men and women learn to read, and to a lesser extent to write? No single factor considered in itself can explain why. Neither economic necessity imposed by commercial or industrial developments nor schools founded by higher order to convert, control, or in some way mould the working classes can explain how literacy became so widespread. The adoption and use of a technology like writing, by large numbers of people is not explicable by institutional or material forces alone. Specific motivations to learn to read and write must instead be seen in terms of the structure of meaning that defined popular culture from the sixteenth century onward. People did not become literate for this or that particular reason but because they were increasingly touched in all areas of their lives by the power of communication which only the written word makes possible. There was, therefore, a motivation to read and write: these skills allowed men and women to function more effectively in a variety of social contexts. This explains why, in the absence of externally provided schools, indigenously supported settings were responsible for the creation and transmission of popular literacy. Laqueur 1976a:255

We conclude that there was an audience for written literature and this audience was a catalyst for the widening of popular culture. This popular culture relied on both social and political material. Broadsheets, ballads, and political tracts provided a key means for political discussion and for recreation (Thompson 1963). These could not have been effective without literate audiences. Economic activity, therefore, was not the only reason for literate development, since it was quite possible to earn a livelihood without literacy skills. Initially, literacy had value in social and recreational areas of life: only gradually did it enter the economic lives of ordinary people in ways that could determine their prospects in life. Robert Altick (1957), in his pioneering study of the mass-reading public, has given many examples of how work and literacy were intermingled in earlier times. For example, a competent reader might be engaged to read to other workers while they worked, in the same way that music is piped into contemporary workplaces.

There existed a literate basis of commonplace culture, before common schooling, which was more widespread than is often assumed. Again, to cite from Laqueur's study:

The popular culture of eighteenth century England was fundamentally literate and thus inexorably bound to the processes and culture of a society beyond the village community. Perhaps as many as 60 percent of men in England by 1754 and 40 percent of women could sign the marriage register and there is evidence that an even higher proportion were probably able to read. 1976a: 255

While literacy was still rudimentary, it did allow for the growth of a popular culture that was an active part of daily life for many ordinary people before the coming of either organized schooling or industrialization. Although the extent of this literacy should not be overestimated, more people did have access to a common literate cultural base than the literacy figures themselves suggest.

The great debate over reform, radicalism and schooling

It is important to recognize the strength of commonplace literacy in early nineteenth-century Britain, to understand the relevance of demands for schooling. Initially, literacy was not taught in separate institutions but was acquired in many different settings such as homes and informal groups.

Literacy was transmitted in much the same way as were traditional occupational skills. Most children learned to read and perhaps to write from their parents, or from neighbors, unlicensed and untrained, in settings which we today and indeed nineteenth century observers would have hesitated to call schools. Laqueur 1976a: 257

During the nineteenth century, however, the various schooling movements increased, and demands for formal instruction came from many sources. At first, schooling was seen as a response to the popular literacy which already existed, and was often associated with radical political causes. However, there were many establishment figures who felt strongly that literacy for the majority of the population, and its strengthening through schooling, was not to be encouraged. In describing the debate developing in early nineteenth-century Britain, Cipolla notes that schooling was seen as too dangerous for working people on the grounds that:

it would teach them to despise their lot in life, instead of making them good servants in agriculture, and other laborious employment to which their rank in society had destined them, instead of teaching them subordination, it would render them factious and refractory, as was evident in manufacturing counties, it would enable them to read seditious pamphlets, vicious books. 1969:65–6

This statement was made during a debate in the British parliament over a bill to provide elementary schools throughout the country in 1807. Opposing this bill, the President of the Royal Society commented that 'the project of giving education to the labouring classes of the poor would in effect be found to be prejudicial to their morals and happiness.' In this statement, one finds the two main arguments used at that time against widespread education: the upper-class fear of running into an uncomfortable shortage of manual labor and the expectation that radicalism through seditious books would cause social unrest and discontent. There were other opinions too: for example, if schooling were limited and controlled, it would serve as a way of bringing popular literacy, and its actual and potential use for social radicalism, under the control of the establishment.

There were many schooling movements, some supported by local sources such as the common-school movement in America; and others initiated by upper-class reformers, many with religious support or backing. The Sunday-school movement was a particularly strong alternative movement in Britain (Laqueur 1976b), where the linking of religiously motivated schooling to a limited literacy was seen by those who viewed literacy as a social danger as providing a suitable approach for educating the working people. Laqueur quotes one such reformer, Hannah More, as suggesting a plan for adult schools which would be that founded on the premise that 'the preservation of the hierarchical social structure was central to their whole conception of the need for literacy education . . . in the achievement of literacy they [the working people] would be taught habits of industry and thrift' through a very restricted program of little writing and some reading of religious texts. However, in other places the religious motivation for popular schooling resulted in a slightly less restricted curriculum for literacy. Throughout the nineteenth century the cause of universal literacy was variously advanced. In Britain, by the time compulsory state schooling was introduced (1870), society was judged, by the standards of a limited or restricted literacy, to be 75 percent literate, since the new act gave legal recognition to what in essence were the many kinds of schools that had existed throughout the nineteenth century. The consequences of this gradual but growing literacy were several and often rather different from those hoped for by many working people; they were even more unexpected to those who had looked to literacy and schooling as a means of improving the quality of life. As Laqueur points out:

> the new cultural meaning of literacy marked a discontinuity. It drove a wedge through the working class. It came for the first time to be a mark distinguishing the respectable from the non-respectable poor, the washed from the unwashed. It served to sharpen a division which was far less clear in the eighteenth century. 1976a: 270

The protagonists in the debate over social unrest did not necessarily foresee the consequences, but with hindsight we can now see how soon the idea of differentiation through schooling achievement, which became such a marked feature of twentieth-century life, was first brought into public debate. (We will return to this issue later in the chapter.) Initially, it was not schooling which developed literacy, but rather the reverse. Literacy led to the growth of a commonplace culture that was part of a movement for social change, thus, the linking of literacy to schooling at its outset was not an historical cause but rather an historical consequence of the growth of popular literacy that had preceded the development of mass schooling. Therefore, nineteenth-century schooling was not set up to initiate literacy acquisition, but for other rather different purposes (Graff 1979).

Not only in Britain but also in other European countries, such as France, Germany, Scandinavia, and in America other changes accompanied, or coincided with, schooling. Altick and Vincent have stressed the rapid cheapening of print after 1850 with a corresponding rapid rise in readership for books, journals and newspapers, along with a large increase in the number of circulating libraries (Altick 1957; Vincent 2000). In their study of the development of schooling in Ohio, Soltow and Stevens (1981) have documented changes in attitudes toward schooling and literacy that took place from 1830 throughout the nineteenth century. They demonstrate how schooling in both Europe and in America was considered as a means of bringing popular literacy under the control of publicly organized school systems; how the making of literacy into a school-based skill changed for ever the relationship of the majority of the population to their own talents for learning and for literacy. Therefore, while the schooling movement was welcomed in the main by ordinary people as a valuable extension to their own literate culture, it also raised questions about the social and political assumptions on which schooling was grounded. Questions commonly raised in the late nineteenth century concerned the kinds of cultural expression and literacy that were suited to the education of a majority of the working population. The systematic development of literacy and schooling meant a new division in society, between the educated and the uneducated (or schooled and unschooled), and a new form of increasingly powerful social control that could be exerted through the school curriculum. In these ways the consequences of literacy for all, promoted through schooling, were not what had been expected in the debates at the beginning of that century.

The reversal of position, from seeing a dangerous radicalism inherent in acquiring literacy to the opposite view that the social and political danger was in having illiteracy in the population, began at this time. We can also see that the selective transmission of knowledge through different conceptions of schooling for different sectors of society became the cornerstone on which the schooling for universal literacy was built.

Harvey Graff, in his study of schooling and industrial development in Ontario, develops this view and shows how it was possible that public schooling came to control rather than expand the life experiences of the working class, while growing modern industrial forms of production made schooling into an important social and bureaucratic force. The major goal of mass schooling was thus to control literacy not to promote it; to control both the forms of expression and the behavior which accompanied the move into literacy. The development of public schooling became based on the need to achieve a new form of social training that made home-based or rural workers into a factory labor force. Thus, while literacy preceded industrial development, it was the needs of the new industrial, capitalist economy that shaped schooling and its institutionalization, as Graff details:

> To 'educate' the workers was necessary. But it was not an education in reading and writing; rather it was 'the need to educate the first generation of factory workers to a new factory discipline, [part of] the widespread belief in human perfectability . . . but one of their consequences was the preoccupations with the character and morals of the working class which are so marked a feature of the early stages of industrialization'. Toward this end – the reshaping of character, behavior, morality, and culture – factory owners and other capitalists joined with social reformers and school promoters (as in North America) seeking alternative, more effective and efficient approaches to socialization. Increasingly, we have seen, they turned to *public schooling, literacy transmission, and mass institutions.*
>
> Graff 1981: 257

In this way literacy became linked to a teaching–learning process that stressed behavioral and moral characteristics, with the ability to decode and encode written symbols as an important but secondary goal. The concerns of school reformers were carried on with a new impetus, for the establishment of the moral power of literacy as self-improvement promoted by the school provided a basis upon which other uses of schooling could be developed. Modern industrial work necessitated a workforce that was able to accept new discipline, and so this became a critical new motivation for schooling and literacy.

In sum, we can identify two currents of social change from the eighteenth through to the end of the nineteenth century. Both of these resulted in widening the growth of literacy and in developing the public provision of education, *but their purposes and goals were generally opposed.* First, the popular, literate culture of ordinary people defined literacy and schooling as individual achievements and as parts of radical, personal development. The expansion of schooling that grew directly out of popular literacy movements can be seen first in the traditions of the common school and later in the workers' educational movements. Secondly, politicians and capitalist employers saw schooling as providing a workforce prepared for increasingly industrialized work with a sense of discipline and what could latterly be called *schooled* competencies. While the former popular traditions were seen as too radical, the juxtaposition of the two views, one to promote and the other to control popular literacy, became the impetus for the historical development of schooling as a social movement that led to publicly provided schools, and to literacy as the essential first step of a proper education. To quote Graff again:

> Literacy, it was grasped, could ease the transition and assimilation of the working class and the poor to industrial and 'modern' social habits, if provided in carefully structured institutions. To destroy traditional attitudes, culture, and habits of work was far from an easy or simple task, as many researchers have discovered . . . To protect society and property, as well as to organize, control, and increase production, they [industrialists, etc.] sought – with the school promoters themselves – more moral, orderly, disciplined, deferential, and contented workers: the expected result of *the hegemony of the moral economy of literacy.* 1981: 258–9

Thus, the institution of schooling brought the popular cultural force of literacy under the control of schooling, and shaped its history through these two contradictory movements. As schooling gradually became synonymous with literacy, the idea grew that schooling should ensure adequate literacy development, which in turn was, or could be, a necessary part of economic well-being at the personal level. Achieving literacy through mass schooling meant, from the viewpoint of the political establishment, making literacy safe for the majority. The long-term consequence was a rising political concern over the failure of schooling and a newly sharpened notion of illiteracy that deemed those lacking schooling and literacy a social danger.

The ideology of literacy

However, these arguments alone do not provide sufficient explanation for either the contemporary or even the late nineteenth-century concern with illiteracy at times when the literacy rates were and are higher than ever previously conceived. That the failure of schooling is judged by such indices of performance clearly has, as mentioned at the beginning of this inquiry, other hidden meanings. Graff's discussion of the moral economy of literacy leads us to look again at the ideology underlying our notion of literacy, and to ask whether we have in fact just one notion or several meanings for this concept. We must go back once more to the eighteenth century where the notion of egalitarianism developed and became an important strand in the ideology of literacy. This view assumed that literate skills for all people would result in equality and the possibility of a new social and political order. Goody and Watt, quoting from John Stuart Mill's autobiography, show how strongly this view was held:

> One of the basic premises of liberal reform over the last century and a half has been that of James Mill, as it is described in the Autobiography of his son, John Stuart Mill:
>
> 'So complete was my father's reliance on the influence of reason over the minds of mankind, whenever it is allowed to reach them, that he felt as if all would be gained if the whole population were taught to read, if all sorts of opinions were allowed to be addressed to them by word and in writing, and if, by means of the suffrage, they could nominate a legislature to give effect to the opinions they adopted.' p. 74.
>
> All these things have been accomplished since the days of the Mills but nevertheless 'all' has not been 'gained'; and some causes of this shortfall may be found in the intrinsic effects of literacy on the transmission of the cultural heritage. Goody and Watt 1968: 56

As Goody and Watt point out in response to this quotation, literacy alone has not brought about a transformation of either human consciousness or social life chances and part of the reason for this may lie with literacy itself; or, as we suggest here, with the ideology of literacy that has developed over the past 150 years. Initially it seems that one of the reasons for the failure of James Mill's vision of a future shaped by universal literacy may be that this view rested on an eighteenth-century essentially pluralistic conception of literacy, as part of a multiplicity of skills for the exchange of ideas and information through written words. The breaking up of the pluralistic concept of literacy led indirectly to the establishment, even by the end of the nineteenth century, of a stratified and potentially standardizable notion of literacy that came to be tied to regular schooling. *Schooled literacy* was thus differentiated from everyday uses of literacy. What was learnt through schooled literacy was no longer part of a local common culture, so that ordinary people had less control over their own cultural products. To quote Goody and Watt again:

> The high degree of differentiation in exposure to the literate tradition sets up a basic division that cannot exist in non-literate society: the division between the various shades of literacy and illiteracy. This conflict, of course, is most dramatically focused in the school, the key institution of society . . . Because although the alphabet, printing and universal free education have combined to make literate culture freely available to all on a scale never before previously approached, the literate mode of

communication is such that it does not impose itself forcefully or as uniformly as is the case with the oral transmission of the cultural tradition.

Goody and Watt 1968: 59

Here Goody and Watt are suggesting that the movement toward equality gained through schooling and by the availability of written knowledge was in effect cancelling out some of the benefits of a previously less systematized knowledge base that existed in an oral and pluralistic literate tradition. Schooling and a pedagogy that was based on schooled literacy assured that knowledge became stratified in its transmission. It is this stratification of transmission expressed in the nineteenth-century ideology of literacy as personal self-improvement tied to personal, social and, moreover, to economic advancement that Graff has called the growth of the moral economy of literacy; that is, linking the attainment of literate skills to an individual's sense of goodness. The development of this moral economy was a major element in strengthening the effectiveness of the schooling–literacy bond, as Soltow and Stevens have shown, for to be literate was to be a good and virtuous citizen:

The normative question of whether literacy itself was to be valued had been settled by the end of the eighteenth century, although reformers knew well the dangers of print presented to young minds without a guiding hand. An ideology of literacy carried forward from the eighteenth century and associated primarily with the spiritual well-being of individual and community alike had been further developed within the contexts of nationalism and the ethic of economic self-improvement. Collectively, literacy clearly was considered part of the social cement which helped to guarantee social stability and adherence to cherished social and political norms. The function of literacy was seen as integrative; its value was to be assessed in terms of social cohesion. Individually, literacy was one attribute which helped to make the good man, that is, it was part of being virtuous, and the better man was the man who would improve his skills in reading and writing. 1981: 85

The impetus for the growth of schooling, however, came not only from social reformers, as we have seen, but also from the industrial capitalists and their need for an industrial labor force. In this way a new element was added to the nineteenth-century ideology of literacy that differed essentially from eighteenth-century egalitarianism. The changes that began in the nineteenth century encouraged an ideology of literacy which provided the linkage and justification for the view that individual effort, economic success, and the advancement of literacy through schooling were necessarily related. This ideology was promoted through many different channels, not only through the schools. Soltow and Stevens again describe this:

> The period between 1787 and 1870 was characterized by rapid institutional development to accommodate and popularize an ideology of literacy . . . The ideology of literacy was promoted by printers; textbook authors and newspapermen also viewed literacy skills as important in the achievement of economic success. Not only were literacy and schooling functionally linked, but both were seen as part of the formula for upward economic mobility. The illiterate person was commonly the disadvantaged one and less likely to make his way upward than the literate individual. 1981:61

In this way the ideology not only linked schooling and literacy to goodness, as the making of the virtuous citizen, but also provided for selectivity in the effects of the transmission of literacy. The literate citizen was not just more virtuous but would also experience greater economic well-being. It is a short step from such arguments to those that see the illiterate as being less worthy and so experiencing less economic prosperity. In other words the poverty of the illiterate was of their own making. As Goody and Watt pointed out, literacy, or rather the ideology on which the achievement of universal literacy was based, provided for the introduction of the distinction between the deserving and undeserving poor which has been such an important feature of social thinking in the past century (Himmelfarb 1984). Thus, selectivity of knowledge transmission was at the center of an ideology of literacy that informed the growth of all public schooling.

From this brief review, we can see that there is, at the center of the equation of literacy and schooling, a tension between the wish for education on the part of individuals and the concept of functional public schooling for a large population. The educational needs of literate development for individuals and those of public schooling have always created conflicts in the development of public education systems. It is these tensions that we inherit in the present concern over the relationship between schooling practices and the achievement of literacy.

During the twentieth century, the idea grew that schooling should not only enable, but ensure, adequate literacy development. This in its turn was not only a necessary part of economic well-being at the personal level but was also an assurance of social stability and economic advancement at the societal level. By the mid-twentieth century the ideology of literacy that had underpinned nineteenth-century schooling took on a new character. The result of mass-education movements, and the achievement of more or less universal literacy in the advanced industrial societies, reshaped the ideology of literacy. First, literacy was no longer only a personal goal for individual citizens, it became institutionally a basic human right. The charter of UNESCO assured all countries that literacy along with political freedoms represented a human right for all people. Secondly, literacy in the form of writing systems is not merely a means of storing and transmitting information, it has become a supra-technology which enables other technologies of information storage, retrieval and transmission to grow (Oxenham 1980). Literacy itself no longer represents progressive development for people and societies but rather, as the fundamental technology on which modern societies are built, it becomes the precondition for any future change or progress. Furthermore, education does not merely promote literacy, and schooling does not just develop it; rather, without literacy there is neither schooling nor education. Once again, illiteracy as the absence of literacy takes on a whole new meaning. How did this shift in the ideology of literacy come about? To understand some of the reasons for this change we need to consider the social changes that accompanied the professionalization of schooling and that promoted a pedagogy based on universal literacy.

The professionalization of schooling

Schooling had, by the mid-twentieth century, come to occupy the preeminent place in society as the institution which ensures its continuation and provides talent for the replacement and expansion of the advanced industrial economy, by selecting and preparing this talent for differentiated social positions and occupations. Through most of the previous century the view became established that educational success, not just literacy, leads to economic opportunity. The view that now predominates is that the school must be the provider of cognitive opportunity for personal development and of a literate, educated labor force for the economy. By reason of its professional status, modern schooling has made school-based learning into a universal and standardized technical skill. In a schooled society individuals undergo a transformation through learning, by virtue of which they become members of the wider society. Educational curricula are a matter of societal decision so that knowledge is now public not personal or oriented toward a specific or bounded social group.

It was the introduction of professional schooling in the early twentieth century that provided the organizational conditions for schools to become arbiters of literacy standards, by making literacy both measurable and evaluative of other abilities. The term 'professional schooling' means schooling which is publicly provided, legally supported within society, and with a consistent curriculum which contains an organized plan of instruction for both learners and teachers. Such an organized system of schooling places increasing emphasis on the provision of new techniques of teaching and learning, which make the evaluation of skills and the measurement of abilities possible (Cremin 1962; 1989). In this process literacy becomes one of the basic components of schooling on which other learning must rest. It becomes essentially a cognitive skill, one that enables other cognitive growth to take place, and its evaluation becomes central to the assessment of other potentialities of student learners. In these schooling terms, a non-literate person counts as an *uneducable* person, not merely an uneducated one. Thus, the nineteenth-century ideology was transformed into the twentieth-century ideology which stresses that literacy may bring, not economic well-being directly, but *equality of opportunity* as a basic value from which other advantages can come.

As the development of primary and secondary education took place the balance shifted in the equation of literacy with schooling. While intended to provide equality of opportunity by allowing all individuals equal access to literacy, bureaucratically organized schooling systems served to divorce people from any local cultural base (Katz 1971). Thus, the professionalization of schooling actually resulted in further differentiation of the school population. Once schooled literacy was seen as differing from everyday uses of literate information, stratification in the distribution of knowledge developed, and, as we have seen in the previous section, differentiation of knowledge was at the core of the 'literacy revolution'. Professional schooling provided a pedagogy that determined what was to be learnt and an evaluation of the methods by which it was learnt. The effect of these schooling practices was the maintenance of a stratified school population through an increasingly diverse set of educational institutions, and with a pedagogy that emphasized the need selectively to develop individual talent for differentiated occupational roles. There was a tendency therefore to equate the differentiation of the distribution of knowledge with the social stratification of a literate society. That is, the knowledge of the *less* literate came to be seen as *lesser knowledge*.

The consequences of a pedagogy of universal literacy

The development of national school systems in Western societies was one of the outstanding and controversial achievements of the twentieth century (Bowles 1977; Cremin 1962; Katz 1971; Tyack 1977). With the growing power of the school it had become appropriate by the mid-twentieth century to speak of a *schooled society* (Illich 1972). The bureaucratically organized educational system that has developed over the past seventy years is accompanied by a pedagogy that stresses improvement of life chances through school learning. In this way schooling becomes the preeminent legitimizing force for entry into, and advancement in, a technological society. In a schooled society, schooling becomes the arbiter of attainment, not just for the period of childhood, but for training and learning throughout any individual's life career. Such a society has been the result of the establishment of universal schooling, accompanied by a shift in pedagogy which emphasized that 'things learnt' could change social life chances for a large majority of the population, in ways that were not previously considered. Central to the development of this pedagogy has been the concept of schooled literacy, stressing the advantages of effectively achieving literacy during the period of schooling. The term 'pedagogy' means, in this context, as it meant for Durkheim, not only 'the formal curriculum but also the way that the knowledge it embodies is transmitted and evaluated' (Karabel and Halsey 1977). In his study of the French education system, Durkheim suggested that any pedagogical transformation is always to be seen as the result and sign of a social transformation. From our brief historical review we have seen that throughout the past century or so the social transformation taking place in

Western society was the movement toward a widening enfranchisement of an entire society into a single, but stratified whole: what is described by sociologists as the transformation of a class-divided society into a *class society* (Giddens 1982).

Literacy served as a mobilizing force in this transformation in which the cultural patterns of small and localized groups were supplanted by allegiance to a wider and more uniform cultural and social base in which all classes appeared to contribute, only in a differentiated form. As part of this transformation, universal literacy, the result of public education, was seen as providing entry into a new social order. The continued advancement of industrial society required an educational theory that focused upon more complicated skills than the limited ability to read, write and do simple calculations. Thus a pedagogy evolved that focused upon the potential development of every individual child. This theoretical standpoint contrasted with the earlier nineteenth-century notions, as Bowles points out:

> The older democratic ideology of the common school – that the same curriculum should be offered to all children – gave way to the 'progressive' insistence that education should be tailored to the 'needs of the child'.
>
> Bowles 1977: 140

It was thus during the early decades of the last century, and with the influence of the new progressivism in education, that the change in pedagogy and in the practices of schooling took place, thus enabling the establishment of a school system in which opportunities for achieving literacy and for the promotion of individual talent could be provided. It was considered that such a system would lead to the attainment in society of a suitable place for every individual according to his or her recognized talents. Such a view presupposes the notion of ideal–typical allocation, in which the working of society models an ideal society in which there is a suitable and available slot for every individual according to their talents (Simmel 1971). How this ideal actually worked in practice is shown by David Tyack in his study of American city schools:

> The explicit lesson of the school taught the doctrine of self-help and equality of opportunity, so that the well-socialized child blamed himself and not the social order if he did not succeed in life. The implicit lessons were perhaps even more important: the requirements of obedience, punctuality,

silence, cleanliness, and ritualistic acceptance of the unreality portrayed in textbooks. Tyack 1977: 406

As I have suggested above, the pluralistic popular literate culture of the eighteenth and early nineteenth centuries did not encourage such a separation or ranking of individuals. Rather, it was the introduction of public education that provided the organizational conditions for the development of such ranking, and it was public 'mass' schooling which selected individuals and separated them from each other, by making the practices of literacy both measurable and evaluative. However, although social mobility was not the goal, it did become the outcome of a system of pedagogy that tried to make literacy and its opportunities available to all, and schooling also had the effect of providing opportunities for individuals' social mobility.

Schooling and the test paradigm

The development of ability and intelligence tests in the early part of the twentieth century also played a major role in altering the literacy–schooling equation (Calhoun 1973; Fass 1989). Ability testing received a major impetus as a result of the military recruitment in the 1914–18 war. The psychometric paradigm that grew out of the early experience with tests lent a scientific management aspect to the practices and attainments of schooling (Resnick and Resnick 1977). This psychometric testing paradigm was based on an assumption that all cognitive skills were acquired through a developmental process that is universal; hence the assumption that if skills were precisely defined they could be satisfactorily measured. Failure in these tests thus came to be seen as an indication of an individual's lack of ability, not merely lack of learning or different social experience. At the same time, the increasing refinement of the technical instruments for selection and placement was part of the increasing bureaucratization of schooling (Katz 1971). The transformation of literacy from a moral virtue into a cognitive skill is the key to the twentieth-century changes in the ideology of literacy. The development of a national system of public education as well as a national standard of literacy has meant that schools have become one of the main channels for a selective transmission of knowledge. In such a situation much more emphasis is placed on increasing technological sophistication of teaching and learning techniques as a means to developing children's cognitive skills. Thus, the school, as Sorokin rather cynically wrote as long ago as 1927, becomes a sifting device for providing an educated workforce. In this attempt,

> the school does not really change people; rather, it sorts, labels and grades children for the labor market. In other words, schools do not make children cleverer; they merely certify for employers which ones are cleverer . . . From this standpoint *the school is primarily a testing, selecting, and distributing agency.*
>
> In its total the whole school system, with its handicaps, quizzes, examinations, supervision of the students, and their grading, ranking, evaluating, eliminating and promoting, is a very complicated 'sieve', which sifts 'the good' from 'the bad' future citizens, 'the able' from 'the dull', 'those fitted for high positions' from those 'unfitted'.
>
> quoted in A. Heath 1981: 25–6

If literacy is seen as a cognitive skill that can be learnt and acquired in specialized settings through individual effort, then the less successful at educational attainment can also be seen as socially less worthy.

Thus, Heath argues that the moral imperative behind social mobility in the twentieth century is that 'it depends upon seeing those left behind as intrinsically less worthy and as lacking in effort' (A. Heath 1981: 27). The effect of linking literacy to cognitive skills acquired through technologically developed schooling is that it reduces the learning of all these skills, including literacy, to a technical process that is regarded as socially neutral. Even more importantly, the technological approach to schooling masks the real influence of its social purpose and content. Nowhere is this more obvious than in the contemporary studies of school curricula (Apple 1979). The history of the creation of a society based on schooling as a legitimizing force has shown that equality of opportunity has been the main concern of modern educational theorists and that literacy skills have been its chief instrument.

Having established the linkage of schooling to literacy, we must now consider the effects of this linkage on the current 'crisis of literacy'. As mentioned at the beginning of this chapter, the broadening of the conception of *functional* literacy provides an insight into some of the changes, from a pluralistic concept of literacy for all to a standardized but multifaceted conception. As a result of these changes we have increased our demands on education, so that what is now seen as a failure of literacy teaching may really be attributable to the failure of schooling to bring about the social improvements that were originally hoped for as a consequence of a wider enfranchisement into literacy.

Hence, there are two strands to the pedagogy based on universal literacy and its influence on our views of society and individual opportunity. *One* strand is the assumption of the progressive value and benefit to individuals of schooling, leading to the development of a basically literate person. The beneficent effect of education is to raise the individual's understanding and ability to appreciate and control a greater amount of symbolic information. This notion of the uses of literacy as a widening of cultural interests is central to the liberal view of education as society's investment in human capital (see A. H. Halsey's (1975) discussion of Marshall's thesis). This is the view of the changing consciousness of education and of the uses of literacy that suggests the value of education was to enable individuals to make better use of their leisure. Education could thus be seen not only to promote industrial efficiency, but also to enable people to make better use of their lives if they became fully literate or, in terms of our initial discussion, developed a 'literate consciousness'. Furthermore, at the level of the reproduction of social relations in an industrialized society, the technological investment in education would provide for an improvement in the standards of work and of culture for all working people. These hopes for egalitarianism (now sometimes termed 'sentimental egalitarianism') have had a strong effect on educational theory and policy (see Karabel and Halsey's discussion in *Power and Ideology in Education,* 1977).

The *second* strand is the growth of technological sophistication within educational practice. It is generally believed that as the result of the refinement of testing techniques and the ability to produce what are seen as *neutral and objective evaluations of individual abilities* the educational system could become an efficient and effective selector of individuals. By this selection mechanism educational goals are differentiated in accordance with different ranges of ability. The development of an educational system based on the principles of the testing and development of individually assessed cognitive abilities has meant an increased emphasis on curricula that focus on 'individualized instruction' and a reliance on the production of test results as the goal of teaching and learning. The influence of these two strands of thinking on the conjoining of literacy to schooling has led to two rather different recent critical views of education.

The argument that the coming of universal full literacy in advanced industrial society should have, and could have, provided a basis for a socially fuller life for ordinary people has revived the concern that the linkage of schooling to literacy performance is not necessarily a beneficent one, and that those of lesser schooling ability are likely to be regarded as of lesser worth (Hoggart 1958; Williams 1961). More recent criticisms suggest that although schooling emphasizes an ever greater individualization of techniques to suit individual talents, there may really be greater control exerted at the social level on the shape and content of education, and therefore on its results and opportunities (Mehan 1996). What looks like greater freedom at the level of the individual in the classroom is, at the level of the 'hidden social curriculum', more likely to result in greater control on cultural understanding and learning, and to promote existing social orders through education (Bernstein 1973).

Criticism of the relationship between literacy and schooling has also been made from the second standpoint, that concerning the influence on cognitive processes. In a set of recent socio-cognitive comparative studies of the relationship of literacy to schooling, Scribner and Cole (1981) have found that the cognitive consequences of greater control over mental processes and symbolic information, attributed to literacy alone, may in effect be attributable to schooling itself. In a socio-cognitive comparative study among the Vai people in Liberia, Scribner and Cole found a society in which literacy and schooling were developed as two differentiated activities within a single social group. This naturally occurring experimental context enabled them to explore the cognitive consequences of schooling and of literacy without the one inevitably entailing the other, which, as we have seen, is an intrinsic part of any Western society. Even more importantly for this study, the tradition of literacy available to the Vai had a long history in a written script developed from the local, vernacular language, the

Vai script. This differed from the newly available medium of literacy in English in which schooling took place. Additionally there was literacy in reading the Koran in the classical Arabic. The results of Scribner and Cole's explorations into the consequences of literacy for cognitive changes showed that it was not literacy itself within the traditional medium but schooling which produced the cognitive changes and reasoning skills which have been thought of as concomitants of literacy. Their studies add a new dimension, from the perspective of the assessment of cognitive abilities, to the debate on the effects of literacy, and clearly demonstrate that schooling provides the essential context in which the skills of analysis and reasoning, often referred to as the decontextualization of language (see Simons and Murphy, chapter 9, this volume), are made available.

Conclusion: the uses of literacy in a schooled society

Finally, what in the present day are the consequences of conjoining literacy and schooling? Although literacy no longer has the moral force it once exerted, distinguishing the truly literate person of the nineteenth century as the good citizen, we have seen that there is still an ideology of literacy that underlies our contemporary ideas about its values. Our views on the uses of education have changed over the past century: whereas fifty years ago, schooling could be seen as providing a set of skills and abilities, which once learnt stood the learner in good stead throughout life, this is no longer the case. The idea of education as an entity with a single fixed value has altered. As historian Eugene Weber (1983) commented, the idea that education provided a fixed intellectual capital which could be depended on, and spent throughout life, has gone the way of the lifestyle in which people depended on a fixed monetary capital. As cultural capital, educational experience in contemporary society has to be both affirmed and demonstrated by educational documents and degrees (Bourdieu and Passeron 1977). Education in our advanced technological society is a process of selection and choice, throughout the years of schooling, and after. The educational selection test paradigm governs much of adult life, not only within schooling itself, but in the selection tests and evaluations that have become a powerful legitimizing force in the bureaucratic organization of contemporary society.

This chapter has shown, through its historical inquiry, that the equation of literacy and schooling is a changing one in which the balance between the values of these two has shifted greatly in the past seventy years. It is still possible, although this phenomenon, as Scribner and Cole (1981) and Street (1984) have shown, is increasingly restricted to 'developing' societies, to have literacy without schooling; but to have schooling without literacy is not possible. While it might seem, therefore, that literacy has the more influential role in public life, its position is mixed. Rather it is contemporary educational systems that, as the institutions of selection and placement for societies with complex labor needs, have made schooling the preeminent force. Literacy itself has become redefined within the context of schooling. And it has turned into what we now refer to as *schooled literacy*, that is, a system of decontextualized knowledge validated through test performances.

What are the consequences of these observations for subsequent studies? When studying literacy in classrooms we need to look not only at the acquisition of printed word, decoding skills but at all the abilities and practices that make up the school-language experience as a whole. We need to consider how the historically embedded and community-specific notion of language as discourse style and commonplace literacy are, or are not, realized in current school practice. It is our knowledge as practitioners of language, and as community members, that discourse skills, not language as an abstract linguistic phenomenon, are at the basis of our everyday knowledge. The emphasis upon grammar and correctness is, as Hymes (1980; 1996) points out, an historical feature of our society based upon the historical accident (common to many other societies) that the written literate language was different from the spoken vernacular at critical historical periods. The evolution of language style in contemporary English-speaking society is toward an ever closer interrelation between spoken and written forms of discourse (Kay 1977). However, this convergence has only served to further confuse our school-based notions of literacy that are still founded upon the earlier nineteenth-century notion of grammatical correctness. If we consider the equation of literacy and schooling we can see that the two elements of the equation are not equal.

We are in a very different position historically than at the beginning of the movement for mass education for literacy; and one which historically is irreversible. If it seems that any of these arguments take a similar line to those made in the early 1970s for deschooling society (Illich 1972), this view must immediately be dispelled, for a very different and opposing set of views is being put forward. As Feinberg commented, 'there is little reason to believe that with the absence of schools other agencies would not be found to reproduce labor and distribute work according to present patterns' (1983: 262); and it is this distribution of opportunity and reproduction that remains at the center of contemporary concern with the literacy and schooling relationship. In fact the rationale for the exploration in this chapter has been to indicate some of the wider social values about learning and literacy that still influence our views of this relationship. The thrust of the argument from the comparative, historical or anthropological, perspective shows that there is little reason to believe that schools, or some form of schooling, and the institution of educational systems will not continue to play an even larger role in the organization of modern societies. The social-reproduction argument made by Bourdieu and Passeron (1977) indicates the possibilities for a spiraling development of increasing power for education as each new generation of educational transmission is further supported by the reflection of its own success. Karabel and Halsey, quoting Bourdieu, argue that:

> To the extent that social hierarchies are transformed into academic hierarchies modern educational systems fulfill a function of legitimation that is more and more necessary to the perpetuation of the social order in societies with a complex division of labour. Education can play this role in that the placing of individuals in social and occupational hierarchies can be based on academic achievement as demonstrably certified through the educational process. 1977: 452

It is this sociological viewpoint that ties our historical exploration of the development of literacy and schooling to a consideration of contemporary uses of literacy both as an educational phenomenon and as an ideology. If it appears from this discussion that the broader, historically founded concept of literacy, owing something to the old pluralistic ideas of literacy expressed in Raymond Williams' notion of the 'long revolution', has been disenfranchised by the increasing power of the schooling paradigm, then it is to current schooling practices, to an examination of the goals and values current in educational practice that we must look to redress this balance. We should also consider that it may be that the need for the homegrown early nineteenth-century modes of literacy disappears in the complexity of our modern environments where communication with others who do not share our background is essential to daily life, and where we need exposure to and contact with other modes of thinking and reasoning, which can be given by modern professional schooling.

However, our conclusion for the present must be that while literacy test scores are the products of schooling, literacy as such is not and cannot be solely the outcome of schooling. In our advanced technological society some of the pluralistic set of skills and understandings that we describe as literacy are part of our common socio-historical heritage. Although the actual stylistic form of this heritage varies according to the social and linguistic history of the social community, no part of any modern society can realistically be called non-literate. Literacy for all purposes surrounds the school career of children (Szwed 1981). However, the purpose of schooling is to transform this commonplace literacy of contemporary society into a formal discipline of literate reasoning that takes the form of a set of technical skills. It is these technical skills that we take to be the subject of literacy tests and literacy rates. If these technical competencies become confounded with normative standards and prescriptive practices based on earlier views of literacy, as we have shown in this chapter, then confusion over the nature of literacy as a product of schooling results. Linguistic differences within the community become seen as sociolinguistic deficits and as the cause and product of the inability to use literate reasoning. It is against such an ideological prejudicial view of literacy that the study of classroom interaction as language practice attempts to produce a detailed and realistic account of the processes by which sociolinguistic understanding is gained and shared. How the conceptions and uses of literacy current in educational practice operate, both at the formal level and at the informal level of personal practice, will be explored in detail in the subsequent chapters.

3

Interactional sociolinguistics in the study of schooling

John J. Gumperz and Jenny Cook-Gumperz

Preamble

In the years since this volume was first published new theoretical paradigms and concepts have emerged, existing ones have been revised and incorporated into research methodologies, and new empirical studies have appeared which significantly add to knowledge. In what follows we will briefly review these ideas, and show they apply to the arguments made in the original version of the chapter as well as evaluate their import for educational communicative processes. We have decided to present the argument as a decade-by-decade progression of ideas and findings, the focus however remains on interactional sociolinguistics in the study of schooling.

The 1960s: from linguistic deficit to cultural and linguistic diversity

Systematic research on language in education began in the 1960s largely in response to concerns with what was then regarded as 'minority group school failure'. At the time it was assumed that while children may have come to school with different sociocultural backgrounds, what counted was how written language was presented in the classroom (Graham 1980). Wherever school failure was attributed to children's language use it was regarded as a matter of innate ability. Attempting to counter the biological determinism, and implicit racism of these views, educators turned to the work of anthropologists (Lewis 1960) and sociologists (Glazer and Moynihan (1963) to argue that the poverty and cultural deprivation of inner-city families had led to 'linguistic deprivation' reflected in non-standard grammar and inadequate reasoning ability, and that these were the major causative factors of school failure (Hess and Shipman 1966).

In the years preceding the publication of the first edition of this book, educational and political debates continued to center on this question. A number of explanations were proposed, some arguing that it was necessary to look to the social/cultural background and personal attributes of individual children for an explanation, others saw the differences as the consequence of culturally different learning styles and some proposed that language differences as such were the main cause of elementary school failure. These arguments together came to be known as the 'linguistic deficit thesis' suggesting that the cultural environment in which low-performing children grew up did not provide adequate exposure to adult talk, resulting in lack of verbal stimulation that in turn impeded cognitive development. Consequently, the argument went that, not having reached their full communicative potential these children lacked the background to profit fully from schooling (Bereiter and Engleman 1966; Deutsch 1967). This 'deficit thesis' was supported by anecdotal evidence based on students' pronunciation and classroom explanations. A variety of programs designed to compensate for the supposed deficiencies were initiated in response to these conjectures. Some sought to provide preschool activities to make up for the lack of verbal stimulation at home, others taught standard grammar on the assumption that children must learn appropriate grammatical rules as a basis for literacy.

Few educators knew that the premise underlying the remedial programs, failure to speak what was regarded as the 'standard language', directly conflicted with generally accepted linguistic findings since the beginning of the twentieth century. Direct field research on a wide range of languages throughout the twentieth century had established that the relationship between speaking and thinking is not as simple as that proposed in the deprivation/deficit thesis. The reasoning that underlay the educational-enrichment programs had truncated and distorted this relationship. The need for greater awareness of these linguistic findings and their consequences for education brought sociolinguists into the arena.

Sociolinguistics, which had come to be recognized as a separate discipline in the 1960s, offered a new approach to the study of language problems in education. Researchers worked in urban-school settings to develop systematic methods for the study of language use. It soon became apparent that the assumptions about minority students' speech underlying the remedial programs were simply unfounded. The very children who were said to be unresponsive and lacking in verbal ability in the classroom were often shown to be extraordinarily skilled communicators in out-of-school, and peer-group situations. The minority varieties they spoke were indeed significantly different from what was regarded as 'Standard English' but many of the forms that had been cited as evidence of verbal impoverishment could be shown to reflect underlying grammatical principles that were as systematic and cognitively complex as those of the school standard. Moreover, as is the case with any other language, these forms could be derived from earlier forms of speech by generally accepted laws of historical linguistic development (Rickford 1999). Notions of linguistic deprivation therefore had no more validity than the nineteenth-century evolutionists' notions of linguistic and cultural primitivity which anthropological linguists like Boas and Sapir and their students have so effectively disproved (Gumperz and Levinson 1996). There is no reason to assume that children whose everyday grammar deviated from the school standard could be judged as lacking the cognitive prerequisites for learning. Educational policies of the time had simply failed to recognize what is involved in situations of language diversity where speakers of distinct speech varieties have separate but equal grammatical and cultural systems.

The consequences of schools' failure to assess cultural minority students' verbal ability were most effectively brought out by William Labov, who in a now-classic paper 'The logic of non-standard English' (1972b) demonstrates the logical consistency of arguments made in everyday, African-American vernacular. Elsewhere, Labov (1982) in reviewing a well-known court case in Ann Arbor Michigan, where African-American parents had sued the school system for depriving their children of the opportunity for equal education, showed that children's language usage had attitudinal consequences that significantly affected not only their treatment in school, but also their academic placement. He argued that what is important about minority speech forms is perhaps not their function in 'conveying referential content', but rather the effect that a child's 'language usage patterns' can have on treatment in school that leads to stigmatization.

As a result, how the language used by students in the interactional environment of the classroom is evaluated and judged in relation to the school system's requirements becomes the major issue. The distinction made here between 'grammar' and 'language use' is an important one that has received a great deal of attention through sociolinguistic research. In the past, linguists had tended to claim that grammatical structure and lexicon alone could account for all that is significant about language, however as post-1960 research reveals, spoken language practices are grounded in additional systematic operational principles that go beyond grammatical rules to constrain interpretation. We will elaborate on this point later, but first a bit more about grammar.

Linguists now look at grammar as an abstract cognitive system that takes the form of internalized processing principles governing individuals' abilities to produce and understand intelligible sentences. There is overwhelming evidence to show that all children, no matter where and under what conditions they are raised, have full command of the grammatical system of their language by the age of four to five. Grammatical knowledge furthermore is used automatically without conscious reflection. It is not readily subject to overt recall and not always directly apparent from the surface form of what is said at any one time. To study a person's grammatical system, therefore, we cannot rely solely on casual observation of speech. Indirect methods of in-depth analysis are necessary and investigators require special training to enable them to test generalizations based on their own initial observation against native speaker assessments of grammaticality so as to guard against the tendency we all have of superimposing our own grammatical presuppositions on our ability to hear the speech of others (Gumperz 1982a). When these systematic linguistic methods were used to reanalyze the American Indian languages that nineteenth-century investigators had dismissed as structurally primitive, overly concrete, and lacking the means to express abstract thought, it was shown that these native languages had grammatical systems every bit as complex as any other. In many cases earlier investigators had failed to perceive key phonological and morphological distinctions, and had thus been unable to analyze the languages in systematic terms.

Educators' failure to recognize the effects of linguistic diversity may compound the very problems that they had originally set out to correct. If they define their task as simply correcting perceived deviations from 'Standard English', without recognizing that there are additional systematic communicative abilities that underlie children's verbal performance, remedial programs are unlikely to succeed. Schooling that does not understand the complexities of language use misjudges the difficulties that children face in confronting the classroom environment, so that in working to correct grammar alone one may end up by reinforcing linguistic and/or social prejudice.

Classroom learning environments

How can we study language effects on classroom learning environments? The bulk of the evaluation measures of classroom performance used in the decades preceding the publication of this paper were methods such as the Flanders System of Interaction Analysis (1970; Bellack 1968) that built on the tradition of small-group studies developed by Bales, Anderson and others, where interaction is analyzed in terms of the overt, referential function of utterances. When applied to classroom situations these methods have been useful in pointing to some important differences between largely middle-class suburban schools and largely lower-class inner-city schools. Leacock (1969) using interaction analysis in connection with her ethnographic work, found teachers in inner-city areas to be more prescriptive, more critical and less accepting of children's learning errors than their suburban colleagues. Although evaluations made in any one instance may seem like momentary phenomena that can soon be forgotten, if they influence formal evaluations and are set down in writing, they are then fed back into the individual children's bureaucratically constructed career profile (Rist 1970).

Useful as small-group measures are in demonstrating that cultural and class differences can create learning problems, conventional interaction measures have been unable to account for the full effects of classroom environments. One difficulty is that the coder's interpretation of behavior, rather than the actual behavior, is the basis for analysis. When interpretations differ, as is likely in socioculturally diverse settings, there is no way to safeguard against cultural bias in the evaluation of performance. As a result, it becomes difficult to distinguish differences in ability and attitude from differences in cultural style. Without reference to the actual processes of interaction, nothing can be said about how participants make sense of particular tasks.

Initial insights into what takes place and what may go awry in the classroom come from the autobiographical writings of teachers themselves that were popular in the 1960s (Holt 1967; Kohl 1967; Kozol 1967). These writings vividly illustrated the problems teachers encountered in going about their everyday tasks of conducting lessons, evaluating performance, keeping order and otherwise organizing proper learning environments. They illustrate how the need to conform to the demands of the school system and to meet established test requirements often limits the individual teacher's ability to deal with students' learning needs and to accommodate differences in students' social background. In this way they draw attention to the gap between official descriptions of curricula and instructional goals and what is actually accomplished on the ground. Teachers' autobiographical accounts are valuable because they focus attention on problems that those familiar with schooling practices know exist but have not been systematically examined. The significance of autobiography is that classrooms are treated as social systems where what is accomplished is not simply the imparting of information, i.e. transferring information from teachers to students, but where the learning process is influenced by the social characteristics of the students themselves. Both, student–peer-group relations and teacher–student relationships, as well as the organizational requirements of the social system of the school, affect the transmission and the products of learning.

The recognition that diversity is as much a matter of language use as it is of culture suggested a need for studies of schooling processes that could provide a better understanding of the role of language in educational achievement, and of the ways in which language entered into the school's social environment. Educational research in various fields had given a variety of different answers to the problem of what causes the so-called cultural difference in school performance. Most policy-makers tended to rely on measures of schooling outcomes such as unsatisfactory test performance in reading, and other literacy skills. Conclusions were based on statistical relationships between these outcomes and macro-social variables such as class, ethnicity and income. Language, if mentioned at all, was cited as just one of these factors. Moreover, in macro-studies language is treated as a unitary holistic variable, not as a context-bound system of linguistic choices carrying social meaning.

Speech communities of all kinds are, as William Labov (1972a) argues, 'intrinsically diverse' and their fissures are linguistically marked by multilingualism, multi-dialectalism or stylistic variability. In conducting their daily affairs, community members must select among the options of the community's linguistic repertoire depending on who their interlocutors are and what they know about them. The principles governing the selection process are therefore both linguistic and social. Since it is this selection process that shapes the judgments and decisions made in school classrooms, it affects what knowledge is passed on from one generation to the next. Literacy acquisition, as several chapters in this book show, is clearly constrained by social/cultural forces.

The 1970s: teaching as a linguistic process and the mismatch hypothesis

In the 1970s, as attention moved away from sentence-level grammar and reference to language use, empirical research on classroom communicative exchanges became a main focus of sociolinguistic attention. Urban schools, it was realized, mirror the society at large, where individuals alternate among the varieties that make up the community's linguistic repertoire in accordance with context-specific norms. Remedial grammar instruction that so far had failed to improve underachieving children's performance could not be the correct solution. Attention therefore shifted to the mismatch between the language of the home and that of the classroom, as an explanation for continued differential performance. The immediate challenge for linguists and sociolinguists became how to design learning activities and curricula, so that culturally different students could benefit, and how to bridge the gap between home and school (Heath 1983). From this point of view the new linguistically sensitive teacher would act as a cultural broker who mediated among the different codes in children's own verbal repertoire so that teaching programs would build on, rather than devalue, what children learn at home (Piestrup 1973). However such research on classroom communicative processes needs to be based on first-hand detailed ethnographic knowledge.

Ethnography of communication and communicative competence

The ethnography-of-communication approach provided detailed evidence of learning processes as systematic ethnographic analysis built on observations in natural interactive settings. The notion of communicative competence is central to this study and was originally proposed in order to account for the fact that to be effective in everyday social settings speakers and listeners depend on knowledge that goes beyond phonology, lexicon and abstract grammatical structure. Language usage, it was argued, is governed by culture and context-specific norms that constrain both the choice of communicative options and the interpretation of what is said (Hymes 1971; Gumperz 1982a).

The significance of this concept and its application to the task of specifying what is involved in the ability to produce and comprehend messages are best understood within the context of the academic atmosphere of the 1960/70s. The then-predominant theories of generative grammar drew a sharp distinction between a) *competence*, defined as the abstract knowledge that enables speakers of a language to identify grammatical sentences and recognize structural relationships among them, and b) *performance*, what is actually said at any one time and therefore is always context determined. Only the former was seen as rule-governed and subject to formal analysis, while the latter was regarded primarily as a matter of personal choice or inter-individual variation, and not part of linguistics as such. By applying the term competence to performance, ethnographers of communication put forward the claim that there exist measurable regularities at the level of social structure and social interaction that are as much a matter of subconsciously internalized ability as are grammatical rules proper. Control of these regularities is a precondition of effective communication (Gumperz 1982a; Hymes 1974).

The difference between generative grammarians' and sociolinguists' view of language is of both theoretical and practical significance. It has important implications for what counts as linguistic data and for the way these data are elicited and analyzed through fieldwork. The generative grammarian's method of operation is basically a deductive one in which linguists, using their own knowledge of abstract grammatical processes, construct sample sentences illustrating significant theoretical issues and then consult native speakers as to whether or not they believe these sentences to be grammatical. Ethnographers of communication, on the other hand, take an inductive, empirical approach by recording natural speech in a specific social group, and then go on to determine how such speech varies from speaker to speaker and situation to situation.

Rather than accounting for their observations by postulating abstract systems of rules and categories, which they assume any one individual must control in order to speak the language, ethnographers of communication argue that while grammar is generally shared, there are in any one human population additional systematic, socially distributed and therefore communicatively significant patterns of language use – or 'communicative practice' – which are not shared by all individuals. The communicative resources of any human collectivity can best be described as made up of a repertoire, that is an overall system consisting of a range of subsystems, not all of which are known by all individuals. The assumption is that in any one encounter participants must select among the repertoire's options in accordance with principles of linguistic and social etiquette specific to the situation at hand. Linguistic variability thus becomes a communicative phenomenon to be accounted for as part of sociolinguistic analysis. Neither the range of linguistic variants nor the grammatical relations among sets of variants, and the norms that govern their employment, can be known beforehand: these must all first be discovered through ethnographic observation and analysis. Thus, on this view any system of linguistic analysis which relies primarily on linguists' use of their *own,* and necessarily limited, knowledge to determine what sentences are significant, cannot uncover new, hitherto unknown facts about variation.

Ethnographies of communication have done a great deal to document the diversity of vernacular, communicative conventions throughout the world. We now have ample evidence to demonstrate the sociolinguists' contention that the criteria by which we evaluate what counts as persuasive, or what is appropriate, or even grammatical speech are always context-bound and can vary from setting to setting. A new fieldwork tradition has emerged which begins with the isolation of identifiable communities or subgroups in a region. Ethnographic observation of everyday activities is employed first, to describe the cultural norms and values that are relevant to speaking, and then to isolate characteristic speech events and activities in which they are realized. Analyses of speech activities concentrate on isolating time-bound sequences of interaction. These are characterized in terms of their sequential structure, participants' roles, rights and duties, and in terms of the communicative and linguistic options employed. Linguistic analysis can then be used to determine the phonological, syntactic and lexical characteristics of constituent varieties so as to isolate both categorical (shared) and variable (non-shared) features. The goal is to determine the context-specific rules or norms that constrain what variants are used when, by whom, and under what circumstances in a community. Viewed in historical perspective, the early work of ethnography of communication was basically descriptive in nature and dealt with economically simple societies and local cultures, but it had significant relevance to more complex urban societies and to diverse educational settings.

The notion of communicative competence (Hymes 1972) was developed to deepen the theoretical response to the complexities and the variety of communicative options that speakers use to signal what they intend to convey. It thus seemed particularly relevant to the educational arena. What the work on communicative competence does is question the common assumption that linguistic regularities must be studied through sentence-level analysis that in the past had shaped most research in education. For example, for African-American groups we now have an impressive series of detailed case studies revealing regularities at the discourse level of performance style that seem to have survived forced-transplantation from West Africa to the Caribbean and to the United States (Baugh 2000; Morgan 2002; Rickford 1999). These regularities take the form of speech routines occurring in formal performances as well as in everyday speech. They play an important role in signaling what an interaction is about, and what is expected at any one point. They enable both analysts and participants to obtain replicable insights into what transpires in school in terms of their own historically based rhetorical traditions.

Ethnographies of classroom language and interaction

The ethnography-of-communication approach led to some of the most revealing of the classroom ethnographies that shed light on the systematic differences between home and school learning experiences. In one of the first and most influential of these, Susan Philips (1972) compared patterns of classroom participation among reservation-reared native-American children and among non-Indian children. She found that the Indian children participated more enthusiastically and performed more effectively in teaching situations which minimized both the obligation of individual students to perform in public and the need for teachers to control performance styles and correct errors. Preferences for these contexts reflected the kinds of relationships that the children were accustomed to on the reservation, where lateral peer networks of children in groups were more important in learning than hierarchical, role-differential networks of adults and children. Philips attributes the generally poor school performance of Indian children to the far greater frequency in conventional classrooms of conditions that for them create unfamiliar and threatening frameworks of participation. She proposed the notion of 'participant structure' to characterize the constellation of norms, mutual rights, and obligations that shape social relationships, determine participants' perception of what has transpired, and influence the acquisition of formal skills.

In a classic, comparative study in cotton-mill towns of the US South East, Shirley Brice Heath (1983) worked in three communities, African-American working class, white working class, and a mainstream community, showing in vivid ethnographic detail how certain aspects of learning activities that outside observers may term deviant or dysfunctional are actually firmly grounded in the interactive practices and learning styles of the home. She finds significant differences in the interactive norms that govern instructional encounters in the three communities. Each has its own rhetorical values, and its conventions are internally consistent. Heath goes on to show through discussions of classroom behavior and teaching strategies how these differences in discourse patterns affect information transfer. This study argues persuasively for new curricula that can account for similar variations in children's home background and language. Thus, the work in the 1970s classrooms, responding to the concern over the mismatch hypothesis, showed that use of what was regarded as stigmatized linguistic forms was not a matter of free choice and that in consequence these led to classroom misunderstandings.

Most of the 1970s ethnographic studies of learning processes cited here directly address the issue of the cultural/linguistic mismatch between home and school language then regarded as a major cause of school failure. However, as the classroom ethnographic studies indicate, the main issue is not one of instructional content and techniques but rather it is the learning environment created through the interaction of setting, student and teacher language use, and course content that then in turn affects the transmission of knowledge. If we accept the basic assumption that teaching and learning must be treated as interactive processes in which language use, both in its referential and connotative meaning, differs between home and school, then the transmission of information is likely to be disrupted as repeated misinterpretations influence motivation to learn. But it is not the disruption per se that causes the problem, rather as some ethnographic studies showed, what is at issue is interpretation. Non-standard language forms become interpreted in such a way that they lead to group stigmatization resulting in prejudice that is difficult to overcome through classroom teaching. What is or is not accomplished in the classroom is a function of what is communicated through the interplay of pedagogical strategies, and how participants perceive each other's sociolinguistic practices (Gumperz and Cook-Gumperz 1979).

As soon as we employ qualitative ethnographic techniques we are led to examine more general questions concerning the acquisition of knowledge, and to notice additional cultural differences in styles of learning. More recent theorizing went beyond the confines of the mismatch hypothesis. Anthropologists and comparative cognitive psychologists working in non-literate and in literate but economically simple societies have called attention to informal or experiential learning processes, and the context-bound procedures by which members acquire the locally valued skills and knowledge they need to carry on their daily affairs (Goody 1983; Greenfield

1972). Scribner and Cole, working in Liberia (1981), demonstrate that in societies where formal schooling is a new experience, even a little schooling – as little as six months or a year – makes a critical difference, both in strategies of learning and understanding. These informal styles differ from known classroom-learning processes in several important respects. The outside observer will note relatively little direct verbal instruction. Skills tend to be acquired through observation and imitation. As with the native-Americans described by Philips (1972), and Erickson and Mohatt (1982), evaluations, criticism, or other types of immediate verbal feedback are rare. It seems to be taken for granted that the child is able to learn and that progress will eventually be made, so that adults do not expect to test for progress at various stages of acquisition through feedback questioning. The details of such experiential learning vary from society to society and in relation to different tasks, yet all experiential learning takes place against a background of specific shared, communicative conventions and understandings of what goals are to be achieved. Strategies for participating in everyday learning situations outside the school context reveal significant discrepancies from traditional psychological models of the learning processes (Lave and Wegner 1991).

Going beyond the mismatch hypothesis we see that the very nature of the interactive situations constraining the acquisition process, and the participant structures by which we recognize that learning is taking place, are all subject to cultural variation. While we can go some way toward recognizing differences of language and cultural norms in classroom practices, if in addition we admit the validity of the claim that strategies of learning differ, then the problem of dealing with cultural difference in schooling becomes more difficult. Differences become apparent when transferring these findings to contemporary urban settings where the schooling paradigm of formal education and universal literacy has existed for over a century. In comparing learners across cultural groups, we are not dealing with a simple distinction between those who *have* and those who *do not* have certain types of abstract knowledge, but rather with systematic differences in notions of what learning is about, and differences in the criteria used to judge what has been learned and achieved. It is this issue that has continued to present a challenge in studies of schooling.

It became evident that if we wanted to deal adequately with linguistic phenomena in classroom interaction we needed to focus on discourse; that is, on how language works as part of an integrated system of communication. Early systems of analyzing classroom discourse such as Sinclair and Coulthard (1975) sought to overcome the objections to the small-group analysts' reliance on counts of isolated content categories by proposing that the structure of classroom discourse arises from sequential constraints on the sequencing of verbal acts, such that one type of act is likely to follow or be followed by other specific types. That is, communication among teachers and students is conceptualized as moves in a Wittgensteinian language game that follows implicit rules of action and takes grammatical form as well as lexical content into account in describing the functioning of classroom moves. Although they constituted an important step forward, both these analyses are limited by the fact that they are based on data collected in formal instructional situations where teachers were encouraged to follow predetermined lesson plans. Only the actual teaching part of the lesson was examined; and individual teachers' styles are described in terms of profiles of utterance functions in which since the function is taken as a given, what is in fact studied is the significance of teachers' and students' moves in relation to the stated lesson goal.

The 1980s: classroom communication as a discourse process

By the 1980s attention had shifted from communicative competence as reflected in phonological and grammatical variability to discourse as a wider frame for the exploration of everyday interaction and understanding at the micro level. Studies of linguistic variability had called attention to the complexity of language issues in education, and highlighted the difficulties and injustices that arise when this complexity is ignored. Yet the mechanisms by which language usage affects learning and the question of how pejorative stereotyping can be avoided were still far from clear. Is it enough to instruct teachers on recent research findings in linguistics or sociolinguistics to expose or avoid pejorative attitudes? Ethnographic studies of classroom processes were successful in calling attention to previously unnoticed features that affect classroom learning, through analysis of interaction processes concentrating on speech acts as such and on speech events as frames that constrain context-bound expectations. Communicative competence, the ability to participate in situated discourse, the knowledge that it requires and how it varies with social background had taken on a new importance (Gumperz and Hymes 1972/86) in which expectations about suitable topics and themes, norms and appropriate styles of speaking played a key role in the interpretation of what was said. By the late 1970s and 1980s micro-ethnographic studies of classrooms (Erickson 1982; McDermott 1974) and their social organization shed new light on these questions.

The analytical point of departure became speech activities as they occur within the context of specific 'speech events' that could be seen as constituting micro-social systems, no longer language usage as such. Certain instructional practices and misunderstanding between teachers and students were found to result from constraints that could only be revealed by in-depth examination of turn-by-turn interactive exchanges, so that learning could no more be treated as a linear information flow where teachers' messages are automatically received and processed by students. Learning came to be seen as an interactive process where all participants must work to elicit attention and the ability of any one individual to do this is constrained by the nature of the group's shared communicative history developed over the course of interaction. The group's participation structures can vary along with communicative structure to make an effective learning environment (Goodwin 2001). In other words learning in a classroom becomes an interaction of several systems or mutually dependent levels of meaning. Erickson (2004), grounding his argument in data from naturally organized classroom interaction, refers to these as socio-ecological systems. In this way the organizational constraints of the group on classroom environments, teachers' interactional strategies and communicatively based evaluations of students' initiations and responses make up the micro-order of the classroom.

Micro-ethnographic studies of discourse and participation in the classroom

Empirical studies based on the ethnography of communication in which culture, contexts, and codes were explored in descriptive detail (Cazden, John and Hymes 1972/85) had questioned earlier simplistic cultural-difference models. Further shifts toward detailed ethnographic work appeared in the next two decades from the micro-ethnographic analyses of classroom-discourse processes such as those of Erickson and his students (Erickson and Mohatt 1982; Florio 1978) and other studies of classroom discourse (Cazden 2001; Green and Wallat 1981). The value of these more detailed micro-studies is that they provide replicable ways of discovering constraints on interaction that while not readily noticeable nevertheless guide interaction and reveal unstated conventions and standards of judgment that may influence teacher evaluation of student performance. While earlier small-group analyses tended to assume that the classroom can be treated as an undifferentiated social system where teacher and students interact as individuals, micro-ethnography indicates that this is not the case. Much of what children do is influenced by home- or school-based peer relationships. In addition, other interactive processes are at work within each setting and at various times throughout the day, and it is the nature of such subgroup relationships (within these varied settings) that determines the contexts which guide and channel behavior. In Florio's study, for example, children move sequentially through different types of participant structures in the course of a typical class session. Some of these structures have established names, such as 'show and tell' (or 'sharing time', which Michaels describes in chapter 5). Each of these learning contexts involves different modes of interaction and learning, and different standards for the evaluation of behavior and for the interpretation of what goes on. As part of the learning process, children must become familiar with what these structures are; they must understand how transitions between structures are signaled, and what behavioral strategies are effective in gaining the teacher's attention or in securing the cooperation of peers. In other words, familiarity with the subtleties of classroom social organization is a precondition for gaining access to learning opportunities. Observations from a multi-year ethnographic study of San Francisco Bay area classrooms on which several of the chapters in this volume are based will illustrate this point. For example, much of the teacher's efforts during the students' first year of school went into developing routines appropriate to particular classroom activities. In carrying out this socialization task, the teacher relied on set formulaic phrases which she used repeatedly and pronounced with special emphasis, both to announce activities or mark transitions from one to another and to sanction inappropriate actions. Accordingly, what she called 'rug time' was announced by: 'OK, everybody come to the rug.' Directions to stop working and get ready for recess or cleanup were prefaced by: 'OK, everybody freeze.' Sanctioning often took indirect forms, such as: 'You can wear a hat in class when I wear a hat,' or 'I can see all the sharks on the rug.' What is special about these phrases is not so much their actual content as the way in which they are spoken and the context in which they are used. It is this manner of articulation that lends them their quasi-formulaic character and their special significance for the class that marks them as routines (Cook-Gumperz, Gumperz and Simons 1981).

In studies such as these we can see that the teacher, by means of what she says, seeks to set up a predictable organizational structure so that children know how and when to recognize a context. Once established, the context creates frames that guide students in interpreting the teacher's utterances. Similarly, Mehan's analysis of data from an ethnographic study of an experimental, multiethnic, inner-city classroom avoids a priori assumptions about message function by studying message content in terms of empirically observable features of the instructional routines of which they are part (Mehan 1979). His work builds on the sociological tradition of conversational analyses of turn-taking and sequencing of conversational moves (Garfinkel and Sacks 1970; Goodwin 1981; Levinson 1983). By treating conversation as an interactive process in which speakers and audiences cooperate to create the conditions that make understanding possible, conversational analysts have shown that speaking is not simply a matter of individuals saying what they want when they want. All conversations follow organizational principles of their own which are in large part independent of the grammatical structure of component utterances. These principles are illustrated by the conversational analysts' concept of adjacency pairs: question–answer, greeting–greeting, request–acknowledgment (Sacks, Schegloff and Jefferson 1974). Although produced by different speakers, the two members of each pair are reciprocally related in the sense that the first sets the condition for the occurrence of the second while the second is dependent on the prior occurrence of the first. Furthermore, once a first member has been produced, the speaker must cede the floor to another who is expected to produce a suitable reply. Following similar lines of reasoning, Mehan argues that instructional talk differs from ordinary conversation in that there are not two components but three: an evaluative rejoinder always follows the response to an initial move, resulting in a tripartite system of initiation–response–evaluation (1979). Successful accomplishment of such interactional routines requires teacher and student to establish an interactive rhythm so as to synchronize their moves. Mehan further argues that what is conveyed by means of these synchronized exchanges significantly affects what is learnt in classroom lessons.

Such detailed work demonstrates that discourse cannot be seen simply as a sequence of semantically independent sentences. Discourse consists of interrelated sequences of moves and countermoves, each sequence being marked by a beginning, middle and end, such that the temporal ordering of arguments and of speaker exchange constrains what can be said, and how it is interpreted. Reliance on such principles of organization enables participants to guide the flow of an interaction and create the conditions for interpretation to occur. Like the action sequences analyzed by micro-ethnographers, the ordering of conversational moves is interactionally achieved without explicit overt instruction, and relevant verbal strategies must be learned indirectly through active participation in the instructional processes. We often become aware of what we do only when something goes wrong. Important as it is in revealing the interactive character of verbal exchanges and showing that information transfer is interactively managed, focus on the organizational underpinnings of verbal communication is not enough. We need a fuller theory of communication to show what it is about participants' linguistic and cultural background and their ideology of learning that affects their ability to get things done in class, and why it is that differences in background can lead to differential learning in apparently similar contexts. What is required is a speaker-oriented approach to interpretation that enables us to look directly at the interpretive processes that underlie the individual's perception of what goes on in the classroom. Research in linguistic pragmatics and speech-act theory provides some basic insights into the nature of interpretive processes (Austin 1962; Cole and Morgan 1975; Levinson 1983).

Interaction as communicative strategy: the interactional sociolinguistic approach

While micro-ethnographic analysis focuses on constraints on interaction, interactional sociolinguistics, hereafter IS, is concerned with interpretation as such and with speakers' and listeners' meaning assessments in interaction. Departing from earlier traditions of semantic analysis that tended to concentrate on the relation of words to referents (that is objects and concepts in the extralinguistic world), IS adopts Paul Grice's (1971) position that meaning must be defined in terms of the effect that a sender intends to produce by means of a message. Thus speech acts and activities defined in terms of illocutionary force or speaker's intent, rather than propositional content or reference, become the main units of analysis. As speech act analysis shows, conversationalists rely on context-dependent presuppositions and other types of extralinguistic knowledge along with referential meaning to make interpretations that often have little direct relation to dictionary meaning. If for example a teacher in class is heard to say, 'I don't see any hands' when she has asked a question and several children call out, her utterance will be interpreted as a request for a show of hands and therefore as an indirect request for silence, rather than as a simple descriptive statement. In other words, we build on our knowledge of what classrooms are like and what the goal of instruction is in order to infer what is intended in any particular utterance or utterance sequence.

Moreover, knowledge of the events and what is accomplished is shared by groups of people. From this perspective, language in the classroom can be seen as part of the language of the school setting. Particular classroom situations are held together through regular speech routines that constitute the daily practices of teachers and students. That is, there are features of these routines that are similar across all classroom contexts, and some that vary as schooling progresses. Classroom-ethnography studies in different age grades, covering interaction in and out of school, show regularity in speech event occurrences and in the norms that govern particular events.

Speech events can be further explored by looking at participant structure, that is, the norms of participation that exist in different cultural settings. The type and quantity of interaction that make up any event can be described as the speech economy of a group or setting (Erickson 2004; Hymes 1996). By examining the patterns of events over time and space (i.e. in different settings, different schools or classrooms) an interactional perspective makes it possible to see that any one set of events, while a critical part of the structuring of social life, does not constitute the whole communicative experience of members of a social group. It can be shown that our knowledge or expectations of these events play an important part in our interpretation of what transpires. We can assume that this knowledge becomes part of the interpretive frames or schemata that channel our understanding. The degree to which frames are known, how framing of information is signaled and learnt, and to what extent learning is a matter of sociocultural background, are crucial to our understanding of the communicative dimensions of the interactional and instructional processes. Schematic knowledge thus provides the overall perspective that enables us to integrate what we hear with what we already know, and to fit individual bits of information into a coherent argument. When such knowledge is not shared the same message, looked at in terms of overt content, may be interpreted differently by different individuals.

The indirect inferencing illustrated here is an inescapable feature of everyday communication. Successful instruction depends on it to a degree that is not ordinarily realized. Although it is the overt aim of school talk, and part of our implicit notion of pedagogy, that all relevant information must be explicitly lexicalized or put into words, it is also true that such explicitness can never be achieved in practice. What teachers and grammarians may see as simple, clear utterances (for example, instructions such as 'Draw a line on the bottom of the page') can only be put into action with reference to a complex set of understandings that must be negotiated in the course of classroom interaction. It is in this context that our discussion, in the earlier part of this chapter, of the teacher's efforts to organize class settings, set up learning environments, and label and define instructional tasks must be understood. Speakers and hearers depend on each other's cooperation in creating such understandings which set the preconditions for effective information transfer. By the above actions teachers create the conditions that make learning possible. The interactional sociolinguistic approach focuses on the interplay of linguistic, contextual and social presuppositions that interact to create the conditions for classroom learning. Analysis highlights key instructional activities that ethnographic observations have shown may be crucial to the educational process and to specific classroom or other settings. These activities are realized through definable speech activities that stand out against the background of everyday conversation; they have characteristics that can be understood and can be described by ethnographers and recognized by participants.

What does schematic knowledge consist of and how is it conveyed? Discourse analysts in the past have tended to treat schemata as matters of extralinguistic knowledge, that is, knowledge that speakers learn to utilize in the normal course of the language acquisition process and which all competent speakers can be said to possess. But if we take an IS perspective on understanding as negotiated through conversational processes, serious questions arise as to the extent to which the requisite knowledge is shared. Conversation of all kinds presupposes active cooperation between producers of messages and listeners who provide feedback, either by means of direct responses or through other forms of back channel signaling. Such cooperation cannot be taken for granted. To enlist conversational cooperation potential speakers must induce others to cooperate; that is, they must somehow convey at least some advance information on what the outcome of the extended exchange may be. Once talk has begun, moreover, initial schemata are subject to constant change, and changes have to be negotiated in the course of the interaction.

Further problems arise with the allocation of turns at speaking. Individuals do not automatically have space to present or develop an argument; they must work to retain their turn by enabling others to predict where their own responses can fit in. In this way we can see that interpretation of all kinds, even in classroom instructional situations which are normally seen as task-oriented instrumental activities focusing on objective (i.e. fact-oriented) information transfer, depends on participants' use of signaling strategies to establish contexts favorable to communicative effectiveness. Work on interaction in the classroom concentrates on these phenomena while taking off from an ethnographic basis that is concerned with the description and analysis of key speech events in classrooms. In order to re-examine in detail the occurrence of events, such methods focus on the processes by which definable events are established as special sequences within the stream of activities that make up daily interaction. For classroom members the daily movement through time, event to event, is part of the essential communicative knowledge of when an event is happening, how a shift in activity is taking place and is recognizable as such, how such a shift becomes a new context which tells what to expect next, and how to interpret what is said. We assume that interaction in classroom settings, like verbal interaction everywhere, is guided by a process of conversational inference which relies on participants' perception of verbal and nonverbal cues that *contextualize* the stream of daily talk activity. By means of these cues participants recognize speech activities as wider sequences of talk through which contexts are recognizable. In this way schemata are created and signaled by participants to act as frames for each other's situated interpretations. These signaling cues together create a nexus of significations by which interaction progresses and through which the moves make up specific events. Although these transitory and transitional conversational phenomena have a situated and localized meaning reference, at the same time they provide a continuing thematic thread by which participants across time build up a specific inferential chain of understandings (Gumperz 1982a). Thus, our task as Interactional Sociolinguists in contemporary educational settings is to chart the process by which models of educability are put into daily practice and to uncover the implicit theory of learning that informs our choice of model.

The studies in this volume are concerned with the different ways teachers and pupils together, in classrooms, construct the day-to-day reality of the social process of knowledge transmission. But the main aim is both to be more specific, by looking at the actual mechanisms of daily communication in school settings, and to show how these processes relate to the wider system of knowledge creation. In what follows, we will explore briefly how this can be achieved in practice. Although not wishing to give a simple answer to a very complex set of questions, we can point to some uses of the notion of communicative competence as a diagnostic tool. If we treat the social transmission of knowledge as a product of communicative experience and interactively created communicative understanding, we can expose some of the hitherto unnoticed complexities involved in learning. We can see that schooling is not just a matter of exposure to classroom instruction. It is significantly affected by how information is made available through the curriculum, how skills are defined and cognitive abilities evaluated; that is, the form that knowledge takes and access to it are both socially defined and interactively constrained. We cannot therefore assume that the problem of cultural variability in the classroom can be solved by changes in the language of instruction or teaching style and strategies, if these are taken as single factors to be manipulated out of context. The task of exploring the cultural transmission of knowledge as communicative competence requires us to see the face-to-face relations of teacher to student as embedded interactively within a context of classroom procedures and practices within schools, which themselves are part of the institutional complex of educational policies and ideology. Ultimately, such a perspective requires the intermeshing of two traditions of research, one, looking at the generation of systems of educational knowledge and two, the more interactional perspective of classroom ethnography and sociolinguistics. It is this issue that is raised in many of the criticisms that were made in the late 1980s of the recently established sociolinguistic and ethnographic traditions.

The 1990s and beyond: discourse, ideology and communicative practice

Why was sociolinguistics that had been so much a part of educational research in danger of being sidelined by the1990s? Much of the work on classroom discourse had come to concentrate on micro-interactional processes like the turn-by-turn mechanics of speech exchanges, and on the context-specific details of interpretation. This focus on detailed discourse processes was criticized for ignoring the broader issues of learning, school failure and the continued reproduction of social inequality. Critics of sociolinguistic approaches to discourse argued that in order to deal with educational problems of equity what should be examined is the structuring of society and its educational selection, not micro-ethnographic studies that required multiple longitudinal investigations to be validated. Critical for any consideration of educational achievement is the need to see the practices of speaking and interaction within the wider context of the educational assumptions and ideologies held by members of the society (Gee 1996). That is, we must provide for the linking of explanation at the level of policy and institutional process with understanding at the more detailed level of daily educational practice. As in sociological research on the transmission of knowledge, critical-discourse analysis began to deal with factors of power, economic resources, and occupational and class division within the broader society (Fairclough 1996; Blommaert 2005). How these tensions are transmitted as school-based learning and manifest themselves through classroom communication is a central theme of Bourdieu's classic work on education and cultural capital (Bourdieu and Passeron 1977). However Bourdieu's notion of language was limited to the established structuralist perspective as Collins shows (1996). Analysis of discourse can provide a further basis for showing how such cultural presuppositions and processes affect interpretation of what is said, and thus the social action that follows. These interpretations are in large part a matter of inferences, along with grammar and lexicon, they rely on context-specific and therefore culturally embedded background knowledge of the social world.

In the 1990s we begin to see a body of work that goes beyond local classroom situations, that shows how insights derived from micro-analysis can shed light on concerns that are beyond the immediate frame of the local situation. It is at this point that some recent studies find their beginning. From ethnographic studies we can see how social factors and the climate of opinion outside the classroom enter into the classroom learning process, and how differences in discourse interpretations establish long-term institutional practices. In other words, prevailing attitudes and preconceptions mediated through discourse affect evaluations of students both in specific classroom situations and as part of an institutional educational record. Mehan (Mehan et al. 1983; Mehan 1996) shows how teachers' educational knowledge and communicative expectations both construct an institutional ideology; and how this ideology in turn is communicated in classrooms through teachers' discursive assessments and interactional strategies that determine students' institutional careers. In a study of school decision-making processes of school referral Mehan et al. established that the complex interaction between communication in the classroom, teacher's evaluation of a student's behavior and the longer-term processes of assembling a school record of demonstrable abilities together serve to constitute a student's school-life career (1983). In the aggregate these careers provide for the social reality of schooling and its outcomes for different social classes and groups. In generating such records the decision-making process is not subject to a simple linear string of decisions which Mehan calls 'centralized rational decision making,' but rather decisions are arrived at through a chain of face-to-face local interactional judgments which are influenced by all the subtleties of verbal and non-verbal cues that have been uncovered in the studies of classroom discourse. The interactional accomplishment of bureaucratic records provides a needed theoretical link between micro-discourse phenomena and the long-term outcomes of schooling.

The more recent discourse studies show that stylistic variation is both inter- and intra-individual relying not just on group discourse conventions, but on an individual's choice of an historically and socially informed selection of discourse options in the accomplishment of everyday communicative tasks (Duranti and Goodwin 1992; Gumperz and Cook-Gumperz in press). For example, by examining the cultural presuppositions that enter into the interpretation of everyday discourse and the range of individually chosen options we can show how stereotypes arise. Where discourse group conventions are shared within a small group it is much easier to speak one's mind or make a convincing argument or let one's hair down and feel at ease. That is peer-group sociability rests on shared discourse conventions established over time in a small group (Goodwin 1990). While intergroup communication may have more risks for misunderstanding and more formal, less relaxed styles the rhetorical effectiveness of in-group communication by contrast is seen as essentially confirming of identity. Other studies such as those by Eckert (2000), Hewitt (1986) and Rampton (1996; 2006) show that minority groups consciously choose to use publicly stigmatized language forms as symbols of resistance to the dominant system and as rallying points for peer-group solidarity.

These selected examples give some indication of the range of issues now a part of the study of language in education. Many questions remain such as: why is it that dialect or language distinctions continue to be preserved in a postmodern urban society? What is the value attached to linguistic diversity? Given the evidence of discourse differences and communicative difficulties in classrooms are there also important shared conventions? Questions that follow from these studies may shape research agendas in language and educational process for the coming decade.

We conclude with a brief comment. In recent years linguistic anthropological thinking on language in human interaction has greatly expanded and sharpened in focus. Here we confine ourselves to just a few remarks. First, our ideas of language use, although they build on insights outlined above, have begun to change. The distinction between formal linguistic structure constituted by abstract grammar and referential semantics and 'language use' is replaced by a new linguistic anthropological paradigm integrating the pragmatics of Charles Saunders Peirce into linguistic analysis (Silverstein 1993). The basic idea here is that verbal communication always involves two distinct types of signs, the symbolic or grammatical and the indexical. While the former signal by means of the well-known grammatical and semantic processes the latter, indexical, processes convey meaning by direct association between signs and context. Both symbolic and indexical signs of signs are always simultaneously involved in communication, and it is on these ideas that interactional sociolinguistics and its core notion of contextualization are built. In his book *Language and Communication* (1996) Hanks integrates the new and the earlier perspectives showing how language structure and language use can be analyzed within a single overall discourse-level framework, where 'language use' as a technical term is replaced by the notion of communicative practice. Our own interactional sociolinguistic perspective is clarified further in Eerdmans et al. (2003). However, apart from terminological issues, the substance of the arguments about the history of the language–schooling relationship and the place of interactional sociolinguistics in the study of schooling processes remain valid.

4

The language experience of children at home and at school

Gordon Wells

Preamble

It is now more than a quarter of a century since the study reported in the first edition of this book was completed. Nevertheless, to the best of my knowledge, no study of comparable scale has since been carried out that casts doubt on the original findings. I shall therefore retain most of the earlier chapter. However, I shall take the opportunity, in the final part of the current chapter, to say something about the collaborative action research with classroom teachers in which I have recently been engaged in the attempt to create richer opportunities for children to construct knowledge together through more dialogic forms of classroom interaction.

It has always been assumed that language plays a major role in formal education. And with good reason. Most of what is taught in schools is transmitted either through teachers' oral presentation or through textbooks and reference works, and when assessments of educational attainment are made they are typically made through the medium of questions and answers in either the spoken or the written mode. It seems self-evident, therefore, that to succeed in school a pupil must have an adequate command of the linguistic skills of listening, speaking, reading, and writing.

Although correct as far as it goes, such a concept of the role of language in education is seriously misleading, since it leaves out of account the essentially interactive nature of linguistic communication. What students learn from what is presented to them depends not only on what they bring to the learning encounter in the form of their linguistic repertoire and associated knowledge of the world, but also on the content and form of what is presented to them and, even more important, on the opportunities they are given to enter into negotiation with the teacher concerning the meaning and significance for them of what they are expected to learn. Where such opportunities to engage in discussion are lacking, unfamiliarity with the specific content or uncertainty about the purpose of the activities they are required to engage in may overwhelm students whose linguistic resources are quite adequate for the task in hand and reduce them to silence or apparent incompetence.

Teachers have, on the whole, been slow to recognize the significance of the manner in which they interact with their students. More than ever, in this age of accountability, they have been so concerned with the overt curriculum, its content and its sequencing, that they have tended to ignore the interactional relationship between the teacher, the learner and that which is taught and learned: the 'I', the 'You', and the 'It' (Moffett 1968; Wells 1981a; 1999). Not explicitly attended to by teachers and, for that reason, only implicitly recognized by students, this aspect of schooling has not inappropriately been dubbed the *hidden curriculum* (Barnes 1976; Mercer 1995). Yet, although hidden, it colors almost all of a child's experience of school learning and, as I shall argue below, is probably one of the most important influences on the success with which students are able to apply their intellectual abilities to the tasks that make up the overt curriculum.

At no stage is this more important than in the child's first few months at school. In the preceding years, as he or she engages in activities of many kinds that arise either within the routines of everyday life at home or from naturally occurring events and situations of interest, children talk and learn largely from an active and spontaneous need to make sense of their experience. To a greater or lesser degree, the adults around them – parents, relatives, and neighbors – support them in their search for understanding, sustaining their interests and providing a resource of skill and information they can draw upon when they need it. The motivation to learn comes chiefly from within, however, and there is little systematic attempt to instruct, except in such matters as safety and socially acceptable behavior. When children enter school, on the other hand, they enter an institution that has been set up for the specific purpose of extending their knowledge and skills in predetermined directions, and they find themselves in a social environment where they are one among many children in the charge of a single adult, who has the responsibility for ensuring that all of them make progress toward goals that are set by society at large, The culture shock of this transition will clearly be lessened if problem-solving strategies that have been acquired at home can be capitalized on at school and if styles of interaction with adults that have served well at home can continue to be of service in the classroom. If that can happen, there is every reason to hope that the active, self-motivated learning that characterizes the preschool years will continue and be extended at school.

What, though, *is* the experience of children as they make this important transition from home to school? What images of themselves as learners do they form from their first encounters with the curriculum, both hidden and overt? Are some children better equipped than others to benefit from the opportunities that school provides and, if so, in what does their advantage consist? How far do differences in linguistic ability and experience, in particular, contribute to their academic attainment?

To answer these and related questions was one of the major aims of the Bristol longitudinal study, 'Language at Home and at School', which followed a representative sample of children from the first observation of them at fifteen months until the end of the primary stage at approximately ten years of age. The preschool phase of the research, concerning the early development of oral language and the influence of conversational interaction with parents and other adults on that development, was reported elsewhere (Barnes, Gutfreund, Satterly, and Wells 1983; Wells 1981a; 1985), as were certain aspects of the relationship between preschool linguistic experience and subsequent school attainment at seven and ten years of age (Wells 198lb; 1986a). This chapter focuses on the results of one specific part of this larger investigation: a comparison of the language experienced by children in the two settings of home and school at the age of five years.

Collecting and analyzing the data

Throughout the longitudinal study, the emphasis was on obtaining representative samples of naturally occurring conversation between the children studied and whoever interacted with them. To this end, recordings in the children's homes were made using a radio-microphone worn by the child, which transmitted to a receiver that, linked to a tape recorder, was pre-programmed to switch on and off at selected times of the day, thus yielding a time-based sample that was equivalent for every child. No observer was present during the home recordings, contextual information being obtained from the parents during a replay of the recording with them at the end of the day.

However, such a design could not be replicated in every detail in the school setting, first because it would have been impossible to distinguish individual children's voices when so many were interacting, and second because a teacher could not be expected to recall in any detail the activities that one particular child had engaged in throughout the course of a day. Accordingly, the decision was taken to introduce an observer into the classroom to take notes on the child's activities and to supplement them with a video recording. The radio-microphone continued to be the main source of recorded data, however, and, as in the home, the actual recording in both audio and video modes was subject to a predetermined time-based sampling frame.

The data for the present investigation consisted of two recordings, the first made a few weeks before the child started school at the age of five years and the second in the second half of the first term (that is, after about six weeks in school). Both recordings consisted of nine five-minute samples recorded at twenty-minute intervals between 9 a.m. and 12 noon. These times were chosen to be within the normal morning program at school – the part of the day, we were assured, when the children would be most likely to be engaged in activities connected with the formal curriculum. Because some of these samples were lost in some recordings – because the children were out of range of the recording equipment, on visits to the local shops, or away to collect siblings from school in the case of the home recordings, or in the playground during the mid-morning break in the school recordings – only seven samples from each recording were used for the purposes of the time-based comparison. Every observation thus consisted of thirty-five minutes of recorded time, with the surplus samples being excluded on a random basis where more than seven had been recorded.

The subjects for the investigation were thirty-two children selected from the original stratified random sample of sixty-four. This larger cohort was selected to be representative of the preschool population of Bristol in terms of sex, class of family background, and season of birth (see Wells 1985, for details).[1] In selecting the present sample, date of entry to school imposed a considerable constraint, as did the need to ensure that the full range of measured linguistic ability was represented. As a result, although the criterion of equal representation by sex was adhered to, there was some overrepresentation of the two extremes of the dimension of family background. However, when this latter dimension is dichotomized, the sample divides into two almost equal groups: fifteen so-called middle-class and seventeen lower-class children. All the children had been judged by health visitors at fifteen months to be showing normal development; they were all singletons, living in their own homes with parents who spoke English as a first language. Their positions in the family birth order varied from only child to last of six; none had suffered any unusual illness or misadventure during the preschool years, although one of them had had articulation problems, which had been treated by a speech therapist. All entered school close to their fifth birthdays, between January 1977 and January 1978. The majority had had some preschool educational experience, either in a nursery school or class, or in a preschool playgroup.

All the parents and teachers were visited before the recordings were made, at which time it was emphasized that the purpose of the investigation was to observe the children's spontaneous linguistic interaction. Parents and teachers were asked to carry on their normal routine and to make no special arrangements to give the child more attention than usual. Although, of course, one can never be certain how representative an observation is of what happens when no observation is in progress, the parents were all very familiar with the experience of being 'bugged' and, as far as one could judge from other non-observational visits to similar classrooms, the teachers behaved normally and without evident self-consciousness. Occasional references were made by the children to the wearing of the radio-microphones but otherwise they seemed to be totally unaffected by the by-then-familiar experience of being recorded.

Following the observations, the sixty-four recordings were transcribed in traditional orthography and coded according to a modified version of the scheme of discourse analysis developed in an earlier phase of the research program (Wells, Montgomery, and MacLure 1979; Wells, MacLure, and Montgomery 1981). The analysis allows for three levels of discourse structure: interaction, exchange, and move, with exchange being the pivotal level. Exchanges consist of two moves: initiating and responding, although it is recognized that some moves may function simultaneously in two exchanges (compare Wells, MacLure, and Montgomery 1981). Exchanges may be combined by means of various links, chief of which is cohesion, to form interactions. Interaction boundaries occur when there are no, or at most only weak, links between adjacent exchanges. Each interaction is categorized according to the context in which it occurs and according to which participant is the initiator. Exchanges are categorized as nuclear, preparatory, reformulating, prompt, or text-contingent. Moves are scored for syntactic complexity and categorized according to semantic content, temporal reference, information focus, and mood. They are also categorized according to the function(s) they perform as conversational acts.

Traditionally (for example, Dore, Gearhart, and Newman 1978; Sinclair and Coulthard 1975) conversational acts or moves have been assigned to one and only one category according to whatever is judged to be the dominant function. However, it has long been recognized that some moves are multi-functional (compare Labov and Fanshel 1977) and various attempts have been made to do justice to this feature of conversation. In the present scheme, following suggestions made by Searle (1977), the meaning of any conversational move is seen as being potentially multi-dimensional. In addition to conveying or requesting information (in almost all cases), a move may also have implications for action, be concerned to express affect, and/or have a bearing on the interpersonal relationship between speaker and addressee. Since a move may 'carry a loading' on each of these dimensions, moves are simultaneously coded, as appropriate, on all of them, with further subcategorization being made on each.

Finally, moves are categorized according to whether they incorporate matter from preceding moves in the discourse and, if so, whether that matter was contributed by self or other. This judgment, however, was restricted in the present investigation to moves contributed by adults.

Coding was carried out by three coders, home and school transcripts for any one child always being coded by the same coder. Compared with the results achieved in earlier phases of the research, inter-coder agreement was rather low. It varied according to category, but overall was between 84 percent and 89 percent. However, this is very similar to the level reported by Tizard and Hughes (1984) in a rather similar study, which will be discussed below. In view of the latitude allowed to coders in deciding how many and which of the dimensions of functional meaning to code, a relatively low level of inter-coder agreement is perhaps not surprising. Such an approach, while theoretically justifiable and intuitively appropriate, is unusually prone to operational unreliability. The consequence is that more than the usual degree of caution must be exercised in setting an acceptable level of significance for all statistical tests of relationships between variables represented by frequencies.

For this study, analysis was carried out only on the total corpus for each child from the two settings of home and school. This report, therefore, will be concerned chiefly with the quantitative and qualitative description of discourse moves – their content and interactional function, and their status within the exchange.

Having coded according to the scheme described above, the coders first calculated raw frequencies for each of the categories and, where appropriate, z-ratios were computed to establish the significance of differences between mean frequencies in the two settings of home and school. However, because the total amount of speech occurring in the thirty-five minutes of each observation varied very considerably across children, more detailed analyses were carried out on the proportions of an individual's total number of moves falling into the different categories. In some cases, inspection of the data revealed the further possibility of differences associated with the sex and/or class of family background of the children. In such cases a three-way analysis of variance, with repeated measures on the setting factor, was carried out; otherwise, z-ratios were calculated. In all cases involving analysis of variance, an arc-sin transformation of the proportional scores was first carried out in order to provide scores more closely approximating a normal distribution.

Before reporting the results, however, it is important to emphasize that this investigation is concerned with the description of patterns of interaction. Scores will be interpreted, therefore, not in terms of the speaker's relative linguistic and conversational competence, but rather in terms of the opportunities that these patterns of interaction can be expected to provide for children to exploit the resources they already have and to develop further competence, both linguistic and intellectual.

Results

Because the primary aim of the investigation was to compare children's linguistic experience at home and at school, the results to be reported will start with those derived from a comparison of interaction in the two settings. Table 4.1 gives the mean values of the absolute amount of speech occurring in thirty-five minutes (seven times five-minute samples) together with a number of indices of length of interaction and relative complexity of individual contributions.

As will be seen, children talk significantly less in the classroom than at home ($p < .001$) and address a considerably smaller proportion of their utterances to adults ($p < .001$). (This latter comparison is based only on the twenty-two children who had the opportunity to talk with siblings and peers as well as adults at home.) By contrast, the amount of talk addressed to the children by adults does not differ significantly from one setting to the other. However, the figure for adult talk in the classroom includes both utterances addressed to the child as a member of a group and utterances addressed to the child in one-to-one interaction. If this latter category is considered alone – and this might be a more appropriate comparison, since the adult speech at home is almost always in a one-to-one interaction – the classroom mean is 76.4 (SD 51.7), which is significantly lower than the mean at home. As the standard deviations indicate, however, there is very considerable variation in both settings; the range at home is 36 – 457 utterances and at school 8 – 229. In both settings two factors influence the amount of speech that occurs: the contexts and activities children choose to be engaged in or are required to engage in, and the number of available

Table 4.1. *Comparison of speech at home and school ($n = 32$)*

		Home	School	Significance level
Mean number of child utterances		189.2	114.9	$p < .001$
	SD	59.4	55.1	
Mean number of child utterances to adults		122.0	45.0	$p < .001$
	SD	64.6	29.0	
Mean number of adult utterances to child		152.7	128.7	n.s.
	SD	101.2	52.6	
Ratio of child to adult utterances		1.13	0.65	$p < .001$
	SD	0.46	0.39	
Mean number of child turns per sequence		4.1	2.5	$p < .01$
	SD	1.4	0.8	
Mean child syntactic complexity in talk with adults		3.1	2.4	$p < .001$
	SD	0.4	0.6	
Mean child syntactic complexity in talk with peers		2.8	3.2	$p < .05$
	SD	0.5	0.5	
Mean adult syntactic complexity		3.5	4.3	$p < .001$
	SD	0.6	0.7	
Mean number of categories of semantic[a] content in child speech		15.5	7.9	$p < .001$
	SD	2.4	2.3	

Note:
[a] This comparison is based on only 16 children

adults. In several homes the father or some other adult as well as the mother was present (although this could lead to less talk with the child as easily as to more), and in a substantial number of classrooms there was a nursery assistant as well as a teacher.

More significant as indices of conversational opportunity, however, are the ratio of child to adult utterances within interactions and the length of the interactional sequences as indexed by the mean number of child turns per interaction. On both these measures the children were at an advantage at home, taking part in longer sequences ($p < .01$) and having a more equal share of the interaction ($p < .001$). A further indication of the conversational opportunity is to be seen in the mean syntactic complexity of contributions in the two settings.[2] The child's is significantly lower at school ($p < .001$) whereas that of the adult shows a difference in the opposite direction ($p < .001$). At least in terms of syntactic complexity, therefore, the children are less frequently exploiting their full linguistic resources when talking to their teacher than when talking to their parents. This is underlined by the fact that their talk with peers in the classroom is significantly more complex than their talk with adults, although this is not the case at home.

The last line in Table 4.1 presents the mean number of different categories of semantic content expressed by the children in the two settings. These categories are based on the scheme for the classification of sentence-meaning relations in terms of case grammatical configurations used in the preschool phase of the research (see Wells 1985, for details). Nine categories are used for the classification of single-clause utterances; these are combined with a further nine categories for the classification of complex utterances involving embedded and subordinate clauses. This analysis is based on the data from sixteen of the children, selected so as to be representative of the sample as a whole.[3] However, the results are absolutely clear-cut. Every one of the children expressed a greater range of semantic content at home than at school and, overall, forty of the categories were used by at least one child at home, while the comparable figure for the school observation was twenty-three. Furthermore, when a comparison is made among the specific categories occurring in the two settings, it is the categories involving the more complex, multi-clause utterances that are absent from the school observations. Only two categories occur markedly more frequently in the classroom: these are giving reasons or motives for possession or change of possession of an object and naming or describing simple attributes of objects. These results amply confirm the picture yielded by the comparison of mean syntactic complexity: children talking with adults at school draw on a far narrower range of their resources of semantic knowledge than when talking with adults at home.

Turning now to what happens within sequences of interaction: Tables 4.2 and 4.3 present the results for child speech and adult speech separately in the form of proportions of the relevant totals for each.

First let us consider who initiates. This can be described at two levels. Each complete interaction can have only one initiator, but within an interaction there can be an indefinite number of exchanges, each being potentially available to either participant to initiate. Table 4.2 shows that, at home, children initiate about two thirds of all interactions with adults, whereas in the classroom the ratio is reversed ($p < .001$). The dramatic decrease in the child's initiation of interactions in the classroom is not altogether surprising when account is taken of the occasions when the teacher is organizing class activities, calling the names on the register, and so on; but even when only one-to-one interactions are considered, the ratio does not begin to approach equality. In exchange initiation, the figures appear somewhat different. However, this is because a substantial proportion of exchanges have no overt response, either because none is expected or because a response is implicit in the next initiation. Here is an example of such an exchange:

Example 4.1

A I'm just going out to the shop. (Initiation)
B Please will you get me an ice-cream? (Implicit response + initiation)
A All right. (Response)

When this is taken into account, it can be seen that as well as there being significant decrease in exchange initiation by the child between home and school ($p < .001$), the ratio of adult to child initiation shifts from near equality at home to a substantial imbalance in the adult's favor at school ($p < .001$).

Table 4.2. *Proportional distribution of child speech at home and school (mean values; n = 32)*

		Home	School	Significance level
Interactions initiated by child		63.6%	23.0%	$p < .001$
	SD	13.1	18.0	
Exchange-initiating utterances		70.2%	43.8%	$p < .001$
	SD	11.2	20.0	
Elliptical or moodless utterances		29.4%	49.4%	$p < .001$
	SD	11.0	20.4	
Complete statements		31.2%	28.0%	n.s.
	SD	8.3	13.7	
Questions		12.7%	4.0%	$p < .001$
	SD	6.1	4.6	
Requests		14.3%	10.4%	$p < .05$
	SD	5.1	9.2	
Requests that are indirect		67.9%	83.2%	$p < .01$
	SD	19.3	25.0	
Utterances in text-contingent exchanges		9.4%	6.3%	n.s.
	SD	5.6	6.8	
References beyond here-and-now		9.1%	6.4%	$p < .05$
	SD	7.0	7.6	

The next set of comparisons concerns the functions of utterances. As explained above, the coding of function was multi-dimensional and involved a large number of distinctions. Tables 4.2 and 4.3 report only some of the most salient superordinate categories because space does not permit the presentation of greater detail. The highest proportion of child utterances by far is elliptical, single-word responses or other moodless utterances, such as exclamations. This category accounts for 29 percent at home and 49 percent at school. The reasons for this relative increase across the two settings will be discussed below. The next most frequent category is complete statements occurring either as exchange initiations or as responses. Here, as indicated by the similarity of the mean values in the two settings, the decrease between home and school is not statistically significant. When we look at the adults' speech, on the other hand (Table 4.3), we find that the proportion of elliptical utterances and of complete statements remains more or less constant across the two settings, with the proportion of complete statements by adults

Table 4.3. *Proportional distribution of adult speech at home and school (mean values; n = 32)*

		Home	School	Significance level
Exchange-initiating utterances		59.9%	78.7%	$p < .001$
	SD	14.3	14.3	
Elliptical utterances		5.7%	5.8%	n.s.
	SD	2.8	6.2	
Complete statements		26.2%	24.5%	n.s.
	SD	8.5	10.3	
Questions		14.3%	20.2%	$p < .01$
	SD	7.8	8.3	
Requests		22.5%	34.1%	$p < .001$
	SD	9.9	13.1	
Requests that are indirect		38.5%	50.0%	$p < .05$
	SD	15.9	18.0	
References beyond here-and-now		10.1%	8.5%	n.s.
	SD	5.6	7.4	
Requests for display		2.1%	14.2%	$p < .001$
	SD	4.0	10.8	
Extending child's meaning		33.5%	17.1%	$p < .001$
	SD	10.9	9.3	
Developing adult's meaning		19.3%	38.6%	$p < .001$
	SD	8.7	9.5	

being rather smaller than the comparable proportion produced by the children.

Where the major differences occur, both between adults and children and between settings, is in the proportion of questions and requests – categories of function, it will be noted – that occur only in exchange-initiating position. At home there is close to parity between adults and children in the proportion of utterances that are questions; at school, on the other hand, there is a very considerable imbalance, children asking only a third as many questions as at home and the teachers asking almost half as many questions again as the parents. These differences between settings are statistically significant alike for the children ($p < .001$) and for the adults ($p < .01$).

A somewhat similar pattern emerges with respect to requests – that is to say, utterances that call upon the addressee to act, or desist from acting, in some way. In this case, however, the reduction in the proportion of children's requests is rather smaller (from 14.3 percent at home to 10.4 percent at school, $p < .05$), while the increase in the proportion of adult requests is somewhat greater (22.5 percent at home to 34.1 percent at school, $p < .001$).

Because it has been suggested that some children may experience difficulty in recognizing the force of the more indirect forms of requests, which are believed to be more common in schools than in some homes (Bernstein 1971; Heath 1983), a comparison was made between the proportion of requests that was direct and the proportion that was indirect in the two settings. Direct requests are those that allow no discretion to the addressee as to whether to comply, being realized through the choice of imperative mood (for example, 'Be quiet'); indirect requests, on the other hand, allow discretion to the addressee, at least ostensibly, by making appeal to his or her ability or willingness to carry out the action, by stating the speaker's wish, or by referring to relevant conditions (Searle 1975) (for example, 'Would you make less noise, please'; 'There's so much noise I can't hear what John is saying'). Given the belief about the relative unfamiliarity of the indirect form of request to some children, it is interesting to note that, by the age of five years, a greater proportion of children's requests are made indirectly both at home and at school, with the proportion increasing significantly on entry to school ($p < .01$). The same trend is seen in the case of the adults, teachers using the indirect form more often than parents ($p < .05$). In neither setting, however, is the proportion of indirect requests as high in the adults as it is in the children.

Finally, a number of comparisons were made of other features of utterances that were considered might indicate the extent to which the occurring conversation provided opportunities for extending the children's learning. First, a comparison across settings was made with respect to the proportion of the children's utterances that occurred in text-contingent exchanges, that is to say, in exchanges that seek to repair breakdowns in communication or to clarify inadequate messages. Such exchanges may be initiated by either adult or child, but in either case they offer the potential for learning more about the language system and about the conditions necessary for successful communication (Robinson and Robinson 1982).

Somewhat surprisingly, the proportion of such utterances showed a trend towards a decrease from home to school that only just failed to reach statistical significance ($z = 1.94$, n.s.). Further inspection showed that this was because the children rarely asked the teachers to repeat utterances they had not heard and never asked them to clarify or elaborate their meanings.

Second, the time-reference of utterances was examined. As is well known, early conversation between parents and children is restricted almost entirely to the here-and-now of ongoing activity. One of the aims of formal schooling is to extend the child's horizons, leading him or her, among other things, to set the present in the temporal context of before and after, and to consider the possible and the hypothetical as well as the actual world of current experience. It might be hypothesized, therefore, that the proportion of utterances referring beyond the here-and-now would increase in the school setting. However, this was not the case. The proportion of such utterances by children actually showed a significant decrease ($p < .05$), and there was a change in the same direction among the adults, although this figure failed to reach significance.

The final comparisons are restricted to the adults' contributions only. The first concerns adult-initiated exchanges that request and then evaluate a display of knowledge or skill by the child. Once again it has been suggested that this function of utterances is relatively unknown to some children (Mehan 1978), although our own longitudinal data show that all children experience such exchanges in the very early stages of language development, as they are asked to name objects, imitate the sounds made by animals, and so on. However, just as important in the present context as the possible differential familiarity of this discourse pattern to children from different family backgrounds is the fact that, in its allocation of the roles of exchange initiator and of evaluator of its content to one participant (the adult), and the role of respondent with minimal discretion as to the form of that response to the child participant, this exchange pattern serves strongly to emphasize the inequality of status and power between the participants in the discourse. With this in mind, it is interesting to note that requests for display are made almost seven times as often by teachers as by parents of five-year-olds, with many children receiving no such requests at all at home at this age. This difference is highly significant ($p < .001$).

Somewhat similar in the picture it gives of the relationship between the discourse participants is the final comparison. All adult utterances were coded as to whether and in what way they incorporated matter contributed to the interaction in previous moves, the most important comparison in the present context being between adult utterances that picked up and extended matter contributed by the child (so-called extending utterances) and those that developed matter previously introduced by the adult (developing utterances). Where the matter incorporated in an adult utterance had been contributed equally by child and adult, the utterance was coded as extending.

Both at home and at school, more than 50 percent of adult utterances fall into one or the other of these two categories (the remainder being either topic initiations, repetitions, paraphrases, minimal responses, or formulaic utterances). But whereas at home twice as many adult utterances are extending rather than developing, the ratio is reversed in the classroom, with teachers developing matter introduced by themselves twice as often as they extend matter contributed by the children. Both these differences are highly significant ($p < .001$).

The results reported so far have all concerned differences between the two settings. However, the design of the study also allowed differences between the sexes and between the two classes of family background to be investigated through analysis of variance. The results of these analyses can be reported very briefly. As far as variables based on the children's contributions are concerned, there were no significant main effects associated with sex and only one main effect associated with family background: lower-class children asked more questions than middle-class children in both home and school settings ($F = 6.47$, 1 and 28 d.f., $p < .05$). There were no significant interaction effects.

There were, however, a small number of significant results from analyses of the adult contributions. The first again concerns adults' questions. Although there were no significant main effects, there was an interesting but non-significant trend: lower-class girls had proportionately fewer questions addressed to them at home and more at school than other groups ($F = 3.96$, 1 and 28 d.f., n.s.). With regard to requests, there was a significant class and sex interaction effect: middle-class girls received proportionately more requests and lower-class girls proportionately fewer requests than either class of boys ($F = 4.50$, 1 and 28 d.f., $p < .05$). Interestingly, when requests were divided into direct and indirect, there was a main sex effect: in both settings a greater proportion of requests addressed to girls was indirect than was the case for boys ($F = 11.08$, 1 and 28 d.f., $p < .01$). Finally, with respect to references beyond the here-and-now, there was an interaction effect: boys received proportionately more such utterances at home than at school, while for girls there was a change, although smaller, in the opposite direction ($F = 7.06$, 1 and 28 d.f., $p < .05$). Apart from this handful of significant results (which, given the number tested, may have been due to chance), there was no indication of differences associated with either sex or class of family background.

The transition from home to school

Although this was to our knowledge the first attempt to compare the language experience of five-year-olds as they make the transition from home to school, it was not the first study to compare the conversations young children have with parents and teachers. In the investigation already referred to, Tizard and Hughes (1984) recorded thirty four-year-old girls, half middle-class and half working-class, at home and in their nursery classes, and obtained results very similar to those reported here. Summarizing their results, they wrote:

> The most striking finding in the present analysis was that, for the majority of variables considered, home–school differences were very large and social-class differences at home very small or absent. That is, at home conversations were more frequent, longer, and more equally balanced between adult and child; further, children of both social classes asked questions at home much more frequently than at school, and answered adults more often.

In the main, our results corroborate theirs, though showing even less in the way of social-class differences. They also extend them to the next stage of schooling, that of the infant reception class at age five, and show that boys do not differ significantly from girls with respect to most of the dimensions of conversation investigated.

Compared with their experience at home, we find children at school playing a much less positive role in conversation with adults and having much less opportunity actively to explore their experience and develop their understanding through interaction with mature speakers who sustain their interests and encourage them to initiate topics, ask questions, and evaluate, or query, the answers they are given. Asking questions, in fact, seems to be very largely the prerogative of the teacher and, although we found children asking a substantial number of questions when talking with their peers, like Tizard and Hughes we found that school conversation tended to take the form of a series of questions from the teacher and answers from the child.

A very similar picture emerges from another study of conversation in preschool playgroups and nursery classes. On the basis of recordings made by twenty-four playgroup leaders and nursery teachers, Wood, McMahon, and Cranstoun (1980) also note the generally subservient role of the children in interaction and the high proportion of terse and even monosyllabic answers given to questions asked by adults. 'Indeed,' they comment, 'the tendency to ignore children, talk over them, and generally dominate the proceedings, was the single most striking feature of the recordings that our twenty-four practitioners responded to when they read their own transcripts' (p. 65). Similar responses have been made by Infant teachers who have listened to the recordings made in the study reported here.

One possible explanation suggested by Wood et al. for the unequal roles played by teacher and child in the choice of topics and in the maintenance of conversation is the far narrower range of options available to children, compared with adults, for the management of interaction. In absolute terms, this is certainly true. But if adults take time and have sufficient interest in listening to what a child has to say and are willing to extend the child's contributions rather than impose their own point of view, a genuine reciprocity of conversational interaction is possible with young children of this age, as many of our recordings of them at home clearly show.

Their second suggested explanation, on the other hand, seems even closer to the mark. As Wood et al. point out, however child-centered teachers may be, they also carry an institutional responsibility to ensure that all children engage in systematic learning within a curricular framework that it is their duty to provide. They also have a responsibility to maintain control, on a social and physical level, of a large number of youngsters who, left to themselves in such a setting, would quickly generate a state of anarchy that would be potentially dangerous as well as inimical to any serious and sustained activity. 'Perhaps,' Wood et al. suggest, 'the paucity of questions and the lack of negotiation in child language reflect the social structure of the preschool (or reception class) as much or even more than it reflects the child's intellectual and linguistic abilities' (1980: 78).

Certainly the problem of how to keep thirty or more children usefully employed without undue noise or commotion is one that faces every teacher, and a strategy employed by most teachers at least some of the time is to work with the whole class at once. In such a context it is obviously even more difficult to be responsive to an individual's train of thought than in one-to-one interaction, so the characteristics of teacher domination might be expected to be particularly apparent here.

In order to test whether this was in fact the case, a comparison was made between one-to-one and whole-class or group interaction for a number of the variables of adult speech for which overall totals have already been reported. The results are shown in Table 4.4.

As can be seen, except for the proportion of utterances that request a display of knowledge or skill, there is a marked increase in the features of adult domination ($p < .001$ in all cases). Requests for display, however, seem to occur almost equally frequently in one-to-one and group- or class-teaching situations, a phenomenon suggesting that this is a staple feature of many teachers' general style of interaction in the classroom.

The hidden social function of display questions has already been mentioned – to emphasize the status difference between teacher and students and to retain control over their attention and participation. But there is an equally important linguistic/cognitive consequence of this style of interaction, of which teachers are apparently also unaware. Most display questions call for an answer in the form of a single word or at most a simple phrase. It follows, therefore, that the larger the proportion of teacher utterances that take the form of display questions, the larger will be the proportion of minimal utterances produced by the child – if the child responds at all. This result is confirmed by the very high correlation between the absolute numbers of such minimal utterances produced by individual children and the number of display questions addressed to them ($r = 0.70$, $p < .001$).

Furthermore, what is particularly detrimental about this relationship is that, where the teacher has low expectations about a

Table 4.4. *Proportional distribution of teachers' speech in one-to-one and group interactions (n = 32)*

		One-to-one	Group	Significance level
Exchange-initiating utterances		68.2%	90.8%	p < .001
	SD	15.5	14.9	
Requests for display		10.4%	13.7%	n.s.
	SD	9.5	16.0	
Extending child's meaning		23.9%	8.5%	p < .001
	SD	10.8	8.5	
Developing adult's meaning		30.2%	45.3%	p < .001
	SD	12.3	14.6	

child's linguistic ability, the child's (entirely appropriate) behavior in restricting responses to single words or phrases may provide the teacher with evidence that serves to confirm those expectations. That this was happening in at least one case in the present study has been argued at length elsewhere (Wells 1986a; Wells and Montgomery 1981).

But even where the teacher has no such expectations, interaction that is restricted to sequences of display questions provides minimal opportunity for children to express their own ideas and to receive feedback that might lead to enhancement of their understanding of the topic under discussion. This is seen very clearly in the following so-called class discussion, which occurred in the context of reading the story *Elmer the Elephant*. It illustrates very clearly how this asymmetric style of interaction effectively reduces the children's participation to the level of single-word responses and turns an opportunity for sharing ideas and feelings into an exercise in guessing what is in teacher's mind.

Example 4.2

T What was Elmer like apart from being patchwork?
Do you remember?

P Yes

T What was he like Paul then?

P Grey

T No I don't mean to look at I mean what was he like as an elephant?

CHN (No reply)
T What sort of things did he do?
CHN (No reply)
T Well was he quiet and silent and - and very sober?
CHN (No reply)
T What did he do when we first - when we first hear about him?
He kept making the other elephants -
CHN Laugh
T So he was a - what kind of an elephant?
CHN Patchwork
T Yes apart from being patchwork -
What sort - what kind of elephant apart from being a patchwork elephant?
Was he a very sad elephant?
CHN No (mumble)
Yes
T Was he? (surprised)
I don't think he was
What was he Simon?
He was a *happy*[4]
S *Happy*
T Happy . good
Can you think of another word?
C Cheerful
T Cheerful yes
Anyone else think of another word?
CL Happy
C2 Smiling
T Smiling
What other kind of word is a happy smiling elephant?
Can anyone think of another word?
He was jolly and gay wasn't he? (Tone of finality)
C Yes

[T. continues with story]

This example may not be entirely typical, but there were many other classroom discussions that shared at least some of these features. On the other hand, nothing like this occurred in any of the home observations.

However, despite the substantial and significant differences between the patterns of interaction observed at home and those observed at school, there were also substantial individual differences among the children and among the adults who interacted with them in the absolute and proportional frequencies with which they produced moves of the various kinds in both settings. One possible explanation for this is that the adults were responding to individual differences in the children in their disposition to initiate topics, ask questions, or even to talk at all. To test this hypothesis, correlations were calculated between the individual proportional frequencies of different categories at home and at school. With the exception of question-asking, already found to be associated with class of family background, no significant relationships were found. It appears, therefore, that if either participant is more responsible than the other for the manner in which the child participates in interaction, it is the adult rather than the child who bears this responsibility (Wells 1986a).

In the classroom, at least, this is what one might expect, since it is the teacher who ultimately determines what opportunities there are for interaction. In so far as individual children participate in different ways and to various degrees, therefore, this may be the result of a deliberate policy on the part of teachers. For example, they may adjust their patterns of interaction according to their estimate of the children's abilities to engage in verbal interaction. As it happens, the teachers were asked, at about this point in the children's careers, to make an assessment of their oral-language ability, using a fairly detailed questionnaire in which, for each aspect of ability asked about, one of a set of alternative behavioral descriptions had to be selected (see Wells 198lb, for details). It was possible, therefore, to examine the relationship between the children's scores on this assessment of oral language ability, based on the teachers' experience of interacting with them, and the relative frequency with which teachers addressed particular types of move to them.

Using a one-way analysis of variance on teachers' speech across all contexts, we found that only two variables showed a significant effect of assessed oral-language ability: '*total number of requests*' and '*talk extending beyond here and now*'. More requests were addressed to children in the middle range of estimated ability than to children at the two extremes ($F = 4.70$, 2 and 29 d.f., $p < .05$), and more utterances referring beyond the here-and-now were addressed to children estimated to be of higher ability ($F = 6.77$, 2 and 29 d.f., $p < .01$). However, in an analysis of talk in one-to-one interaction only, there was also a significant tendency for teachers to extend a smaller proportion of utterances from children of lower estimated ability ($F = 4.47$, 1 and 29 d.f., $p < .05$) and a trend for them to engage in shorter interactions with the same children. However, in assessing these results it must be borne in mind that the children were all, with two exceptions, taught by different teachers. It is impossible, therefore, to make a systematic comparison of the ways in which individual teachers interacted with children of differing estimated ability.

A further reason systematic differences in teachers' treatment of children on the basis of ability might fail to emerge from this analysis, even if they existed, is that when only one observation is made, the sample of teacher–pupil interaction that is observed is probably unrepresentative as far as individual children are concerned. In any one morning a child can engage in only a limited number of activities, and the interaction that is actually observed will be to a considerable extent determined by the particular activities selected by child or teacher.

In the seven five-minute samples that provide the data from the morning's observation, Darren, for example, was in school assembly for one sample, listened to a story in a second, sat waiting and chatting desultorily with peers while administrative tasks were completed in a further three, and played alone or with other children in the remaining two samples. Olivia, by contrast, was observed in instructional contexts in six out of the seven samples, in three of them as a member of a part- or whole-class group and in the other three working for and engaging in one-to-one interaction with her teacher about the writing and drawing she was doing. Not surprisingly, the interactional profiles of these two children are very different, though subsequent observations suggested that they were nevertheless not altogether unrepresentative of these two teachers' different styles of classroom management.

Tantalizing though these hints are of possible systematic differences between individual teachers, what this investigation has shown is that there are large and systematic differences between teachers in general and the parents and other adults at home in the opportunities for learning they provide in their interactions with the children in their care. While our observations in the classroom provide ample evidence of the children being systematically introduced to the content of the overt curriculum, the results of the analyses reported above must make us question the price at which this advantage is bought. And when we consider that it has often been claimed that one of the chief functions of the first school is to compensate for the linguistic deficiencies believed to be characteristic of many lower-class homes, it is ironic to see just how restricted are the opportunities provided in many classrooms for children to exploit the linguistic resources they already show evidence of possessing in their interactions with adults at home.

What can teachers do about it?

Before attempting to answer this question, it is important to pay tribute to the very real efforts that all the teachers we observed made to plan their work so that children would make progress in mastering the basic skills of literacy and numeracy and to ensure that the tasks the children were given were appropriate to their level of ability. Moreover, the teachers all gave a high priority to spending time with individual children, getting to know them, providing individual instruction, and monitoring their efforts and achievements. This is clearly demonstrated by the fact that, on average, 62 percent of the utterances addressed to the children studied occurred in one-to-one interactions.

Nor should we lightly discount the difficulties under which the teachers labored: the large number of children for whom they were responsible, often unaided, with the attendant problems of physical control already alluded to, their limited knowledge about the children's lives outside the classrooms, and the mounting pressure to ensure coverage of the basic curriculum. It is hardly surprising, therefore, that many of them seemed to have evolved a style of working to cope with the problems of classroom management that reduced the linguistic strategies available to them and gave rise to the patterns of interaction that have been described above.

However, while sympathizing with the teachers and recognizing the heavy demands made on them, we should also try to put ourselves in the place of the children. This is their introduction to formal learning, and the lessons learned at this stage will influence the whole of their subsequent careers at school. Of course, teachers are aware of the importance of getting off to a good start, but what needs to be emphasized is that what children are learning in their first year or two at school is as much about what it is to be a learner in the classroom setting as it is about the ostensible content of their learning. Few, if any, teachers would wish their students to come to expect that schools are places where their individual initiative in thinking and speaking is disvalued, where the asking of questions is the sole prerogative of the teacher, and where the best answer is short and preferably expressed in exactly the words that the teacher already has in mind. Yet, on the evidence presented above, this seems to be the message of the hidden curriculum.

It might seem that all that is necessary to improve this situation is to bring the facts to teachers' attention for, once pointed out, the evidence will speak for itself. However, experience shows that this strategy is not particularly successful. To begin with, teachers are unaware of the manner in which they interact with children, at least in the sort of detail investigated in the present study, and even when they become so by recording themselves and then transcribing and analyzing the resulting tapes, they do not find it easy to change interactional strategies built up over many years. Indeed, simply to suggest that they try to reduce the number of display questions they ask, for example, may actually be counterproductive (compare Wood, McMahon, and Cranstoun 1980) for, like the proverbial centipede, when asked to think about how they talk with children, some teachers find that they become so self-conscious that they can no longer interact in a natural manner at all.

The reason for this, I suspect, is that, under normal circumstances of interaction, the focus of our attention is not on the verbal and nonverbal messages through which we communicate our intentions, but rather on the intentions themselves in relation to the specific activity in which we and our co-participants are engaged. Without giving deliberate attention to it, we modify our style of interaction to suit the requirements of the situation. If this is correct, then it seems that it may be more profitable to focus attention on the sort of tasks that are set and, in particular, on the relationships they call for between the learner, the teacher, and the problem to be solved or activity to be engaged in. Asking children to make up their own endings to a story left unfinished would probably give rise to a very different sort of interaction from that which occurs in the sort of quiz about names, attributes, and main events of the plot that we so often observed to follow the reading of a story. Similarly, inviting children to speculate about specific causal relationships, such as, for example, those involved in plant growth, and then to carry out experiments to test their hypotheses, would probably lead to a different pattern of interaction from that which occurs when a teacher deliberately teaches the facts in question and then questions the students to ensure that they have understood and remembered them.

But even attending to classroom organization and, in particular, to the kinds of task that are set, important though this is, will not inevitably lead to the more reciprocal and exploratory kind of talk that occurs quite frequently in the observations we made in the homes. For, as in any interaction, the ultimate determiner of the way the participants behave is not the situation as such but the way in which they construe it, and in particular the way in which they relate to each other in that situation (Ervin-Tripp 1980). As far as the classroom is concerned, there seem to be two major impediments to interaction that is really conducive to the exploitation and development of children's resources for talking and thinking.

The first is the teacher's limited familiarity with individual children – their interests and abilities. Despite their obvious attempts to find time to interact with children on a one-to-one basis and to individualize instruction, teachers frequently seem to find themselves seeking to match individuals to a preexisting scheme of what children of a given age should be like and, as a result, they almost invariably underestimate what individual children are capable of doing on their own. The pressure to behave in this way seems to have two different but related origins. The first is the prevalence of graded schemes of work for the teaching of reading and mathematics, which assume that all children will go through the same predetermined progression in learning, although at different rates. However, by accepting that assumption, teachers effectively minimize the contribution the child can make to his or her learning through the particular interests and existing skills and knowledge that he or she actually has (King 1978; Walkerdine 1982).

The second is the teacher's conception of his or her own role in the facilitation of children's learning. Despite the almost universal acceptance of a philosophy of early education that emphasizes growth from within and the active, constructive nature of learning, teachers in practice are so concerned to teach what they believe children should learn that they allow very little opportunity for them to take responsibility for their own learning and, as a result, they almost invariably underestimate children's true capabilities. What I am suggesting, therefore, is that, as teachers, we need to start with the recognition that children are already active, self-directed learners outside the classroom and that, on this basis, we should first seek to find out more about the particular interests and abilities of individual students, by listening to what they have to say and by encouraging them to ask the questions they want to ask, and then try to develop a style of collaboration and negotiation in the planning of learning activities to which both teacher and pupil contribute and for which both take responsibility. A really important question, therefore, is how to achieve this goal.

Postscript: collaborative research with teachers and students

In 1984, I moved to the Ontario Institute for Studies in Education (now the Faculty of Education at the University of Toronto) and, from then on, my work was to be with practicing teachers rather than with young children. Very quickly, I realized that, without some first-hand experience of working in Canadian classrooms with children and their teachers, my observational research in England would cut little ice with the teachers who took my courses. And so I began to learn a new form of research, which involved collaborating *with* teachers and students rather than carrying out research *on* them.

For all of us this was a new experience and it took some time to establish a relationship in which there was mutual trust and a research agenda with which everyone was comfortable. In the first few years, the common focus was on the development of literate thinking and involved teachers from Kindergarten to Grade Six who were participating in a longitudinal study of language and learning in multilingual classrooms, in which video-recorded observations were being made of children with Cantonese, Greek, Portuguese or English as their first language. What we learned was that both English Language Learners and those for whom English was their first language became most engaged in learning when at least some parts of the curriculum were addressed through group projects in which the precise questions to be investigated were negotiated between teacher and group members. In this context, reading and writing became critical means for obtaining information and for communicating the knowledge constructed in the group to other members of the classroom community; but just as important, we found, was the talk about written texts, while books were being perused, journals being written, and posters reporting their investigations were being prepared. In these contexts, students had meanings they wanted to share with each other and the teacher in an attempt to arrive at common understandings about the overarching curriculum topics they were studying. Talking about texts in these ways involved them in literate thinking and provided effective ways for them to appropriate the register of written language (Chang-Wells and Wells 1992; Langer 1987).

So successful were these first attempts at collaborative inquiry with teachers that, between 1988 and 1991, I was invited to work with two large school districts, one in Ontario and the other in British Columbia, in which a program of staff development concerning the role of talk in the classroom was conducted through teacher research. As in the previous project, teachers chose their own topics to investigate and received assistance in recording and analyzing the classroom interactional data that was appropriate for their individual projects. At the same time, teachers in the participating schools formed research communities with their colleagues and prepared presentations on their findings for district conferences that were held each year.

There was no doubt about the invigorating effect that participation in these projects had on the teachers and school administrators involved. Clearly the same principles applied for teachers as we had found for elementary students who were encouraged to become inquirers. Very significant, too, was the effect of encouraging participants to form 'research communities', whether this was in school staffrooms or in individual classrooms, since this provided the impetus for a more collaborative form of interaction in which all ideas and opinions were taken seriously and attempts made to work toward a common understanding.

Through taking part in these various projects, I became convinced that teacher inquiry was the most effective form of staff development, particularly with respect to changing the traditional mode of teacher–student interaction, since teachers discovered for themselves that their students became more engaged and seemed to learn more effectively when opportunities were provided for collaborative knowledge-building through talk and literate modes of communication about topics in which they were truly interested. I decided, therefore, to carry out more systematic research about how to create communities of inquiry in classrooms and about how this affected teacher–whole-class interaction.

The 'developing inquiring communities in education project' (DICEP)

Once again, the approach adopted was one of collaborative research. Teacher participants (grades one through eight) volunteered to join the group and, very quickly, the organization of the project became a shared endeavor, with all members taking turns to chair meetings, keep minutes, and plan the agenda for future meetings. We also began to collaborate in making conference presentations and preparing papers for publication (Wells 2001).

The questions that, individually and as a group, we set out to address were: how can classrooms become communities of inquiry, and what part does language play in this process? Initially, we focused on the learning and teaching of science because that is a school subject that lends itself to an inquiry approach. But soon the effects began to spill over into other subjects and, after two years, we officially broadened the scope of the project to include all aspects of classroom life. In fact, at that stage, several new members joined the group, one of whom chose to start by investigating the question of community-building through a focus on class meetings.

Each member, then, chose their own particular focus and decided how to approach it. For the classroom teachers – as their chosen title for the project suggests – the predominant focus was on strategies for community-building and the different approaches to inquiry that were appropriate in different areas of the curriculum. What all agreed to, however, was that video-recorded observations of group and whole-class interaction should be a major source of data, together with samples of students' work and the teachers' own fieldnotes and reflections. In the majority of classrooms, a project officer operated the video camera when an observation was planned and arranged for selected portions of the tapes to be transcribed. These materials were then available for discussion at our monthly meetings, at the majority of which one member updated the group on the progress of her or his inquiry and the remaining members offered comments and suggestions. As the project progressed, more and more of these individual investigations were presented at teacher conferences and several were written up and published in a variety of educational journals and books.[5] Interestingly, while almost all of their presentations drew on transcribed excerpts from the observations, the focus was rarely on language per se; rather the discourse data were used to illustrate ways in which students were becoming more engaged in learning and more adept at carrying out group inquiries in the process.

In the final year of the project, the university members of the group began to carry out linguistic analyses of the corpus of transcripts that had been prepared, using a coding scheme based on the same theory of linguistic interaction as used in the Bristol Study, but substantially revised to place more emphasis on the sequential organization of the discourse, which extended over much longer episodes than had been typical in the home recordings.

The first analysis focused on episodes of teacher–whole-class interaction, comparing the ways in which the style of discourse varied according to the curricular topic (science v. arts) and according to the role of the discourse in relation to the curricular activity in progress (management of activities v. exploration of ideas). In a nutshell, what we found was that the interaction became more dialogic when the class was engaged in the latter (e.g. planning, interpreting or reviewing student inquiries). By contrast, episodes of teacher-led instruction, classroom management and checking on what had been learned tended to be characterized by shorter sequences of talk on a particular issue and a higher proportion of evaluative responses to student contributions. In this respect, there was little systematic difference between science and arts topics (Nassaji and Wells 2000).

As a result of this first analysis, we decided to refine the coding scheme to enable a more detailed investigation of the relationship between the type of move that initiated a sequence of interaction and the way in which the teacher followed up on student contributions. For this purpose, we first distinguished whether a teacher initiation was a question or an informing move and, second, if the initiating move was a question, whether it asked for information supposed to be known or posed a problem and invited suggestions, conjectures or explanations for open-ended discussion. At the same time, we divided the coded observations into two sets: those that were made early in each teacher's participation in the project and those that were made later.

The final report of this second phase of analysis has been completed and the major findings are quite clear. As a consequence of joining the project and attempting to create communities of inquiry in their classrooms, every teacher made significant changes in his or her style of interaction. In particular, they more frequently encouraged students to initiate topics of discussion, asked more questions which called for negotiation to arrive at the best answer, and less frequently responded by evaluating student contributions, instead incorporating them into their own next comment or asking the student to extend or further explain what he or she had said. As a result, sequences tended to be sustained over many more exchanges as students developed their ideas in more detail and offered supporting arguments and as they more frequently picked up on and responded to what their peers had said. These changes in style of interaction seemed to follow quite spontaneously from the attempt to adopt an inquiry approach to curriculum; at the same time the more dialogic nature of class discussions made the practice of inquiry more engaging for the students and led them to think more deeply about what they were doing and learning (Wells and Mejia-Arauz 2006).

Conclusion

What these recent studies show, then, is that teachers can modify their style of interaction in the classroom in ways that more closely approximate the reciprocal nature of the majority of interchanges that occur in children's conversational experience at home. Of course, teacher–whole-class interaction is necessarily more highly structured than the latter, both because it is oriented toward the achievement of required curricular goals and because interaction between the large number of participants necessitates more deliberate management than casual conversation among friends or family members. However, what is most important for students' intellectual development, I believe, is not so much the informality that characterizes interaction in the home as the opportunity to express their ideas and opinions and to have them taken seriously and responded to in ways that help them to extend and deepen their understanding.

In this respect, classroom discussion, when effectively managed, can provide even richer opportunities than conversation at home just because of the diversity of life experiences to be found in any classroom community. For example, when a class of students have all been engaged in investigations of the same topic or listened to the same story, they have a variety of different perspectives to offer and, by attempting to explain their own ideas in ways that others can understand and by listening to their peers' responses and their alternative points of view, they are led to reconsider their own ideas and often to modify or extend them. In this context, while the teacher has the responsibility for ensuring that the discussion remains focused and that less vocal students are enabled to offer their contributions, she or he does not need to be the sole arbiter of what is important and relevant since, with guidance, students can gradually learn to share in fulfilling this responsibility (Gallas 1994; 1995; Wells 1999).

In recent years, there have been a number of other attempts to develop a more dialogic mode of interaction in the classroom: through lessons explicitly helping students to engage in 'exploratory talk' (Mercer 1995); through the support of reasoning in classroom discussion (Pontecorvo and Sterponi 2002); and through the use of 'instructional conversation' (Tharp and Gallimore 1988).

Interestingly, this latter term, 'instructional conversation', was first introduced to describe a form of teacher talk with small groups in the Kamehameha project in Hawai'i, that aimed to support the learning of native Hawaiian children and it has since been used in schools serving 'at risk' children in many parts of the United States. What is significant, however, is that this style of interaction has been found to be equally beneficial for mainstream children (Dalton and Tharp 2002), largely because, as its name implies, it combines the dialogic quality of conversation with the instruction that supports the attainment of curricular objectives.

However, what makes the work of the DICEP teachers somewhat different from these other initiatives is that, in their case, the improved quality of classroom interaction was not achieved by focusing on the talk but rather on the exploration and understanding of the topics that the talk served to mediate. In this respect the DICEP teachers were building on the dispositions learned in the preschool years when learning to talk and talking to learn (Halliday 1975) are inseparably linked in children's desire to participate in and understand the practices of their family and local community. As the Bristol Study showed, inquiry is a major motivator of sustained and thoughtful conversation in the early years and, if it is given its rightful place at the heart of formal schooling, it can continue to enable students not only to learn about the prescribed topics of the curriculum but also to develop those dispositions that are necessary for them to become lifelong learners.

Now, perhaps more than ever before, what our society needs is citizens with an exploratory attitude to the situations they find themselves in and with a versatile ability to recognize problems and to collaborate in the formulation and testing of possible solutions, both symbolically, in words, and also practically, in action. If these attitudes are not fostered in the early years of schooling, it will become progressively more difficult for them to develop and flourish in the later stages of education and in the wider world that our children will meet beyond the walls of the school.

Notes

1. The total sample studied in the preschool years numbered 128 children, selected as just described, the additional 64 children being observed from 39 to 66 months of age. Since observations of the two age-based samples overlapped at 39 and 42 months, it was possible to make comparisons between them. No significant differences were found (Wells 1985).

2. This was calculated by scoring 1 for each clause constituent and 1 for each clause in addition to the main clause. For each child, a mean value was then calculated, from which the sample mean was derived.
3. I am grateful to Maggie Turner for carrying out this section of the analysis as part of her M. Ed. dissertation at the University of Bristol.
4. Italicized words were spoken simultaneously.
5. A full list of the group's publications can be found as an appendix in Wells 2001. Since the publication of that book, the group members have been investigating how to involve their students as co-researchers in their inquiries; the results of this phase of research can be found in the on-line journal, *Networks*, 6 (1), February 2003.

5

Narrative presentations: an oral preparation for literacy with first graders

Sarah Michaels

Sometimes the world doesn't need to know about everything, right?

First-grade teacher at sharing time

Preface

This study of 'Sharing Time' in a first-grade classroom was part of a larger effort to address the problem of differential access to learning opportunities in ethnically and socioeconomically diverse classrooms. The work was written at a time when many teachers implicitly or explicitly subscribed to the 'cultural deprivation' theory for explaining school failure among ethnic and linguistic minority students. It was not uncommon to hear teachers talk about children who came from 'nonverbal' homes where 'the TV is always on but no one ever talks to the children', or about children who don't speak standard English, use double negatives, and thus don't reason logically. Challenges to this view were developing from work in linguistics by Labov (on the logic of non-standard English) and from the tradition of ethnography of speaking by Hymes, Heath, Erickson, Cazden, Philips, and others. This study drew on this work but was centrally informed by work in interactional sociolinguistics, pioneered by John Gumperz and Jenny Cook-Gumperz, which emphasized the systematic resources speakers from diverse

Acknowledgments: I would like to thank Jenny Cook-Gumperz and John Gumperz for their comments and suggestions on earlier drafts. Special thanks to Mrs. Jones and her first graders, Deena in particular, for making this study possible.

cultural groups used to signal intent and interpretation of intent in managing conversational inference in face-to-face encounters. Taken together, all of this work has come to be looked at as supporting a cultural or linguistic 'mismatch' or 'difference' hypothesis – emphasizing difference rather than deficiency in linguistic and sociocultural tools for interaction, and the ways these differences influence access to instruction and evaluation of competence in academic settings.

Perhaps, not surprisingly, this work has been understood by some in an overly simple fashion. Critics of the cultural-difference position point out, correctly, that not all culturally or linguistically different students fare poorly and argue that other factors must therefore explain the phenomenon of differential success in school. But as we revisit this study of sharing time, it's worth noting what was and what was not claimed. It was never assumed that cultural or linguistic differences posed insurmountable barriers to understanding. Children are amazingly adept learners of language and demonstrate robust abilities to code-shift or style-shift from context to context, under certain conditions. Nor was it assumed that other social factors such as economic disadvantages or institutionalized barriers to advancement played no role. Rather, it was argued that subtle communication differences can play a kind of cascading role in the interactional accomplishments of building relationships of trust and collaboration, making it harder for teachers to recognize and then build on students' cultural and linguistic strengths. Differences in discourse style – narrative style in this case – are invariably interpreted within a larger societal context where differential expectations of intellectual competence can be either reinforced or interrupted.

Focusing on conversational inference in situations where expectations of ability and judgments of competence are inextricably intertwined helps us examine how it is that even well-meaning teachers, with high expectations for all children, might nonetheless have a hard time establishing conversational cooperation with certain students, and how it is that negative expectations can seem to be confirmed and reified in the students' own performance, leading to decreased expectations, and a downward spiral. Intersubjectivity, competence, and intelligence must be presumed in order to be jointly produced. This work helps us to unpack the role of language and culture in the complex dance involved in presuming intersubjectivity and competence in the first place.

Sharing time in a first-grade classroom

For children, entry into the adult conversational world requires a lengthy apprenticeship which is developed partially through the ways in which adults interpret and respond to messages from children and partially by direct teaching of skills such as narrative or other forms of descriptive accounts. Such skills, although first learned at home, begin to be taught formally when the child enters school in speech events such as 'show and tell' sessions, where an object is used as a focus for a single child to present an account to the whole class. From observations, we can see that the child's problem in these sessions has several facets. First, he or she must select from the multiplicity of things to tell about, that is, find a realizable theme. Second, the child must develop a sense of how to highlight key information so that the presentation is interpretable to others who do not share the child's background knowledge. It is these two problems of topic selection and the organization of discourse structure which I will explore in this chapter, as they occur in sessions of 'show and tell', which is called 'sharing time', in a particular first-grade classroom.

Sharing time – some ethnographic background

Sharing took place every morning in the first-grade classroom which I studied within the context of a larger episode which I refer to as 'rugtime' – a time when the children assembled on the rug for various teacher-structured activities such as taking roll and doing the calendar. The children were expected to sit quietly on the rug, engaged in what has been called 'attentive listening' (Cook-Gumperz, 1978/82). From repeated observation, it can be shown that sharing time was a clearly bounded speech event, opened formulaically by the teacher, saying 'OK, who has something important [interesting, special] to share?' or simply offering the floor to the person whom the teacher designated the 'special person' (this was a different child each day). To get a turn, children raised their hands and waited to be nominated by the teacher, but while another child was sharing, anyone could call out short, topically relevant comments from the rug. In anticipation of sharing, some of the children brought in objects from home to talk about, ranging from books or toys to a new article of clothing worn by the child. The children were not required to bring in things to share (as is the case in some classrooms with organized sessions of 'show and tell'), and many children simply shared about a recent experience. The only explicit rules for the topics at sharing time were: (1) no sharing about TV or movies (because it takes too long), and (2) no sharing about private family matters, such as quarrels. Very early on, children were urged to tell about events that had already taken place.

When a child was called on, he or she went to the front of the rug and stood next to the teacher who was seated on a chair. The teacher, whom I will call Mrs. Jones, was actively involved in each turn, holding her arm around each child as he or she talked, holding the floor for the child (e.g. 'Excuse me, it's Merle's turn.') and freely interjecting questions or reactions to the child or group at large.

Sharing as a unique speech event

That the children saw sharing time as a completely unique speech event was evidenced by their use of a highly marked intonation contour. This 'sharing intonation' was an integral feature of sharing discourse and occurred in no other classroom speech activity (other than role-playing sharing as a part of 'playing school'). In this particular classroom which was half white and half black children,[1] I have identified two contrasting, but very comparable intonation patterns, both clearly identifying the talk as sharing-talk. The contour used primarily by the white children was a gradually rising contour, stretching over the last word or two of a tone group. The accompanying utterance was often a syntactically complete, independent clause where an adult speaker would often use falling intonation. This particular curve seemed to indicate 'more to come' and was almost always followed by a significant pause. This perhaps served to ward off comments from peers or teacher, allowing the child some extra time for planning.

Example 5.1

AHAB I got this Chinese Checker's game . . .

for my birthday . . . and . . .

The second intonation contour was used exclusively by the black children and very pronouncedly by some of the black girls. It occurred in exactly the same environments (independent clauses), and can be characterized as a lilting high-rise–mid-fall contour, also generally followed by a pause. The contours were used primarily at the beginning of a turn (as the child introduced the topic), where perhaps more planning was required, of the talk most ritualized as sharing talk. For some children, especially for those who use the second contour, this sharing prosody involved rather sharp pitch modulations, giving the talk an almost sing-song quality.

Example 5.2

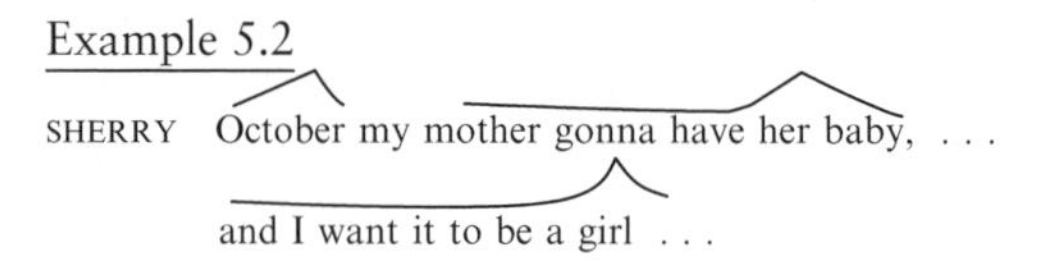

There was also evidence of the use of a lexical formula. In telling about past events, children very commonly begin by saying:

Yesterday . . . or Yesterday . . .

depending on which intonation contour they generally used. That this was formulaic (rather than simply a function of the fact that children want to talk about the immediate past) could be seen in the cases where children corrected a false start.

Example 5.3

BOB Yesterday . . . I mean . . . I mean . . .
When I went to Arkansas [which happened a year earlier].

DEENA Yesterday . . . I mean it was last night . . .

It turns out that using such a formula served several discourse purposes. First, it served to ground the talk temporally, the importance of which was repeatedly emphasized in Mrs. Jones' comments. Secondly, it established a frame that helped the child in structuring, and the listeners in interpreting, the discourse as event- or person-oriented 'accounting'.

Sharing – narratives or not

There is no clear-cut answer to the question of whether sharing-time turns are narratives. The literature on narratives does not usually treat narratives as a part of everyday conversational exchange but as speech events somewhat separate from other kinds of talk. There are, however, exceptions to this position, and children's narratives embedded in conversational sequences have recently been studied (Umiker-Sebeok 1979). The most influential work done on narratives embedded in ongoing talk is Labov's model of narrative structures. Labov suggests that there are six syntactically and semantically organized elements to a story: (1) abstract, (2) orientation, (3) complicating action, (4) evaluation, (5) resolution, and (6) coda. These elements (some of which are optional) represent the necessary temporal sequence of any story and must occur in their designated order with the exception of evaluative devices which can occur in any of the segments. Many other models of narratives similarly take the form of a structured organization of elements which account for temporal sequencing but vary in the degree and extent to which the structures compose necessary and definable parts of the narrative. In studying children's conceptions of story form, Applebee (1976) found that children from the age of five can recognize the main sequential components of a story's structure.

However, these approaches can be seen as having something of a literate bias, in that they assume that narratives whether orally presented or written will follow the same rules of form. Moreover it is assumed that oral narratives can be analyzed from a written transcript showing at best only hesitation phenomena and the rudiments of intonation afforded by punctuation. Folklorists, however, who have worked more specifically with the oral presentation of narratives usually within a ritual storytelling context, have found that oral narratives are built around formulas of content, syntactic form and meter which allow for the rapid production of sequences necessary in oral composition (Finnegan 1981; Hymes 1982). This work has shown the difficulty of translating into writing an oral performance, which depends upon the paralinguistic presentation (stress, intonation, and pitch) to carry essential information (MacClendon 1977). These findings have influenced my study of the materials from the children's sharing time.

Sharing time, as an activity, provides children with experience in presenting an organized sequence of discourse within a recognized speech event frame. In the cases where the child does event-oriented accounting or tells where he or she got the object presented, the order of reported events conforms to the presumed order in which the events occurred. In this way, such a presentation follows the canonical form of narrative discourse, evidencing features of temporal sequencing that are considered basic to narrative discourse, but are lacking in other discourse genres. For this reason, it seems appropriate to treat this talk as a particular variant of narrative discourse.

Example 5.4[2]

1	MARTIN	Yesterday/
2		. . . Burt / . . and I was at Burt's house /
3		and um / . . this dog was running across the street /
4		. . . and uh /
5	T	What did?
6	BURT	[This dog [
7	MARTIN	[was running a cross the street /
8		and a car runned him over /
9		and / . . and he / and he fell / . . down
10		and he was screeching /
11		then he died /
12		and then him mom / put him on a board /
13		and then the bus came /
14		and he [and he got
15	BURT	[called / called for help //
16	MARTIN	called for help //
17	T	I'm sorry. Life isn't all fun and pleasantry is it?
18	MARTIN	It was a lost dog //
19	T	That's a very [sad –
20	BURT	[It was a lost dog // (f)
21	MARTIN	So the guy who owned him / doesn't know / [he was dead // (pp)
22	T	[Really? Right,
23		that's very sad. That makes me feel very bad. But
24		life's like that. We can't pretend it isn't can we?
25	Cs	No.
26	T	'Cause things like that do happen. Sorry

Martin's discourse, produced collaboratively with Mrs. Jones and Burt, shows a great deal of rhythmic synchronization. The discourse in example 5.4 can be analyzed as containing an *orientation* section (lines 1 and 2), *complicating action* (lines 3–11), a *resolution* (lines 12–16), and a *coda* (lines 18, 20, and 21), which also serves as Martin's evaluation of the discourse. Mrs. Jones provides her own evaluative comments (lines 17, 19, 22–24, and 26), which differ in form from Martin's. Martin's comment 'It was a lost dog' (line 18) adds additional information about the dog, which ties lexically back to line 3, where Martin originally mentions 'this dog'. His comment, then, serves several purposes. It adds new and important information about the dog, brings the narrative to a close (also indicated by pronounced falling intonation), and evaluates the discourse implicitly, as if to say, 'It's especially sad because it was a lost dog.' Mrs. Jones does not overtly respond to this comment, perhaps because she interprets it merely as additional detail rather than as Martin's evaluation and point in telling the story. The comment is then repeated, more loudly and with emphasis by Burt, and then further elaborated on by Martin (line 21), who again evaluates by means of providing additional information. Mrs. Jones then makes explicit the 'point' of Martin's story (lines 22–24). She accomplishes this by referring to the event as a whole, standing outside the actual account, whereas Martin's and Burt's evaluative comments are an integral part of the account, and hence remain indirect.

Labov has noted that a common trait of middle-class narrators is that they often use explicit evaluation. That is, they interrupt their narrative mid-stream, turn to their listener and explicitly state their 'point'. Mrs. Jones, who uses this strategy in evaluating the children's talk, often fails to see the implicit evaluative force of the children's remarks and even, on occasion, misses their point entirely.[3] In providing explicit evaluative comments (as with Martin) or prodding the children to produce their own (as will be seen later with Walter), she may be providing the children necessary training in making their talk more explicit and hence less dependent on context, shared assumptions, and background knowledge for correct interpretation.

While clearly a narrative account in structure, this kind of discourse deviates systematically from narratives generated in a normal conversational setting in the following ways:

1. The floor is held for the child by the teacher, as a rule of sharing etiquette.

Example 5.5

DEENA Today, when I go home um. . . and u- . . .and I see my baby sister. . .

TEACHER Excuse me. Walter, it's Deena's turn right now. Could you please listen.

DEENA When I go home tod. . . today and see my baby sister. . .

Once a child has the floor, he or she is allowed to finish (in general), so that 'boring the audience' is not an overriding concern of the speaker. It does happen on occasion that when a child is considered too longwinded or unfocused, a child on the rug may comment on this (e.g. Walter: How many of them rocks is she gonna show us?) or more commonly, Mrs. Jones intervenes and quickly brings the turn to a close.

2. The child is not expected to tie his or her topic to the previous discourse. The relevance constraint requires only that the discourse topic be 'appropriate' to sharing, that is, some kind of personal account or description of an object. Thus the constraints on demonstrating relevance and topic tying are far looser than is normally the case in conversationally embedded narratives.

3. The child's talk does not have to stand by itself as a fully formed narrative. Rather, as example 5.4 shows, sharing turns are highly collaborative. Mrs. Jones interjects questions, comments, and reactions, often providing slots for orienting or evaluating the discourse, if this information is not explicitly provided by the child spontaneously. In this way, the teacher builds a scaffolding for the child's achievement of a narrative (McNamee 1979).

Example 5.6

1	WALTER	I went to the - / beach /
2		. . . and I found / this little thing / in the water //
3	T	For goodness sake. What is it?
4	WALTER	Huh?//
5	DORAL	[A block /
6	CS	[A block / a block /
7	T	A block. W[hen did you go to the beach?
8	CARL	[I-
9	WALTER	[I went to—
10	CARL	[I have tons of those blocks [–
11	WALTER	[I went to- / the 'Santa Cruz beach //
12	T	You did? When? O-Over the weekend?
13	WALTER	[Nods]
14	T	Oh wow. I bet it's nice down there. Wasn't it?
15	WALTER	Yeah // (breathy)
16	T	Was the water cold?
17	WALTER	Yeah //
18	T	It's always cold down there, thank you.

In this example, Walter holds up a weather-beaten wooden block and says he found it during a trip to the beach. Mrs. Jones then asks a series of questions that structure his presentation for him so that it contains the following pieces of information (and no more):

1. the name of the object found in the water,
2. the name of the beach,
3. when his visit took place,
4. that it was nice there, and
5. that the water was cold.

Walter here begins his account with an orientation that could easily lead into a narrative. The teacher's contributions, while designed to help him develop this narrative, in fact serve to turn his performance into a restricted account that contains explicit orientation and evaluation but no complicating action whatsoever. In this respect, it is closer to object-focused, 'show and tell' type discourse than to event-oriented narrative accounting. Furthermore the teacher's responses seem to throw Walter off balance so that the descriptive information which is part of this limited account ends up being supplied by the teacher. The child does not get the kind of practice that the previous child did. In this case, collaboration looks more like 'appropriation' of the child's topic (Cazden, personal communication).

The teacher's model: providing a scaffold for learning

Examples 5.4 and 5.6 demonstrate that the child's discourse cannot be analyzed in isolation. The teacher plays a crucial role in structuring the child's discourse and providing a scaffold which provides slots for the child to provide the form of discourse that the teacher considers appropriate. In analyzing Mrs. Jones' comments in response to the children, it becomes evident that she has an underlying model of what constitutes 'good' sharing, and that this implicit model draws upon the Western story-form model which might be called the canonical story form (Cook-Gumperz and Green 1984). In this underlying model the teacher looks for a simplified version of the canonical form in which importance is attached, not to content per se, nor to the sequentially ordered structure of an account, but rather, as in simple descriptive prose, to clarity of topic statement and explication. What the teacher seems to be looking for is an approach to any topic, whereby:

1. objects are to be named and described, even when in plain sight;
2. talk is to be explicitly grounded temporally and spatially;
3. discourse is to be tightly structured so as to highlight one particular topic (which then makes it sound 'important');
4. thematic ties need to be lexicalized if topic shifts are to be seen as motivated and relevant.

In these requirements, the teacher seems to be encouraging, in an oral mode, the discourse forms that could provide the beginning of an expository prose style. The teacher's notion of sharing is far removed from everyday accounts which depend upon their situated character for much of the detail. In the teacher's model this kind of detail must be fully lexicalized and explicated. The teacher's expectations thus seem to be shaped by adult notions of literate description. It is probable that such an implicit model puts many of the children at a disadvantage, because they are, relatively speaking, less familiar with such a 'prose-like' oral style. Many of the black children, in particular, have a way of doing narrative accounts that approximates a highly developed oral narrative tradition which does not require the restricted temporal and causal chain-ordering conventions of literate narrative.[4] It is when such a community-based discourse style directly differs from the teacher's implicit model, that her provision of a scaffolding for story development is less than successful. Furthermore, the fact that the discourse model is implicit makes the children uncertain as to why their offerings are deemed less successful, as I will illustrate below.

Children's discourse style

I now turn to a more detailed analysis of the discourse style used by the children in doing sharing, in particular as it conforms to, or violates, the teacher's underlying model of what counts as appropriate and adequate sharing.

Just as there is an identifiable difference in sharing intonation used by the black and white children, I have found corresponding differences in discourse style. The discourse of the white children tends to be tightly organized, centering on a single topic or series of closely related topics, with thematic development accomplished through lexical cohesion, and a linear ordering of events, leading quickly to a punch-line resolution.

Example 5.7

1	JENNY	Yesterday/
2		my mom,
3		. . . and / . . my whole family/
4		went with me / . . . um / . . . to a party /
5		and / . . . it was a Thanksgiving party /
6		. . . [where . . . and . . . we . . um . .
7	STUDENT TEACHER	[mm
8	JENNY	my mom /
9		. . . we had to / um . . get / . . dress up as Pilgrims /
10		. . . and my mom made me this hat / for a Pilgrim //
11	STUDENT TEACHER	Oh great.
12	T	Try it on model it for us. Let's see how
13		you'd look as a [Pilgrim.
14	JENNY	[I don't want to //

Structurally and prosodically, example 5.7 evidences characteristic patterns of topic-centered discourse. It begins with temporal grounding ('Yesterday', line 1) which remains unchanged throughout the turn, and uses lexical repetitions and thematically related nominals ('party', line 4; 'Thanksgiving party', line 5; 'Pilgrims', line 9; 'hat for a Pilgrim', line 10) to advance the theme, with topicalization as a device for elaboration ('party' in line 4 becomes 'it' in line 5). Prosodically, the turn begins with sharing intonation (sustained rising tones and vowel elongation) and rising tones, shifting to complex tones as complicating information is provided (rise fall rises (lines 3 and 8) and rise falls (line 9), with falling tones and a shift to a lower-pitch register in closing).

In contrast to a topic-centered style, the black children are far more likely to use a 'topic-associating' style, which consists of a series of segments or episodes which are implicitly linked in highlighting some person or theme.

Example 5.8

1	SHERRY	Yester day /
2		. . . I went / . . . yesterday /
3		. . . yesterday when I came home from school
4		my grandmother was over there / . . and my auntie /
5		. . . and / . . . my grand mother /
6		. . . we goin' / to stay down / at . . . her house
7		when my mother have her baby //
8	TEACHER	[Oh.
9	SHERRY	[And um my bther cousin / . . . and my / um . . . uncle /
10		he gon' to pick up his / . . . son /
11		a . . and / we goin' trick 'r treatin' //
12	TEACHER	Oh that sounds like fun, [OK, Thank you.
13	CELENA	[Uh, we gon' go
14		trick 'r treatin' [too.
15	STUDENT TEACHER	[OK Peter.

In example 5.8 we see shifts both in topic and temporal orientation in lines 1–7, moving from the past (who was at Sherry's house when she got home from school) to the future (associating her grandmother with the time in the near future when she would be staying at her grandmother's house). At the point of the topic change, there is a 1.5 second pause (after the word 'auntie') and a high, level pitch on 'and', features which for some children regularly accompany a topic shift. While there are no explicit lexical or syntactic markers to indicate a topic shift or to relate the two topics, the repetition of 'my grandmother' is intonationally marked, indicating the semantic association across topics. However, a literate adult, telling a similar story, might indicate the shift to the new but related topic lexically, by saying, 'And speaking of my grandmother'. The further shift in perspective that occurs in line 9 (the shift in focus away from her grandmother to other relatives) is not marked overtly in any way. The juxtaposition of the two pieces of information (staying at her grandmother's and going trick-or-treating) and the use of the same tense indicator ('goin' to') forces one to infer that the two activities are related temporally. This relationship might be marked lexically by an adult as 'And while we're at my grandmother's, my uncle is . . .'.

Interactive consequences of sharing style

Given that sharing-time accounts were collaboratively produced, the kind of discourse style used by the child (whether topic-centered or topic-associating) influenced the kind and amount of teacher/child collaboration that occurred. The effects of narrative style and expectations on teacher/child collaboration and the systematic nature of the interactive processes underlying both successful and unsuccessful instances of sharing-time turns will be explored in the following examples.

Topic-centered

With children who used a topic-centered style, Mrs. Jones was highly successful at picking up on the child's topic and using the child's offering as a scaffold on which to build. By means of a series of statements/questions/responses (or vertical-construction sequences), she was able to elicit more explicit, descriptive elaboration on the same topic. Her questions were rhythmically synchronized (usually occurring after the child paused on a falling tone), and hence were not seen by the child as interruptions. For these children, working collaboratively with the teacher, sharing time provided the interactive support and extended practice necessary for learning to do prose-like narrative accounting.

In example 5.9, a single topic, making candles at day camp, is introduced and elaborated upon. Both teacher and child have a similar narrative schema and a shared set of signaling conventions. They are able to agree on what the topic is and collaborate in rhythmically synchronized exchanges, maintaining a high degree of cohesion within and across turns. The teacher is able to build on the child's contributions and help her produce more focused and explicit discourse.

Example 5.9

1	MINDY	When I was in 'da:y camp / we made these / um candle:s/
2	T	You made them?
3	MINDY	And uh / I-I tried it with 'different colors / with both
4		of them but / 'one just came out / 'this one just came
5		out blue / and 'I don't know / what this color is //
6	T	That's neat-o // 'Tell the kids 'how you do it from the
7		very start // Pretend we don't know a thing about candles //
8		. . . OK // What did you do first? // What did you use? //
9		Flour? //
10	MINDY	Um . . . here's some / hot wax / some real hot wax / that
11		you / 'just take a string / and tie a knot in it // and
12		'dip the 'string in the um wax //
13	T	What makes it uh have a shape? //
14	MINDY	Um / you just shape it //
15	T	Oh you shaped it with your hand // mmm //
16	MINDY	But you have / 'first you have to 'stick it into the wax /
17		and then water / and then keep doing that until it gets to
18		the size you want it //
19	T	OK // Who knows what the string is for? // . . .

In example 5.9, Mindy introduces her topic with temporal and spatial grounding (line 1), while holding up two small candles in her hands. She uses distinctive sharing intonation, pausing after a low rising tone on 'candles'. Mrs. Jones comes in at this point, saying 'You made them' with a high rising contour on 'made', signaling pleasant surprise, in the form of an echo question, as if to say 'Oh my, did you really make them (by yourself, by hand)?' Mindy does not overtly respond to the question (i.e. she does not produce the canonical Yes/No response to a Yes/No question). Instead she continues her discourse beginning with 'and' in line 3, which suggests that this turn is directly linked to her previous turn. Nonetheless, there is some evidence of cohesion across turns in that Mrs. Jones follows up on something that Mindy had mentioned first ('making' candles). Mindy's talk about the color of the candles is, however, only tangentially related to Mrs. Jones' comment. In lines 3–5, Mindy relies heavily on anaphoric pronouns ('it', 'them') and deictic forms ('this', 'this one'), which are by definition rooted in the context of speaking. There is minimal lexical elaboration, but because she is holding the candles up for everyone to see and gesturing with one hand and then the other, one would have no problem filling in the semantic information.

Mrs. Jones waits until Mindy pauses on a low falling tone (on 'color') and reiterates her interest in the actual process, but this time, does so more explicitly. She provides a clear and elaborate set of guides for how she wants Mindy to talk about making the candles. 'Tell the kids how you do it from the very start. Pretend we don't know a thing about candles.' The last remark is of course an instruction to assume no shared knowledge and to be as explicit as possible, Mrs. Jones then pauses and gets no response. She rephrases her instruction as a question, 'What did you do first?' She pauses again and follows with an additional clue by offering an obviously wrong answer to the question, which nonetheless suggests to Mindy an example of the type of answer she has in mind. 'What did you use? Flour?' At this point Mindy responds, building upon the base which the teacher's questions have provided. She describes what she used ('hot wax') and the steps involved. In addition to a description of the sequencing of activities involved in the business of making candles, this passage introduces several context-free lexical items ('some hot wax', 'a string', 'a knot'). The use of lexical items provides explicit information about the activity and the materials used in candle making. This contrasts with the use in the preceding turn (lines 3–5) of anaphoric and deictic items which rely on context for interpretation. Additionally the use of definite and indefinite articles grammaticalizes the distinction between new and old information: 'some wax' and 'a string' became 'the string' and 'the wax' (lines 10–12).

When Mindy pauses on a low tone, Mrs. Jones asks a further question about how she had shaped the candles (which had an unusual rippled shape). Mindy responds somewhat uninformatively saying, 'You just shape it.' The use of 'just' and the low falling pitch on 'shape' (giving the utterance unmarked declarative force), implies that how you shape it goes without saying. Mindy thus relies on her listeners to 'fill in' what she left unsaid, that she simply shaped the candles with her hands. Mrs. Jones evidently has no problem making the correct inference. She begins line 15 with 'Oh' as if to say, 'I see', and then repeats the gist of Mindy's utterance, this time making the conversational implicature fully explicit.

Mindy does not overtly acknowledge Mrs. Jones' contribution (that is, she does not say, 'That's right, with your hands'). However, there is tacit acknowledgment in that Mindy begins her next turn with 'but', used not as a contradiction or denial marker, but rather to mean something like 'Yes, that's right, but there's something more to add to that.' Thus Mrs. Jones' comment 'with your hands' now stands as part of the account and is referred to by Mindy as if she herself had uttered it. Mindy then builds on Mrs. Jones' contribution to round out the description of the process, filling in several important steps that come before the shaping of the candles. 'But you have, first you have to stick it into the wax, and then water, and then keep doing that until it gets to the size you want it.' In this way, we can see how this procedural account is a joint production. Mindy's comments in lines 16–18 acknowledge and build upon Mrs. Jones' contribution in line 15, which in turn builds on and fills out an earlier contribution of Mindy's.

There are several notable points about this episode as a whole. For one thing, most of Mrs. Jones' questions occur when Mindy pauses after a low falling tone. Such pauses indicate some kind of closure. Hence Mrs. Jones' questions occur at the end of a complete unit and do not sound like interruptions. Furthermore, her questions descend from general to specific, until a level is reached at which Mindy can and does respond appropriately. Lastly, the teacher's responses and clarifications build on Mindy's own contributions.

It is important to note that Mindy's discourse in response to Mrs. Jones' questions and comments is far more complex than the spontaneous utterances produced without Mrs. Jones' guidance. Thus we can see in this example how a shared sense of topic and a synchronization of exchanges with the teacher, in a series of vertical constructions, enable the student to develop a lexically explicit and coherent account of a complex activity.

Topic-associating

With many of the black children, who tended to use a topic-associating style, the teacher was markedly less successful at providing a scaffold, via her implicit model to structure and clarify their discourse. Her questions were often mistimed (due it appears to a misreading of prosodic cues) and often interrupted the child mid-clause. Moreover, the teacher appeared to have difficulty discerning the topic of discourse and anticipating the direction of thematic development. As a result, her questions were often thematically inappropriate and seemed to throw the child off balance, interrupting his or her train of thought. In cases where the child continued to talk, undaunted, these turns were often cut short by the teacher, who jokingly referred to them as 'filibusters' on occasion.

Mrs. Jones was sincerely concerned about helping topic-associating children develop what she considered to be a more appropriate sharing style. She successively introduced two specific pedagogical techniques to curtail topic associating. Early in the year, she began to emphasize the notion of 'importance' (as in the example below), indicating that topics for sharing were events that were 'really, really very important and sort of different'. Later on in the year, Mrs. Jones began regularly to invoke a new sharing principle: that the children should tell about only one thing, saying, for example, 'Celena I want you to tell us about one thing that's very important.' It is important to note that both these rules of thumb are glosses for topic-centered discourse. They made sense only if one used a topic-centered style to begin with.

Example 5.10 is a sharing turn where trouble arises, due to the mismatch between the child's style and the teacher's implicit model. In this case, Deena moves fluidly from topic to topic without making explicit the thematic ties connecting (or separating) the various topics.

Example 5.10

1 DEENA Um . . . I went to the beach / . . Sunday/
2 and / to MacDonalds /
3 and to the park /
4 . . . and / . . I got this for my / . . birthday //
5 . . . My mother bought it for me/
6 . . and um / . . . I had / . . um / . . two dollars for my birthday
7 and I put it in here /
8 . . and I went to where my frie-nd /
9 . . named Gi Gi /
10 . . . I went over to my grandmother's house with her /
11 . . . and um / . . . . . she was on my back /
12 and I / . . and we was walkin' around /
13 . . . by my house /
14 . . and um / . . . she was hea-vy /
15 She [was in the sixth or seventh grade //
16 T: [OK I'm going to stop you. I want to talk
17 about things that are really really very important.
18 That's important to you but tell us things that are
19 sort of different. Can you do that? And tell us what
20 beach you went to.

In example 5.10, Deena begins with explicit temporal and physical grounding by telling without much descriptive detail what she did on Sunday. She then shifts gears radically to object-focused discourse about a small purse she had brought from home, embedding it in person-oriented talk that shifts focus away from her birthday present to playing with a girlfriend (an activity related only temporally, or through association with the purse, to her birthday). She begins to tell about her activities with her friend but is stopped just before she gets to what, on the basis of her prosody, appears to be the 'point' of her discourse, the fact that she was able to carry her friend, fully twice her age, around on her back (and Deena was, at the time, a tiny six-year-old).

Topical shifts are indicated prosodically through emphasis and vowel elongation on key words which introduce a new topic (on 'Sunday', 'birthday', and 'friend'). Moreover, she uses exaggerated emphasis and lengthening on the word 'heavy', which suggests that she is building to the main point. However, the lack of any lexicalized markers other than 'and' between topics makes the discourse difficult to follow, for someone expecting the account to focus on a single event or object. It sounds as if there is *no* topic, and no point, and that Deena is simply rambling on about trivial occurrences. If we take a closer look at this turn, we see that the topics of discourse themselves are not inherently trivial or uninteresting, but rather that the rhetorical style used makes it 'sound' as if there is no topic whatsoever. Taken by themselves, each separate topic discussed by Deena above would have counted as highly appropriate: activities on a Sunday, a birthday present, and acrobatics with a friend. The problem with Deena's presentation was more one of discourse form than of content. However, simply reminding the children to tell about important events does not provide them with the criteria for either topic selection or discourse form centered around a single topic.

For the white children in this class, who already had more elements of the schema for topic-centered discourse, the teacher was better able to collaborate with them and so build on their narrative intentions. With the black children, on the other hand, the teacher's questions lacked rhythmic synchrony and therefore must often have been seen by the children as interruptions. Typically, the teacher's questions resulted in asynchronous exchanges, a fragmentation of topics, and frequent misinterpretation of semantic intent. Most importantly, the teacher's comments did not build on what the child already knew and so provide the extended practice and assistance that would lead to an expanded, lexicalized narrative-accounting style.

Deena as informant

One year and four months after this sharing turn was recorded, Deena, now a second grader, was asked in an informal interview what she thought about sharing time in the first grade. She expressed a keen sense of frustration about being interrupted during sharing time. She saw this as an indication that the teacher was simply not interested in what she had to say, explaining, 'Sharing time got on my nerves. She was always interruptin' me, sayin' "that's not important enough" and I hadn't hardly started talkin'!' Her older sister (also present during the interview) recalled similar frustrations from her sharing experience five years earlier, in both kindergarten and first grade.

Interestingly, when I played specific sharing turns of Deena's, she was able to verbalize and clarify many of the unstated connections in her discourse.

Additionally, when I asked Deena during the interview what she thought Mrs. Jones meant by 'tell about one thing', Deena said, 'she meant tell about one thing, not 35,000 other things. Like, don't say, "Yesterday, I had a fight (pause) I saw some roses."' I take this as a further indication that Deena did indeed have a sense that some topics were related and others were not, and that she was not simply moving from topic to topic in an arbitrary, unmotivated manner.

Finally, when asked what she thought Mrs. Jones wanted the children to do at sharing time, Deena offered the following example of 'good' sharing talk.

Example 5.11

DEENA ˈShe just wanted us to ˌsay like / well

well yesterday,
blah blah blah /
blah blah blah /
blah ˌblah blah blah/
blah ˌblah blah blah /
blah ˌblah blah blah //

Deena begins with the sharing-time formula, 'yesterday', using pronounced sharing intonation. She then provides an account without words which is segmented prosodically into what sounds like a beginning (orientation), middle (elaboration), and end (resolution). Interestingly enough, this captures precisely the intonational patterns of topic-centered discourse. This indicates that Deena had a sense of what topic-centered discourse *sounded* like and knew this was what Mrs. Jones wanted, but did not impose this prosodic framework on her own narrative style and presentations.

Sharing time might have provided Deena with the extended practice she needed to internalize a new narrative schema and a new set of strategies. But during sharing time, Deena and Mrs. Jones seemed to be working at cross purposes: Mrs. Jones was looking for topic-centered discourse (which she glossed as 'telling about important things' or 'telling about one thing only') while Deena was building up a topic-associating narrative account whereby the overall point had to be inferred from a series of concrete anecdotes, without any explicit statement of the topic. Each was working within her own sharing-time schema; without a shared sense of topic and narrative style, and a shared set of signaling conventions, collaboration was unsuccessful. Mrs. Jones' indirect attempts at instruction were misinterpreted and Deena's occasional use of topic-centered discourse was not appreciated, nor was her discourse seen as organized and well-planned. Misevaluations such as these, on the part of both teacher and child, may explain in part why topic-associating strategies persisted over time, despite the fact that children like Deena got frequent opportunities to share and were generally able learners, as shown by their improvement over the course of the year in other literacy-related skills, such as handwriting or spelling.

Moreover, Mrs. Jones' perception of topic-associating children as having difficulty planning their discourse in advance, *selecting* an appropriate topic, and sticking with it accounts for her emphasis on 'importance' and 'telling about only one thing'. The fact that these children *did* have an 'important' theme in mind and a systematic set of strategies for thematic development (albeit different from hers) explains in part why these sharing principles were not particularly informative or effective with topic-associating children.

Conclusion

These examples are not isolated instances. Rather, they are illustrative of stable patterns of differential treatment, characteristic of sharing-time interaction over the course of the entire school year. On the basis of these recurring patterns of interaction, the following conclusions emerge: a shared sense of topic and a synchronization of questions and responses in a series of vertical constructions enable teacher and child collectively to create an account that is lexically and grammatically explicit, and in many cases more complex than what the child would be likely to create on his or her own. On the other hand, differing narrative schemata, lack of a shared sense of topic, and apparent misreading of prosodic cues result in asynchronous pacing of teacher/child exchanges, less rather than more talk, and misevaluation of intent on both teacher's and child's part.

It is important to note that, in this classroom, a child's general discourse style did not in any neat way reflect or predict reading achievement. Among the children in this class, Deena, who had consistent problems doing appropriate sharing, was one of the very best readers (she had been taught to read by her older sister while still in kindergarten). Furthermore, while Deena's reading, mathematics, and spelling skills all showed marked improvement over the course of the school year, her sharing discourse style remained unchanged. And so, while sharing can be seen as an oral preparation for literacy, its influence on children's reading ability remains unclear. However, Deena's topic-associating oral-discourse style may, in time, greatly interfere with her ability to produce literate-sounding descriptive prose. What effect Deena's non-prose-like oral style will have on her participation in school activities such as sharing or creative writing, and correspondingly on the teacher's evaluation of her performance in class, remains to be seen from what she does in the second, third, and fourth grades, where discourse style and ability to write cohesive prose assume increasing importance.

In this study, I have attempted a careful description of a highly collaborative classroom activity, and have uncovered systematic communicative mismatches that result in unsuccessful collaboration and misassessment of children's ability. The question then is what can be done to improve the quality of teacher/child interaction in activities such as sharing time.

For one thing, it is important to recognize that learning is not a simple transfer of knowledge from the teacher to the student. Rather, learning is mediated through complex interactive and interpretive processes and whether learning takes place is a function of the way an activity is structured, the amount of contact, practice, and instruction allowed for, and the quality of the contact. For this reason, the problem of differential access to practice in activities such as sharing time should not be seen as a problem with individual teachers or individual children, using particular discourse strategies. Instead the problem lies with schools as complex social institutions, embodying decisions at the level of school-board members and educational policy committees to track and evaluate children, as well as the pressures of overcrowded classrooms and severe cutbacks in support staff. Given this state of affairs, ethnic differences in discourse style introduce an additional factor into an already complex social arena, creating interactional constraints that make learning more difficult.[5]

Secondly, the communicative processes that I have identified are completely automatic and not easily accessible to conscious scrutiny or control (Silverstein 1981). Becoming attuned to different devices for signaling thematic cohesion, or monitoring and modifying one's own discourse style or timing would require more than a handy in-service workshop or two. It would be akin to learning to touch type on a completely rearranged keyboard, or learning to talk with a foreign accent.

However, simply becoming *aware* that there is a logic and regularity to what sounds like 'rambling' discourse is the first step to improved collaboration with children who use a topic-associating style. One last anecdote will illustrate this point. I recently had the opportunity to do a follow-up study of teacher/child collaboration in a first/second grade classroom in the Boston area. The teacher in this class was very interested in the work and had asked to read the research proposal. Included in the proposal was a detailed description of topic-centered and topic-associating narrative styles. The next time I visited her classroom she mentioned to me that she had found the proposal very interesting because she knew 'just what I was talking about!' Several of the black children in her classroom, it seemed, used topic-associating discourse strategies in group discussions and sharing-time sessions. She said that she had never quite known what to make of it, or do about it, and admitted that she had often interpreted it as rambling and unfocused. Nothing more was said at that point.

One week later, I was again observing in her classroom. Her children were engaged in a free-writing exercise, on the topic of 'a pet I have or would like to have'. I noticed that Antonia, a quiet black girl, had written the following in her writing booklet:

> I have a cat and my cat
> never go to the bathroom
> when my cousin eating over
> my house and we went to
> the circus my cousins
> names are LaShaun Trinity
> Sherry Cynthia Doral,

The writing looked suspiciously like topic-associating discourse (in that it included a shift in scenes and temporal orientation and seemed to highlight key relatives). I therefore paid special attention to what happened when the child approached the teacher, notebook in hand, to show her what she had written. The following interaction ensued. The teacher asked Antonia to read aloud what she had written (a standard practice during a teacher–student writing discussion in this classroom). The child read in a slow, staccato style, saying each word carefully. The teacher's first response was, 'Boy, you've got a lot of cousins!'[6] She chatted with Antonia for some time about her family. And then the teacher paused and said thoughtfully, 'Just one more thing, what do your cousins have to do with the circus and your cat?' Antonia answered very matter of factly, saying, 'Oh, my cousins always eat over my house, and they sleep over my house too. And one day last week, we all went to the circus.' The teacher nodded her head, smiling, and said, 'Ooooh, I see.'

Later that day, the teacher came up to me and mentioned the episode (which I had watched at a distance, and even managed to tape record). She said she thought that what Antonia had written was an example of topic-associating discourse, and seemed very pleased. And then she added, 'You know, it's a whole lot easier to get *them* to make the connections clear, if you assume that the connections are there in the first place.'

It is this level of 'awareness' that can be of practical significance to teachers. They may still not be able to figure out 'on the spot' just what the connections are, but in starting out with the assumption that the child has an important point to make, there is at least a common ground to build upon.

Postscript

Following the original 'Sharing Time' study, Courtney Cazden and I did a follow-up study in four Boston-area classrooms, and explored teachers' implicit judgments of both topic-centered and topic-associating styles. A general summary of this work is reported in Cazden 2001. But the most interesting development of the sharing-time work in the past two decades has come from urban elementary-school teachers who read the article and recognized the many Deenas in their midst. A number of these teachers tape recorded sharing-time sessions, examined the way they structured sharing time, characterized the stories children told (and didn't tell), and analyzed the impact of their own talk (and evaluations) on their students' later performances. In a number of cases, 'teacher research' on sharing time led teachers to alter the structure of the event, the norms for participation, and even what counted as a 'story' in the first place, expanding the possibilities for storytelling in their classroom. Perhaps best known are articles published by members of the Brookline Teacher Researcher Seminar, a group of teachers who met weekly for over ten years, tape-recording their classroom interactions and using tools and techniques of interactional sociolinguistics to examine language and literacy. Work such as Karen Gallas' *When the child takes the chair* (1994) or Steve Griffin's *I Need People: Storytelling in a Second-Grade Classroom* (2004) show the power of these tools in the hands of teachers in helping to work with cultural and linguistic differences so that they become intellectual resources rather than barriers. (See also

Cazden, 2001 for a discussion of the ways teachers have taken up the work.)

In a number of these reconfigured sharing-time events, teacher and students took on new roles and rights for telling stories. These changes opened up the classroom conversation so that more voices could be heard, making it easier for teachers to recognize students' narrative and academic abilities. Most impressively, teachers used this expanded discourse space to support all of their children to take on new 'ways with words', in both speaking and writing.

Notes

1. This study was carried out in an elementary school located in Berkeley, CA. At the time of the study (1977–79), Berkeley's hills and 'flatlands' neighborhoods were largely segregated by class and ethnicity (white professional families tended to live in the hills and black working-class families in the flatlands). The city had a voluntary bussing program so that all schools were integrated. This particular school was located in the Berkeley hills. All of the white children were from upper-middle-class families and walked to school. All of the black children came from working-class families, lived within a radius of eight blocks of one another, and were bussed to school. Class and ethnicity, as influences on discourse styles, are thus confounded. In the original article, the children were referred to as black or white rather than black working-class and white middle-class, and I have left these labels (however problematic) in place.
2. Prosodic and paralinguistic cues are transcribed using a simplified form of a system developed by John Gumperz and his collaborators, based on Trim's work. In this system, speech sequences are first divided into tone groups or intonational phrases. A phrase can be marked by a minor, non-final boundary '/' or a major or final boundary '//'. Within a tone group we indicate: (1) location of the nuclei (i.e. the syllable or syllables marked by change in pitch): '\' low fall, '\' high fall, '/' low rise, '/' high rise; (2) other accented syllables in the tone group, '|' high, '|' low; (3) paralinguistic features such as (a) shift to high pitch register '⌈' or shift to low pitch register '⌊' (both applying to the entire group), (b) pausing: '. .' indicating a break in timing and '. . .' indicating a measurable pause, (c) speech rate: rate:"acc." indicating accelerating tempo and 'ret.' indicating slowing down, (d) loudness over an entire tone group is indicated by 'p' (soft) or 'f' (loud). Doubling of one of the above symbols indicates extra emphasis.
3. The following is an example of a case where the implicit evaluative force is missed altogether by Mrs. Jones. Here Sherry uses 'internal'

evaluation, putting 'the point' of her account in a non-narrative descriptive clause, between two narrative clauses.

1	SHERRY	Yesterday I 'went to the dentist /
2		and this my ˌlast appointment /
3		goin' ˌto the dentist //
4		I ˌjust got two ˌcavities //
5	T	And what did the dentist say to you?
6	SHERRY	(puzzled) . . . He say 'this my last appointment //
7	T	So you don't have to go back for a while //
8		Not for a while.

In this example, the crucial point (for Sherry) is the good news that she is done with the dentist (for the time being). However, the force of this information is carried through the parallel rhythm of 'last appointment' and 'goin' to the dentist' (both said with sustained pitches on appointment and dentist and each with a regular three-beat tempo). The use of parallel rhythm and intonation as cues of salience, is missed by the teacher for at least two reasons. For one thing, Mrs. Jones was probably expecting the evaluation to occur at the end of Sherry's account, following the action itself (where she is typically inclined to add it). Secondly, the strategies Sherry used as evaluation were not the ones that Mrs. Jones typically used, and hence, perhaps were not salient to her. Thus it may be that Mrs. Jones would have been more likely to correctly interpret Sherry's evaluative comments as such if the point had been made explicitly (as she herself does in lines 7 and 8) or else if Sherry had used stress or sharp contours (rather than level pitches and rhythmic marking) to make these comments stand out as evaluative.

4. I feel confident in speaking about children's sharing-time styles approximating an adult standard, because similar features of black adult narratives have been described by others, and used by black authors such as Zora Neal Hurston. The black linguist Geneva Smitherman, in her book *Talkin and Testifyin*, writes:

> Black English speakers will render their general, abstract observations about life, love, people in the form of concrete narrative . . . This meandering away from the 'point' takes the listener on episodic journeys and over tributary rhetorical routes, but like the flow of nature's rivers and streams, it all eventually leads back to the source. Though highly applauded by blacks, this narrative linguistic style is exasperating to whites who wish you'd be direct and hurry up and get to the point. (1977: 147–8)

5. It is important to note that it is not the use of topic-associating strategies per se, or the reliance on prosodic cues rather than full lexical items that makes it difficult for these children to acquire 'prose-like' discourse strategies. Rather, I am suggesting that their use of a discourse style that is at variance with the teacher's own style and expectations decreases

the *quality* of interaction in key classroom activities that might otherwise provide these children with the practice needed to develop a more expanded, prose-like discourse style.

6. Commenting on, or questioning the child about, the very last thing mentioned is a strategy commonly used by teachers in responding to topic-associating children at sharing time. See Michaels and Cazden (1986) for another example. These questions or comments generally only relate peripherally (if at all) to the child's underlying theme, but may be the only thing the teacher can get a handle on if unable to infer the theme implicit in the series of episodes.

6

Differential instruction in reading groups

James Collins

Preamble

In revising work conducted many years ago, it is appropriate to comment on original intentions and highlight aspects of the analysis that might now be obscure. It is also appropriate to assess the value of this work in light of what has followed. Accordingly, I comment on general intentions and analytic approach in this preface and comment on subsequent work of relevance in the afterword. The desire to revise, update, and improve is insatiable, author and text rarely being reconciled, but I have tried to resist this impulse, restricting changes in the chapter below to spelling and punctuation corrections and occasional rephrasing to clarify a sentence or passage.

The research presented in this chapter concerns different instruction strategies found among ability-ranked groups of first-grade students. It reports differences that are similar to what we now call 'phonics' versus 'whole-word' literacy instruction (Coles 2000; Collins 2003; Lemann 1997), but the terms of that current controversy are too polarizing. The different groups below are having their lessons with the same teacher, and they are working through the same basal reader. It is the contention of this chapter that the differences found are not the result of a fixed and unchanging 'teacher expectation', nor the result of some set of reading traits or skills that distinguish the two groups of students. Rather, the differences discussed below are the result of interactions occurring and recurring over the course of a school year: the face-to-face micro-order of adults and children talking to each other as part of the enterprise of teaching and learning. A concept used to orient the analyses is that of *conversational inference*, perhaps most simply described as the process through which people understand one another's utterances in given circumstances, responding on the basis of those situated understandings, provoking, in turn, responses from their co-conversationalists, which engender further responses from them, and so forth (Gumperz and Cook-Gumperz, this volume; 1982a; Michaels, Campbell, this volume).

My use of this concept reflects two general research commitments. First, there is a sociolinguistic insistence that *interaction matters*. In the case at hand, this means that it is necessary to study teachers' language and students' language together, as influencing and motivating one another, and not, as is often the case, as two parallel series that can be analyzed in isolation as containing this or that preferred or dispreferred feature of teacher talk or student language (see other chapters in this volume; Cazden 2001; Nystrand et al. 1997, ch. 3, on this point). Second, there is an ethnographic insistence on talk in context, that analyzing the back and forth of talk as the back and forth of teaching or learning is also the study of *situated action*. To be sure, there are aggregate, cross-contextual patterns in the reading lessons described below, and some of those patterns are reported in Table 6.1, which presents frequencies of kinds of instructional activities. But the crux of the argument is that those differences must be understood as emerging from situated communicative events. For instance, a teacher talking with students about given texts both influences and responds to how students read on a given occasion and throughout the school year. Secondly, students read aloud from a given text in ways that reflect their talk in other settings and how they respond to their teacher and their peers, enacting in the occasion, and over the course of a year, differing views of what reading is.

As one case study in a broader sociolinguistic ethnography of schooling and literacy, this chapter attempts to address a question of social justice – what are the implications of differential instruction for persisting inequalities of educational achievement and attainment? – along with questions of cognition – how do subtleties of prosody and pacing, of word selection and framing, influence the inferences interlocutors draw about one another and the task at hand? It is a virtue of theoretically informed ethnography that it enables a wide-ranging yet focused inquiry on social structure and classroom communication (Rampton 2006); it is a strength of conversation analysis that it insists on the here-and-now of language, talk together, as an essential aspect of both mind and society (Ochs 1996).

Introduction

In acquiring and mastering the skills of literacy young students must gain access to situations that allow them to learn and practice a variety of interpretive processes under the guidance of an adult. The following study is concerned with the way the language used by students and teachers influences the learning opportunities children encounter in formal classroom settings.

The way school children are organized into social groups and the linguistic means by which they communicate in those groups have an obvious bearing on the linguistic and cognitive skills they show as adults. This fact motivates the recurring concern in the United States with the way social and linguistic factors influence achievement in a stratified educational system. In the past three decades there has been a good deal of language-oriented research concerned with the effects of family background and teachers' expectations on educational achievement. Using a variety of coding schemes, discourse analysts and educational psychologists found that teachers' elicitation strategies and students' response patterns vary with students' classification as high-ability or low-ability (Brophy and Good 1974; Cherry-Wilkinson 1981; Mosenthal and Jin-Ma 1980). While rigorous in isolating linguistic and behavioral variables for analysis, this research suffers from two defects. First, it fails to situate ability classification in a historical and institutional framework that would shed light on the observed patterns of behavior and achievement. Second, it concentrates on small discourse units (for example, question–answer pairs) and so fails to provide a processual account of the communication found in high-ranked and low-ranked classroom activities. What is needed is a precise account of the way the typical social organization of classrooms constrains the communicative options available to students and teachers, and does so in such a way as to produce the different patterns of linguistic behavior reported in the literature. It is in an attempt to provide some answers at this level of analysis that this study of differential reading groups is made.

An important part of the organization of most early-primary classrooms is the ability group. The ostensible justification for ability grouping is that it permits instruction to be tailored to student aptitude and that, being flexible, it can be adjusted to the given student population and to changes in that population. In practice it represents a very inflexible classifying procedure, permitting little movement into or out of groups, once ability status has been assigned. This chapter demonstrates that individual aptitude is not the sole determinant of continued placement in an ability group, particularly a low group.

Once groups are set up, the group patterning takes on its own organizational life. Teachers and administrators are reported to believe strongly in the necessity and effectiveness of ability grouping, despite accumulating evidence to the contrary. In short, ability grouping represents a powerful a priori classification that restricts mobility, because groups are not added, deleted, or changed, despite the initial heterogeneity of or change in student aptitude.

One result of such practices is that students perceived as less prepared or less attentive in early primary grades are grouped together as low-ability. But these decisions are made when children are five and six years old, an age when ability is very difficult to determine. The negative result is that once ranked, low-ability students are given instruction different from that given to their high-ranked counterparts. The difference is due in part to teacher expectations, but also to the organization of activity. Microethnographic studies of reading groups have shown that in low-ranked lessons there is more apparent inattention and distraction (both from inside and outside the groups), with the result that less time is spent actually reading. Students most likely to have difficulty learning are thus assigned to groups where the social context is much less conducive to learning. There are clear and well-known effects of this assignment on achievement.

The phenomenon of differential treatment has been recognized and studied, in its various aspects, for over thirty years. Leacock (1969) approached the issue in terms of the differences between inner-city and suburban schools. Her work describes the differences in socializing processes that are transmitted in the school: in the inner-city minority schools, instructional activities and student–teacher exchanges emphasize discipline and respect for authority; in suburban middle-class schools, instructional activities and student–teacher exchanges emphasize individual initiative and self-learning. Rist (1970) studied differential treatment as part of the tracking system that is characteristic of most American public schools. He examined the criteria used in setting up ability groups, the effect of group membership on the quantity and quality of instruction received, and the long-term effect of group membership on educational performance. Piestrup (1973) studied differential treatment in reading instruction and focused on the teacher's reaction to the presence of dialect features in students' speech. In her study of reading instruction in fourteen classrooms, she described how the teacher's reaction to dialect features, stated in terms of teaching styles, helped to determine the quantity and quality of instruction that took place in a given lesson and, cumulatively, students' ability to read.

McDermott (1976; 1978) studied reading groups in detail and clarified a number of important aspects of reading instruction and the way it differs across ability groups. First, he showed that much less time was given to the actual tasks of reading with the low-ranked group (approximately a third of the time that was spent by the high-ranked group). Second, he showed that structural aspects of differential interaction resulted in a different pattern of turn-taking strategies and in inter-group rivalry. Third, and most important, he was among the first to see that the instructional process is collaborative: both teachers and students build upon one another's verbal and kinesic signals. This collaborative process unconsciously creates a pattern of interaction that is either harmonious and directed at reading or disharmonious and filled with interruptions. In the high-group sessions McDermott studied, the sequencing of turns proceeded smoothly, and questions about the readings usually concerned semantics, or meanings; conversely, in the low-group sessions, turn-taking was less orderly, consuming time that could have been spent on reading, and questions about the text usually concerned grapheme–phoneme correspondences and rarely addressed the more synthetic issue of overall story line.

In this study we decided to focus on language use in reading-group instruction, looking at the process as a verbal analogue to the kinds of nonverbal structuring of the classroom environment that McDermott studied. Since we examined language, we expected to be able to show how the kinds of interaction patterns McDermott observed are linked to communicative background and interactional history. The situation is different from the one studied by McDermott, because the reading groups in this study frequently used the same procedure for turn-taking (round robin). However, the more subtle forms of interactional harmony and disharmony were evident on videotapes of the reading lessons: lively engaged reading occurred during the high-group lessons, with frequent praise from the teacher; distracted and inattentive reading occurred during the low-group lessons, with frequent admonitions from the teacher to pay attention.

Recent work in the analysis of natural conversation has shown that nearly all successful communication is a process of exchanges in which conversationalists build upon the contributions of previous speakers. In our attempt to study the influence of community-based discourse styles on classroom interaction and reading instruction, we assumed that learning is an interactive process requiring similar sorts of collaboration between students and teachers (a perspective supported by research on language learning, such as Snow and Ferguson 1977; on preschooling by McNamee 1979; on classroom learning by Mehan 1979; and by Wells 1981b).

It followed that the collaborative learning process could be studied profitably by using concepts and techniques developed for the analysis of natural conversation. Because much research has shown that inferencing processes are crucial in language comprehension, and especially crucial in conversation, we relied upon a notion of *conversational inference*. This concept refers to the situated process of interpretation by which participants in a conversation assess other participants' intentions and respond on the basis of that assessment (Gumperz 1982a). It concerns two levels of communicative intention: (a) the perception of activity; and (b) the chunking of information into units and the signaling of given versus new information. Because it refers to signaling what the activity is, as well as utterance-level signaling of intention as part of an activity, the concept offers some purchase on the issue of the way differing interpretations arise and in turn contribute to patterns of differential interaction.

On the basis of our ethnographic work we knew that the reading-ability groups of the first-grade classrooms we studied had been subjected to differing sorts of instruction from the very beginning of the school year. The low group received much more instruction in phonics drill than the other groups. The relation of this difference in instruction to known or perceivable ability was problematical. Although the results of K-l reading readiness tests showed clear differences between the ability groups, these scores were unavailable early in the year and hence could not have informed the teacher's decision as to the right ability groups into which students should be placed. Additionally, when the participant-observer took the two groups aside and gave them informal tests of letter recognition, high- and low-group readers performed equally well on the tests. But the latter were nonetheless given extensive drill in letter recognition, while the high-group counterparts were beginning to read sentence texts. It was also clear from a cursory inspection of audio- and videotapes that what was superficially the same behavior, a hesitation or mispronunciation, prompted very different student–teacher exchanges in the high- versus low-group lessons. Thus we had strong indications that there was differential treatment across the ability groups, both in terms of the overall emphasis of instruction and in terms of particular corrections of errors, but we did not know how extensive and systematic the differences were, what the causes were, and what the effects would be.

We decided to focus on first-grade reading lessons because reading aloud in ability groups occurs most extensively in the early-primary years. We wished to have control over participants – both teachers and students – and to be able to contrast differing participants throughout the school year. We had initial hypotheses concerning the effects of community-based discourse conventions on student–teacher exchanges and had noticed that these differences appear to be related to ethnic-group and social-class membership.

Lesson selection

The first-grade classroom had a total of four different reading-ability groups: the low, mid, high, and extra-high groups, for whom we had a collection of thirty-six audio- and videotaped lessons. Of these, we selected sixteen lessons in which the senior teacher or the regular teacher's aide worked with high- or low-group readers. This selection allowed us to study the same teacher working with different groups and the same group working with different teachers at the beginning, middle, and end of the school year. Since the two groups were homogeneous with regard to ethnic-group and social-class membership – high-group readers were from white professional families, low-group readers from black working-class families – we could expect maximal contrasts in community-based speech styles and in such things as implicit teacher expectations. The lessons excluded from the corpus to be analyzed were those sessions when readers of the mid and extra-high groups were working alone, since we lacked comparable lessons through the year, or were lessons taught by temporary assistants, substitutes, or visiting reading specialists.

The reading lessons we analyzed had a teacher-to-small-group participant structure, in which the teacher initiated and directed the sequencing of activities and controlled who would participate and whether participation would be individual or collective. Each teacher organized turn-taking somewhat differently: usually children were nominated in a round-robin fashion, but occasionally they were allowed to bid for a turn. The act of reading aloud meant that a given student had the floor and that he or she was the recipient of any questions and had the obligation to respond, unless the teacher indicated otherwise. The teacher usually signaled the end of a reading turn, or indicated that the floor was open to group participation, by some evaluative comment and by turning to face the entire group and slightly raising the pitch register on questions. Reading lessons could be further segmented into activities, such as naming letters and words from flash cards, dictation, reading from reading books, and so forth. And each of these activities could be subdivided into a sequential patterning of tasks. For example, for the high-group reading lesson, the activity of passage reading (reading in the reading books) could be divided as follows: one child is nominated to read; that child reads an entire page; the teacher then asks comprehension questions of the entire group; and the pattern repeats. In the comparable low-group lesson one child is nominated; the child reads a sentence, or a page, if it is very short; instead of comprehension questions, frequently the whole group reads the same material in unison.

An initial transcription and analysis of the selected reading lessons showed that the differential emphasis in instruction noticed by the field researcher continued throughout the year. Comparison of the groups revealed a two-tiered structure of differential treatment. On one level, the more general one of amounts of time spent at the various types of instructional activities, low-group readers were given extensive sound–word identification drill, with little attention paid to the meaningfulness of the reading task, while their high-group counterparts were given much more practice in passage reading and the answering of questions about the material being read. On the other level, that of specific instructional procedures, correction of oral reading errors for low-group readers focused on grapheme–phoneme correspondences and word recognition, while corrections for the high-group readers focused more on the semantics and pragmatics of text comprehension – in short, on meaning.

Of the sixteen lessons selected for analysis, five were of the high-ranked group, eleven of the low-ranked group. These lessons were segmented into five activity groups: dictation, sound–word drill, sentence completion, passage reading, and comprehension questions.

Dictation consists of drill in transcribing letters, words, or sentences, either copying them from a written sample or in response to an oral sample given by the teacher. It is done both at the blackboard and by individual students in their workbooks.

Sound–word drill is a part of what is known in the educational literature as decoding skills. It consists of (1) exercises in giving the sounds for letters, in isolation, in prompt words, or in the names of things pictured in the workbooks; and (2) exercises in identifying isolated lexical items, perhaps in association with a picture, but not embedded in sentences or a connected text.

Sentence completion consists of drill in supplying the appropriate lexical items to complete prompt sentences. It tests the students' knowledge of co-occurrence restrictions operating between prompt sentence and available lexical choices – in the most general sense, the student's native-speaker awareness of lexical contribution to sentential meaningfulness.

Passage reading (or 'reading in the reading books') consists of reading aloud from connected texts, under the guidance of the teacher, and usually in a round-robin style of turn-taking. This is the most advanced sort of reading: the high-ranked group begins the last month of the first term; the low-ranked group does not begin until late in the fifth month of the school year.

Comprehension questions consist of the teacher asking questions of fact and interpretation about the passage being read or about the preceding lesson. Such sessions train memory and teach students to regard written materials evaluatively and in accordance with a notion of literalness, plausibility, and coherence.

The sixteen sessions contain a total of 217 minutes of reading activity on tape and transcribed. The five high-ranked group lessons comprise 61.5 minutes; the eleven low-ranked lessons comprise 155.5 minutes. Table 6.1 presents the number of minutes and percentages of total time for each category, for the high- and low-ability groups.

A quick inspection of the aggregate percentages by category shows the differing emphases in instructional activity. Where the high group spends 70 percent of its time at passage reading and comprehension questions, the low group spends only 37 percent of its time at the equivalent activities. Conversely, where the low group spends nearly half its time, 47 percent, at dictation and sound–word identification, the high group spends less than a fifth of its time, 17 percent, at the equivalent activities.

Thus we find that differential instructional strategies are reported by independent ethnographic sources as well as by systematic comparative studies of ability groups and their reading instruction. If we view cognition and ability as the outcome, at least in part, of social interaction, then we must inquire as to the cognitive consequences of the differing emphases. In other words, what conceptions of the task of reading are being formed by the differing

Table 6.1. *Time on task*

	High group		Low group	
	Minutes	Percentage of time	Minutes	Percentage of time
Dictation, penmanship	0	0	24.5	16
Sound–word identification	10.5	17	48.5	31
Sentence completion	8.0	13	24.5	16
Passage reading	29.5	49	49.0	31
Comprehension questions	13.5	21	9.0	6

emphases (on decoding versus meaning), how are they being formed, and how will they be realized or occur in actual reading lessons?

The existing literature on children's conceptions of reading consists of interview surveys of good and bad readers and more recently of experimental studies probing the abilities that seem to underlie the differing conceptions of reading that children profess. The interview literature reports a simple and consistent dichotomy: for poor readers, the final purpose and hallmark of proficiency is fluent and rapid reading aloud, with little concern evinced for possible meaning; for good readers, however, the goal of reading is extraction of meaningful content – and usually they view reading instrumentally, as a means of attaining further information (Downing and Ollila 1975; Edwards 1958; Glass 1968; Johns 1974; Mason 1967; Weintraub and Denny 1963). The experimental literature shows that good readers have a practical sense of lexical, syntactic, and semantic contribution to the overall meaning of a text; additionally, good readers will attempt to map spoken language prosody onto a text (Carney and Winograd 1979; Kleinman et al. 1979). In short, they readily apply their knowledge of spoken language to the task of reading.

Hallmarks of reader ability

Our main concern was with the mutual influences of communicative styles and learning opportunities. We narrowed this by concentrating on the relationship of the reading-aloud style and correction strategies. We treated the two as mutually reinforcing cues for conversation-inferencing processes: the children's reading-aloud styles influencing the teacher's conception of their reading abilities, the teacher's corrections, in turn, influencing the students' conception of the task, their 'schemata for reading' (Carney and Winograd 1979).

In order to have material with which to examine the relationship of reading-aloud styles and correction strategies, we selected passages in which the same teacher worked with high-group and low-group readers as they read from texts of equal complexity. The texts were transcribed with a detailed prosodic notation, which enabled us to analyze how different readers divided the text into 'information units' (Halliday 1968), that is, how they segmented the text into breath groups and signaled intonational prominence within groups. Because of our concern with the place of conversational inference in classroom interaction, we analyzed the placement of tone group (that is, breath group) boundaries and tonal contours for their predictive value: that is to say, analysis sought to establish the language units being demarcated by tone groupings and nuclei placement. This goal requires simultaneous attention to two discourse levels, both (a) the phrasal and sentential constituencies of the text being read and (b) the teacher–student exchanges occurring during a turn at reading.

By studying these transcripts we were able to infer certain things about the way instructional interaction is linked to reading-aloud styles. In particular, we found that members of the two groups segmented a text intonationally in different ways, and further that these ways of prosodically organizing a text, which we have variously called prosodic text-processing strategies or reading-aloud styles, appear to be related to oral narrative styles. The differing prosodic strategies provoke differing correction strategies: although low-group readers do make more errors, the extreme emphasis on isolated decoding cues in their lessons would seem to be partly the teachers' response to the students' reading styles. It should be kept in mind that the groups are reading from equivalent texts, taken from the same basal reader; presumably, they are at the same level of reading ability, yet they receive very different instruction. The differing approaches to error correction in their turn create a context in which queries designed to elicit or reinforce comprehension succeed differentially.

To the casual adult observer, both groups read in a staccato or word-by-word fashion, that is to say, with slight hesitations after each word and even stress on most lexical items. However, the staccato quality is more noticeable with low-group readers. Members of this group read with long pauses between words and frequently place equivalent stress on all items in a passage. The process is comparable to reading single items from a list: to the listener it sounds as if each word is a breath group or tone group unto itself. High-group members, on the other hand, are more likely to have some of the intonational characteristics of fluent, adult reading aloud. In particular, even when they read in a halting, word-by-word fashion, they finish sentences with falling tone. Both traits are typical of the fluent reading aloud of declarative sentences.

The differences between relatively staccato and relatively fluent reading styles can be seen in examples 6.1 and 6.2. The story being read is entitled 'A Visit to Grandmother's'. The actual sentence being read appears as follows in the text: '"What did you cook for Grandma?" asked mother.'

Example 6.1

		Low reading group (staccato)
1	C	'what/ . . 'did/ . . 'you/ cook/ . . 'for. . gran'ma//
2		. . . asked / mother
3	T	asked right //

In example 6.1 each item receives equivalent stress, and there are lengthy pauses between items; effectively, each item is treated as a minor tone group, an isolated information unit: 'what/ . . 'did/ . . 'you/ cook/ . . 'for. . gran'ma//. The reader pauses and the teacher supplies the next word. The sentence is completed, but it is as if the final segment, which attributes speakerhood, 'asked mother', is a sentence separate from the preceding material. As regards our earlier stated concern with the predictive value of tone grouping, we should note that this pattern of stress and hesitations makes it difficult to ascertain clause or sentence constituency in the oral reading signal. Instead, each item sounds like an isolated element, and there appears to be no larger language unit (namely, the sentence). In addition, the relationship between quoted material and attributed speaker is not clearly signaled. The teacher's correction cues attend to the isolated word ‘asked’ and do not attempt to improve the word-by-word reading style.

When we look at example 6.2 we see a more fluent style of reading aloud. The story being read concerns a man who lives in a house in the woods. The passage read by the student is treated in the reading book as an entire paragraph: ‘He saw the fishes and the birds. And he saw his green rock. The man was happy. “What a day!” he said.’

Example 6.2

		High reading group (fluent)
1	C	He ’saw the ’fishes and the birds //
2		And ’he saw his green rock //
3		the ’man was happ- //
4		What a ’day he said //
5	T:	very good // ’So he had a happy day / right //

In the first sentence there is a high, even tone on ‘saw’ and a low falling tone on ‘birds.’ Similarly, in the second sentence there is a high, even tone on ‘he’ and a low falling tone on ‘rock’. The effect on the listener of this use of contours and tone group boundaries is that sentences are identified easily in the oral reading signal; it is easy to predict which elements go with which because one has a clear perception of larger language units (sentences) that encompass the word groupings. Additionally, the second line is said with a slightly lower pitch register than the first, which signals an inter-sentential connection between the two. The third line is prosodically odd, with a high, even tone on the final word, and with elision of a final syllable (‘happ-’ instead of ‘happy’). But in the fourth line ‘what’ and ‘day’ are strongly stressed, as is correct for an emphatic quotation of this sort. Low, atonal stress on ‘he said’ clearly separates the quoted material from the attributed speaker. Despite an error in the third line, the reading is notable for its clear demarcation of sentence boundaries and quotations. Overall, the oral reading gives a sense of coherence because it is easy for the adult listener to identify constituents above the word level; it is as if an intonational template were provided with which to arrange phrases, sentences, quotations, and speakers into some sort of meaningful whole. The teacher responds favorably, does not correct the slight misreading of 'happy,' but instead follows with comprehension questions about the man's feelings, what he saw, and so forth.

Examples 6.1 and 6.2 are intended as typical instances of general reading styles that are characteristic of the low- and high-group readers. What we have contrasting the two groups are different strategies for handling a text. One strategy seems to treat individual words as independent elements, or at least places tone groups and contours in such a way as to make it difficult to ascertain clause and sentence constituencies. The other strategy places tone groups and contours in such a way as to make identification of constituency relatively easy, or at least uses falling contours utterance-finally, thus making it easy to identify sentence boundaries. The different strategies seem to indicate differing conceptions of the task of reading: the one perspective views reading merely as pronunciation, the other views it as meaningful. As we shall show below, teachers' correction strategies seem tacitly to assume the differing conceptions and to respond accordingly.

Reading styles and discourse styles

But there were suggestive similarities between the reading styles and what we considered to be community-based discourse styles. An analysis of oral narratives (by Collins and Michaels, chapter 10, this volume) provides evidence that the use of prosody in reading was related to other aspects of oral discourse. In particular, high-ranked readers tended to place tonal nuclei at the ends of clauses, near tone-group boundaries. Low-ranked readers, on the other hand, tended to place tonal nuclei in the middle of clauses, away from boundaries. While both ways of organizing narrative discourse are communicatively effective, the results sound different. The high-group members talked in such a way that sentence boundaries were more easily discerned by the casual adult listener. Additionally, their habit of placing tonal nuclei in clause-final position translated more easily into the strategy of using falling intonation on sentence-final words when reading aloud. The result sounded proficient, even when the reading performance was broken and halting, because it was easier to hear the sentence boundaries. Conversely, the low-ranked readers' habit of placing nuclei mid-clause translated less easily into a strategy of using falling intonation on sentence-final words when reading aloud. The result sounded less proficient because it was difficult to hear the sentence boundaries in the text being read aloud.

Given the exploratory nature of the research and the novelty of the hypotheses, it is difficult to say whether the placement of nuclei in clause-final position is a formulaic habit of language learned in the home and community or a result of advanced text comprehension. Similarly, it is difficult to say whether the placement of nuclei in mid-clause is an oral discourse convention (that is, a community-based habit) or an index of inferior text comprehension. We do have initial evidence that community background and reading style are related, but more controlled study of oral narratives and passage reading is needed, comparing prosodic strategies in tasks of differential complexity. Nevertheless, although causes of differing performance are complex, our evidence suggests that there is an interaction of communicative background and pedagogy that, through a process of cyclic reinforcement, helps produce one or the other reading style.

When we examined the correction strategies used with one or the other group, it appeared that the teacher was socialized to the differing reading strategies. She responded to the different prosodic chunking of texts by handling equivalent errors in very different ways. Numerous examples taken from the entire corpus of sixteen lessons had shown that identical miscues prompted either decoding-focused or comprehension-focused corrections. The four lessons used for controlled comparison confirmed this picture. With the low group, corrections concentrated on low-level linguistic instruction about phoneme–grapheme correspondences and lexical-level composition of texts. But with the high group, correction referred to a broad range of text elements and processes. Instruction was provided about orthography and lexical items, as with the low group, but information about clauses, sentences, expressive intonation, and textual inference was also brought into play.

The descriptions that follow of differential treatment of reading errors should not be construed as a condemnation of individual teachers. When we study conversational interaction in multiethnic situations we are analyzing the effects of unconscious habits of organizing talk (prosodically, lexically, and syntactically) on the unfolding interaction. But a participant, as an actor present in the situation, either as a teacher or student, cannot be expected to employ the analyst's detached perspective. Instead, he or she is busy in the process of assessing and responding to another's contributions. The differences described below should not be regarded as the result of overt decisions to consign one group of students to a year of decoding drill. Rather, the prosodic reading strategies described above should be seen as influencing the teachers' engaged perception of students' performance, and hence their use of correction cues.

In examples 6.3 and 6.4 we contrast the context provided for decoding cues. Example 6.3 is taken from a story entitled 'A Day in the Park'. In the story one character, Debbie, has called to her friend Ann, inviting her to come out and play. Ann replies with the sentence that is being read: 'I'll be out, wait for me.'

Example 6.3

No context provided for decoding cue

1	C	'I'll be out . . .
2	T	a-i says a / . . . wait / . / . . say it / way-
3	C	wait for me //
4	T	'Go on //

As we see in example 6.3, the student reads 'I'll be out' and then pauses. The teacher prompts 'a-i says a . . . wait. . . say it, way-'. The student finishes the sentence 'wait for me'. There is no further instructional interaction; the decoding cue is provided and received in isolation.

A very different situation obtains in example 6.4, taken from a high-group reading lesson. The story being read from is entitled 'John's Afternoon'. It concerns a young man who has fallen out with his mother and his friends; he has walked to the local park, where he sees some other boys playing with a cardboard box; he suggests that they make a house out of it. The passage being read from is as follows: '"(I'll paint the house) and you can make the windows. Let's make big windows!"'

Example 6.4

Context provided for decoding cue

1	C	And 'you can make . . .
2	T	the . . . what's w-i-n //
3		Put your finger over it / everything but w-i-n //
4		Sound out w-i-n with a short i // wind- what //
5		Window // I'll paint the house / and you can make
6		the windows //
7	C	'Let's make big windows //

The student reads 'and you can make' and pauses. The teacher provides a word and then begins spelling out the following word: 'what's w-i-n? Put your finger over it, everything but w-i-n. Sound out w-i-n with a short i. Wind what? Window!' She provides the word and then inserts it in a repeat of the entire sentence. 'I'll paint the house and you can make the windows!' The student then reads the next sentence. Contrasting examples 6.3 and 6.4, we can see that the context provided for the same instructional cue – a decoding cue – is different: in the former it is an isolated word; in the latter the word is situated in a full sentence, and a model of expressive intonation is provided.

In examples 6.5 and 6.6 we can see similar differences in correction strategy. In these examples the cue consists of providing a word or phrase when the reader hesitates. Example 6.5 is taken from the same story as example 6.3; a new character has been introduced. He calls out to the two girls and then approaches them. The passage being read is 'The boy ran up to the girl.'

Example 6.5

Cue provided after hesitation; single word

1	C	The boy run		ran up to the girl //
2	T		ran	
3	C	Do you...		want to come to the park //
4	T		want	

In example 6.5 the student reads 'The boy run' and the teacher corrects 'ran'; the student corrects and finishes 'ran up to the girl'. The student continues 'Do you . . .' and pauses, the teacher provides the word 'want', the student continues 'want to come to the park'. During this and the continuing reading, there is no correction of the staccato, halting intonation used in reading. Instruction consists solely of providing isolated words.

Example 6.6 is taken from the same lesson as example 6.4. The main character's mother has come upon the boys working on their cardboard house, expresses her satisfaction, and offers to help them. The passage being read is as follows: '"I'll make you a doorway," said mother.'

Example 6.6
Cue provided after hesitation; circumlocution and quotative model
1 C I'll make you. . .
2 T a // and here's another compound
3 word / what //
4 C doorway //
5 T: beautiful // I'll make you a doorway //
6 C: I'll make you a doorway / said mother //

In this exchange, the student reads 'I'll make you . . .' and then pauses. The teacher supplies the following word, 'a', and then proceeds to the item that presumably is causing the hesitation. She continues, 'and here's another compound word, what?' The reader responds, 'doorway'. The teacher praises the student and then models the full sentence with proper intonation, 'I'll make you a doorway'. The student mimics the teacher's example flawlessly and finishes the sentence, correctly de-stressing the attributed speaker ('said mother'). As in 6.3 and 6.4, the context provided for what is ostensibly the same instructional cue is different: in 6.5 an isolated word is the cue; in 6.6 information about the word is provided and then the word itself is situated within a model of the full sentence. Contrasting the low-group episodes (6.3 and 6.5) with the high-group episodes (6.4 and 6.6), we see that the former are given isolated decoding cues, whereas the latter are given decoding cues situated within the sentence context.

We should emphasize that examples 6.3, 6.4, 6.5 and 6.6 are representative examples taken from transcripts of complete reading lessons. The episodes were selected to illustrate the ways in which error-correction strategies were sensitive to what we have called prosodic-reading strategies. This was done by showing how identical errors prompted either decoding cues or meaning cues. In the complete lessons it is also clear that different kinds of instructional interaction are taking place. With the low group, correction consists predominantly of low-level linguistic instruction about the grapheme–phoneme correspondences and lexical-level composition of texts. With the high group, correction refers to a broad range of text elements and processes. Instruction is provided about orthography and lexical items, as in the low group; however, information about clauses, sentences, expressive intonation, and the attribution of speakerhood are also brought into play. The differing interactions provide very different contexts for the business of learning to read. Furthermore, what these examples do not indicate is the way in which high-group reading lessons are winnowed with comprehension questions – questions about the inferences that can be drawn from the sequencing of events in two sentences, about speakers and addressees, about emotional states as revealed by expressive quotations. Such inquiries, which frequently use sentence frames like the models found in 6.4 and 6.6, are rarely encountered in low-group lessons. Instead, the context of reading in low-group lessons is usually so fragmented by hesitations, corrections for mispronunciation, dialect, and failure to recognize words, as well as distractions from within and without the group, that synthetic comprehension is difficult to achieve.

The differential effects of reading styles and correction strategies on the context for questions can be seen in the examples below. In 6.7, although the student is able to answer the question correctly, the fragmentary and distracted character of the reading-aloud process can be seen to be making comprehension difficult. In 6.8, corrections and questions attend entirely to meaningful levels of text structure, and as a consequence more material is covered and comprehension is enhanced by a series of questions.

In episode 6.7 the passage being read is from the story 'John's Bad Morning' (the story preceding 'John's Afternoon' [6.4], [6.6]). The main character has just had an argument with his mother. The passage appears in the text as follows:

> He ran out of the house with his things. And then he threw his boat into the garbage can. Liza was there. And she saw what John did.

Although in example 6.7 there are many corrections and several questions, as we shall see, only one of them concerns comprehension of a language unit larger than a single word.

Example 6.7

Minimally effective comprehension questions

1	M	Here he / . . ran / . . out / . . of / . .
2	T	he
3	M	the house . . . wuh- 'with 'his 'things //
4	T	with
5	M	And then . . . he . . . threw his
6	T	sound it out / thr:ew:
7	M	bu- (boat)boat / . . into the . . gahbage can //
8	T	guh-
9		gar:bage // Say 'garbage //
10	M	gahbage
11	T	Don't say gahbage / 'look at me // Say ga:r:bage / gar: / Say it //
12		Everybody say it //
13	CC	gar:bage
14	T	Celena / say it //
15	Ce	gar:bage
16	T	Right // Marlon / Liza
17	M	Liza . . was . . there and she was
18	T	where are we / Sherrie / there
19		What
20	M	she was saw what . . .
21	T	no // sss . . . how does -j- sound //
22	M	juh //
23	T	What's the boy's name // . . John
24	M	John . . said
25	T	did // She saw what John did // Marlon / what did he do //
26		She 'saw what he did // Now what did he do //
27	M	He threw his things in the gahbage
28	T	gar:bage // Right // Go on //

In lines 2 and 4 we see corrections for incorrect recognition of words. In line 6 we find the decoding instruction 'sound it out', followed with a stressed and exaggerated pronunciation of the word. Then in lines 9 through 15 we see a long and embroiled attempt to correct dialect pronunciation. In lines 17 and 18, as the reader is beginning to resume, there is a distraction to correct an inattentive group member. In lines 21 and 22 there are two phonics cues. The student responds to the second of these, 'how does -j- sound', literally, and the teacher is forced to rephrase her question. She then provides the answer. Finally, on lines 25 and 26 the passage is finished and a content question is asked. The final sentence is modeled twice as a frame for the question. The student is able to answer the question – no mean feat considering the number of distractions and interruptions that have occurred during his turn at reading. He is then corrected again for dialect pronunciation before being instructed to proceed.

This can be contrasted with the following episode in which all of the teacher's instructions and cues are concerned with text structure above the word level, with the prosody (pitch register) of sentence-initial position, with inferences deducible from the use of a lexical idiom, with the way an invitation sounds, and finally with consulting the pictures that accompany the text. Example 6.8 is taken from the same story as that in example 6.7. John and two boys he encountered in the story have made a toy house and have gone inside it. John's pet frog has joined them. Then John's friend Liza looks inside the toy house. John, still angry and suspicious, informs her that she cannot come in because his frog, which she supposedly does not like, is inside the house with him. The printed passage reads as follows:

'John, I have your boat,' said Liza.
'And I have a fly for your frog, too
'But you can't have your boat or the fly if I can't come in!'
John looked at his frog, and he looked at Liza.
Then he said, 'Come in, Liza. Come in.'

Although the passage read is much longer than that in example 6.7, the sequence of student–teacher exchanges is shorter and, as noted above, the teacher's correction cues attend to elements of linguistic structure above the word level.

When the passage is being read the teacher focuses on how the material sounds and on the inferences that can be drawn from the occurrence of certain phrases and the overall turn of events.

Example 6.8

Maximally effective meaning cues and questions

1	C	'John I have your boat / said Liza and
2	T	and
3	C	And I have a fly for your frog too //
4	T	'What's she mean by that
5	C	'For the 'frog to eat //
6	T	Okay //
7	L	but . . I . . but
8	J	Wait a minute till she gets through //
9	C	but but
10	J	watch your books watch your books
11	C	'But you 'can't . . have your boat / or the fly / if I can't come in //
12		John 'looked at his frog / and he 'looked at Liza / . .
13		Then he said / come in Liza
14	T	What did he say //
15	C	Come in

16 T How'd he say it //
17 C Come in Li-
18 T Did he say come in Liza . . come. . in // Or did he say . .
19 C Come in . . Liza / come in //
20 T Come in / Liza
21 Here is the other little boy and I didn't see it in Fanny's book. The little boy is kinda caught in the middle of the page, but here he is. Here's one little boy and here's the other little boy and here's John and here's Liza. I think John is in a much better mood, don't you?

In line 1 the student has read the sequence 'said Liza and' with little pause and no perceptible change in pitch level. The teacher corrects by providing the correct pitch level for the initial segment in a declarative sentence. In line 3 the student changes her intonation and reads the next sentence. In line 4 the teacher asks 'What's she mean by that?' In line 5 the student demonstrates that she understands that the apparently declarative sentences are in effect offers by responding 'for the frog to eat'. The response indicates that she has made certain assumptions about flies, frogs' eating habits, and the frame 'to have x for y'. In line 6 the teacher accepts the response. Then in lines 7 through 10 there are several distractions, and the student repeats the initial word several times. The student begins anew on line 11 and finishes the passage. The fourth exchange occurs in line 13 when the student reads the final part of the passage very softly and fails to separate the request 'come in' from the addressee 'Liza'. The teacher interrupts, asking 'what did he say'. The student responds by repeating the material in the same expressionless manner. The teacher interrupts again and asks *how* it was said. Although the student has apparently gotten the drift of the queries and begun to change her intonation, the teacher continues 'did he say' and repeats the material with an exaggeratedly low voice and extra pausing. Then she proceeds to give the alternative. In lines 19 and 20 the student responds, overlapping with the teacher, and finishes the quotation with expressive contours and a clear separation of request from addressee. The teacher finishes the exchange by pointing out and discussing the characters in the story as they appear in the pictures that accompany the text and by making the judgment that John's mood has changed. We can see from these illustrations that different teaching styles provide very different contexts for learning to read.

Some causes and consequences of differential treatment

An instructional process that consists primarily of children reading in a word-by-word fashion and teachers providing isolated decoding cues will leave the beginning readers without much practice in applying their knowledge of spoken language to the task of reading. This difference in application seems to be a major distinction between high- and low-ability readers. The former are much more prone to apply their knowledge of spoken language to the task of reading, and good readers are likely to attempt to map spoken intonation onto a string of non-stressed syllables in order to make sense of them, where poor readers will not. Furthermore, Carney and Winograd (1979) show that good readers will reject a text that does not make sense. It is useful in this light to reconsider examples 6.7 and 6.8. In 6.7 decoding cues predominated. At times they were of such a low linguistic level as to impede effective instruction (lines 21–23, where the student responds literally to the cue and the teacher is forced to rephrase the query). Comprehension questions occur rarely and in the context of a fragmented reading process. In 6.8 knowledge of spoken language and of the world is frequently evoked: in one instance the query concerns knowledge of animals (line 4); in another it concerns knowledge of the way heartfelt invitations sound (lines 13–20); and finally, the students are encouraged to consult the pictures accompanying the text when engaged in reading. The consequences of these differential experiences in reading may have longer and greater effects on children's continuing school performance than the initially small and subtle differences suggest.

By using methods of conversational analysis we can explore more fully these apparently small differences, which in the long term can have a significant effect on educational processes. Analysis of processes of conversational inference provides insights into the ways in which communicative mismatches reinforce the effects of institutional categorization of ability: they feed into students' and teachers' perceptions of their interlocutors' communicative intent and of the reading task at hand. In this way we can see that teaching and learning are collaborative processes in which the use of language provides various long-term interactive options on the part of participants. Teachers appear to have implicit models of what literate behaviour sounds like, as do most people brought up or educated within the Western literate tradition (Bloomfield 1933; Fowler et al. 1979). As a consequence of this, they appear to have differing expectations about students' readiness or ability to assimilate the skills necessary for literacy. Although non-linguistic criteria are also used in setting up ability groups, interactional history is an important confirming influence. The beginnings of this history can be shown in the early reading lessons and in closely related classroom activities, like the oral presentations of sharing time (Michaels, this volume). In the early lessons the teachers' expectations helped to produce, and were in turn reinforced by, the students' conceptions of the task of reading. Taken together, these differences – in teacher expectation, student models of reading, instructional approach and reading-aloud style – indicate the complexity of the communicative events involved in acquiring the skills of literacy. If analyzed, they can enrich our understanding of the social, linguistic, and cognitive variables that play a role in these communicative events and in the long-term process of schooling.

Afterword

The research reported in this chapter is supported and elaborated by other studies which address specific questions, such as the effect of ability grouping on schooling processes and the effect of language difference on teaching and learning. It also implicates broader issues, such as the nature of cultural dilemmas intrinsic to modern (American) schooling and the nature and role of identity in teaching and learning.

As noted in the text above, ability grouping is pervasive in American schooling and has been since early in the twentieth century. As Eder (this volume) demonstrates, grouping as an organizational practice is characterized by rigidity: whatever the initial range of social, linguistic, and skill differences, and whatever changes occur over the course of a year, there are standard numbers of students in a classroom and limited ideas about ability classes (three to five groups per classroom is the standard assumption). This rigidity is systematic, as Rosenbaum (1980) showed in a wide-ranging survey of ability grouping and curriculum tracking. It also has cultural roots, as Varenne et al. (1998) point out in a study of middle-school grouping: everyone in a group lower than the top wants to be raised, but no one wants to go down. Ability groups are status groups within classrooms, as is revealed by any first-grader who knows that the Robins are the 'good readers' and the Sparrows are the 'bad readers.' Status has effects. It influences how teachers view students and how students view one another, and one result is that some groups are more likely to be interrupted in their schoolwork than others. McDermott (1978) showed that in first-grade reading lessons there was more time off-task in low-ability than in high-ability groups. Collins (1982) shows that low-ability groups are more likely to be interrupted, from outside their groups, during their reading lessons. Paralleling the findings about differential instruction reported above, Allington's (1980) survey of twenty primary classrooms in New York reported that low- and high-grouped readers received different kinds of corrections and prompts during oral reading (see also Cazden 2001, ch. 7; Nystrand et al. 1997; and Oakes 1985, for clear evidence of differential instruction in tracked secondary literature lessons). There is also a survey literature on ability grouping and reading instruction, as part of the move to 'phonics' and 'systematic' instruction, which argues that grouping can benefit medium-ability students, but is deleterious for low-ranked students (Lou et al. 1996; Savin 1987; see Gamoran 1987, for a critical response to Savin 1987, advocating a context-sensitive approach).

One response to such findings is to seek causes in teacher expectations or student traits, but I suggest a different view: that the activities of groups and the differences they engender should be understood as *interactional outcomes*, with the proviso that we must also examine how *language difference* influences interaction. Various studies have shown that perceptions of language difference influence how people think about themselves, the institution of schooling, and the educability of children. Morgan (2001), for example, shows that the African-American community is deeply divided and conflicted over the relation between American Standard English and African-American Vernacular English. Many of the articles in Perry and Delpit's (1998) volume on the Ebonics controversy testify to teachers' efforts to reconcile the imperative to 'teach Standard English' with the need to build upon their students' own varieties of English. Linguists such as Labov (1995) and Long (2003) argue that dialect differences per se are not the key issues in differing education outcomes, but that the social meanings attached to such differences influence educational policy and teacher practice as well as language minority students' identification with, and against, the school.

In order to understand better how large-scale cultural–historical and institutional orientations to language impact conditions of teaching and learning, it is necessary to examine how language attitudes – language ideologies by another name – influence classroom interaction. Some work has been done. Bigler (1998), for example, shows that attitudes to dialect variation in English, as well as to Spanish/English difference, influence both curriculum and pedagogy in middle school literature lessons in a multiethnic urban school. Rymes (2001) demonstrates that subtle responses to Spanish/English difference can signal whose knowledge is appropriate for school reading and whose is not. Collins (1996) analyzes how interruption behaviors in third-grade reading groups correlate with dialect use and other features of reading instruction. Briefly, I found that the *salience of dialect* as an instructional issue was a function of the amount of interruption occurring, but that dialect corrections themselves, as in example 6.7 above, could disrupt the activity of reading. In short, it was not a question of language attitude or dialect difference in isolation, but rather of the way in which prescriptive attitudes were triggered, and responded to, in the ongoing interaction of teaching and learning.

7

Organizational constraints on reading group mobility

Donna Eder

While allocation to ability groups and curriculum tracks is ostensibly based on students' aptitude for learning, previous research has found that student aptitude explains only a small portion of the variance in curriculum placement. Likewise, while ability grouping has been described in curriculum theory as being very flexible, studies have found that, in practice, little movement occurs between groups. This study examines ability grouping in a first-grade classroom in order to increase our understanding of the factors which influence ability group formation and maintenance at the very beginning of children's school careers.

I will show in this chapter that time and management constraints influence the number and size of groups formed independently of the range of aptitude in the classroom. Since these factors remain constant throughout the year, they also limit the amount of movement that occurs between groups. These group assignments over time become a part of the record that follows individual children throughout their institutional life careers (Mehan et al. 1983). Placements made in elementary grades, where aptitude boundaries appear more flexible, then become even stronger determinants of potential placement in later schooling. Although at the high school level, other constraints are likely to affect allocation decisions by virtue of the degree of selectivity throughout schooling, early placement decisions are likely to influence later outcomes. While it can be argued that these constraints represent a general problem which

Acknowledgments: An earlier version of this chapter appeared in *The Sociological Quarterly.*

exists whenever there is an attempt to match individuals with positions in society, it is on schooling, as the legitimized preparation for future life career chances, that concern over allocation is likely to concentrate.

In discussing the relationship between the individual and society, Simmel described a conceptually perfect society as one in which there is complete harmony between individuals' characteristics and positions in society. In such a society 'an individual is directed toward a certain place within his social milieu by his very quality. This place which ideally belongs to him actually exists' (Simmel 1971: 20). Much of the current thinking regarding allocation to social positions has been based on the assumption that such harmony exists in our society, or at least is attainable.

At the societal level, allocation to occupations is ostensibly determined by individuals' aptitude or ability. There is a persistent belief that people with more skills and ability have professional and managerial jobs while people with less aptitude and ability are engaged in non-skilled work. Underlying this belief is an assumption that there are as many available professional jobs as there are individuals with high aptitude and ability.

Allocation decisions are also made in educational institutions. By allocating students to different types of training such as non-college versus college tracks, schools are supposedly preparing students for adult roles in line with their ability and aptitude. Since allocation decisions at the high-school level are often based on previous academic performance, considerable selection occurs in elementary grades (Parsons 1959). And this selection has a continuing influence on future outcomes of selection.

In some elementary schools students are actually assigned to different classrooms representing different levels of aptitude (Borg 1966). An even more frequent practice is the allocation of students to ability groups within classrooms for instruction in reading and/or mathematics (Austin and Morrison 1963; Weinstein 1976; Wilson and Schmits 1978). Thus many individuals in our society are first matched with available positions in a social structure (i.e. ability grouping) in the first grade.

As with occupational positions, it has been assumed that the prime determinant of allocation to ability groups and curriculum tracks is student aptitude for learning. Indeed, early advocates of ability grouping emphasized the importance of basing allocation decisions solely on student aptitude, claiming that the actual number of groups needed in any particular class can only be determined on the spot (Burton 1956). Since student aptitude may change, especially in the early grades, flexibility was also stressed: 'They [ability groups] are exceedingly flexible and pupils are constantly shifted from one group to another depending on the extent of their growth' (Burton 1956: 508). Nor should group membership only change regularly, but according to Durrell the number of groups should also be flexible: 'Six groups may be needed one day, three the next, and only one some other day' (Durrell 1940: 69). This flexibility in group assignment is considered important throughout a student's academic career. Indeed, Turner (1960) argues that a system of 'contest mobility' is one in which the race is open until it has run its course. Thus it is important to 'keep channels of movement between courses of study as open as possible' at the high school as well as the elementary level (Turner 1960: 861).

These comments suggest that there should be a one-to-one correspondence between students' aptitude and their ability-group assignment or curriculum placement. However, recent studies of curriculum tracking at the high-school level have found that student ability, as measured by tests of verbal ability or abstract reasoning, has been found to explain less than a fifth of the variance in placement (Alexander and McDill 1976; Hauser, Sewell and Alwin 1976; Heyns 1974). Since it could be argued that curriculum placement at the high-school level is determined by students' interests and actual achievements in school as well as by their native ability, these and other related variables were included in a recent study (Alexander, Cook, and McDill 1978). However, even when ninth-grade achievement, curriculum plans, educational expectations, peers' college plans, and parental encouragement were added to their model, it still explained less than 40 percent of the variance in eleventh-grade curriculum placement.

Likewise, while the flexibility of ability grouping and the continual movement of students between groups or tracks has been emphasized in theory, empirical studies report different findings. In a study of second- to fourth-grade classrooms Groff (1962) found that only 16 percent of the students changed reading groups during the first semester. Another study of first- to sixth-grade students reported that only 9 percent of the students changed groups during the first semester, with the fewest changes occurring in the later grades (Hawkins 1966). Finally, in a study of across-classroom grouping, Jackson (1964) found only 1–5 percent of the children were moved to different groups during the year.

While the studies suggest that factors other than student aptitude influence reassignments as well as initial assignments to ability groups or tracks, they do not indicate what these factors might be. In order to increase our understanding of the factors which influence ability-group formation and maintenance, an in-depth study of ability grouping was undertaken. A first-grade classroom was selected since it is at this point in students' educational careers that they are systematically assigned to ability-based groups. Also, even though within-classroom ability grouping is extremely common in American elementary schools, little attention has been given to determinants of ability-group allocation at this level.

The results of this investigation will show that ability-group formation was strongly influenced by factors unrelated to student aptitude. Specifically, time and management constraints will be shown to influence the number and size of groups formed independently of the range of aptitude in the classroom. Since these factors remained constant throughout the year they also limited the amount of movement that occurred between groups. At the high-school level other, more stringent, constraints are likely to affect allocation decisions, explaining some of the previously unexplained variance in curriculum placement. Finally, it will be argued that these constraints represent a general problem which exists whenever there is an attempt to match individuals with positions in society.

Methods

Because little is known about the factors which affect ability-group formation and limit movement between groups, an in-depth study is most appropriate. Observation of the formation and operation of ability groups was an essential aspect of this study since administrators' and teachers' descriptions of ability grouping are likely to be incomplete. By combining in-depth observation and teacher interviews, it was possible to identify routine procedures that the teacher may have neglected to report, as well as to obtain information from the teacher about the reasons behind the use of these procedures.

Two main criteria were used in selecting a classroom. It had to be a first-grade classroom, since it is at this point that students are systematically assigned to ability groups for formalized instruction.[1] In addition, the classroom had to be typical of other classrooms in the community. The classroom which was selected had a female teacher and twenty-four students (thirteen males and eleven females) who were primarily from middle-class backgrounds.[2] While it would have been desirable to have data from a number of classrooms, the fact that teachers tend to form ability groups at the same time in the year, i.e. during the first two weeks of school, precluded close observation of this process in more than one classroom. To offset this limitation, information from other studies of within-classroom ability grouping will also be presented. In particular, results of similar studies with students from primarily lower-class backgrounds will be included to determine if these results are also representative of other types of classrooms.

Classroom observation was begun in the teacher's previous class in order to develop rapport with the teacher and obtain all possible information about procedures related to ability-group formation. The class which was studied intensively was observed four days a week during the first month of school. On the second day of school the teacher was interviewed and asked specifically about the initial ability-group assignments. Two other formal interviews, in which she was asked to describe each student, and several informal interviews also took place during the first month. The formal interviews with the teacher were tape-recorded and notes were made on informal conversations immediately after they occurred.

During this stage of in-depth observation and interviewing, the impact of time and size constraints on initial ability-group formation was discovered. In order to examine their effect on movement across groups the classroom was observed approximately twice a week for the duration of the year. While the amount of actual movement was determined through observation, information about potential candidates for reassignment was obtained through the interviews with the teacher. Formal interviews, in which the teacher was asked to describe each student's progress, were conducted in the ninth and twenty-second weeks of the year and informal interviews took place throughout the year. Finally, reading-readiness test performance scores were obtained from the school records. These tests were given at the end of kindergarten and measured knowledge of letter sounds, alphabet skills, visual discrimination of letters, and other pre-reading skills.

Factors influencing ability group formation

As mentioned earlier, advocates of ability grouping stressed the importance of basing allocation solely on student aptitude. Indeed, the number of groups to be formed was to be determined on the spot as it should reflect the range of aptitude in a given class. Thus one would expect that, if there was considerable variation in aptitude, more groups would be formed than if the range of aptitude was narrow; in which case fewer groups would be needed.

However, in this classroom the number of groups to be formed was determined independently of the students' aptitudes. On the first day of school the teacher informed me that she was planning to have four groups since there was not enough time to meet with more than four groups and still have time to supervise the students' independent work. I asked her if she had looked at the students' files yet and she said no, but that she had discussed the students' reading aptitude with their kindergarten teachers.

Most of the discussions with kindergarten teachers occurred two weeks prior to the beginning of school, while some took place on the morning of the second day of school. According to her, the purpose of these discussions was to get some idea of how the student would do in reading. During these discussions the kindergarten teachers indicated how they thought each child would do by giving him or her a ranking of either 'one', 'two', or 'three', with 'one' indicating a good reader who could begin in a top group, 'two' indicating an average reader who could begin at a normal first-grade level, and 'three' a slow reader who would need a review of material covered in kindergarten. In addition, four students received a ranking of 'two plus' and one student received a 'three plus' ranking.

If group assignments were solely to reflect students' aptitude, at least as perceived by their kindergarten teachers, one would have expected three groups to be formed, with the five 'ones' being assigned to the high group, the thirteen 'twos' to the middle group, and the four 'threes' to the low group. Or, since the teacher wanted to have four groups, one might expect that two middle groups would be formed, one consisting of the four 'two-plus' students and another consisting of the students ranked 'two'.

However, when the teacher was interviewed on the second day of school she produced a different set of assignments. Some of the students who had received 'two' rankings were in one group and some were in another. When asked about the change in the rankings she said. 'You see, there were too many twos, so I separated the twos.' Altogether, three of the nine students with 'two' rankings had been assigned to the medium-high group along with the four students with 'two-plus' rankings. The decision as to which of the students with 'two' rankings to assign to the medium-high group was based on her own observation of ability and interest during the first day of class. For example, in reference to one of these students she said, 'He seems to be more eager and with-it.'

After this discussion it became clear that the teacher had predetermined requirements for the size of groups as well as for their number. Later on she explained that seven was the maximum number of students that she liked to have in a group as it was difficult to listen to more than seven students read during a group meeting and still maintain the attention of other group members. In general she felt that groups larger than seven presented too many management problems.

The division of children with 'two' rankings resulted in seven members in the medium-high group and six in the medium-low. During the second day of class two boys were added to the medium-low group.[3] At the beginning of the third day of school the groups had the following members: high 5; medium-high 7; medium-low 8; and low 4. Three days later the teacher decided to move two students. Explaining that the medium-low group was too crowded, she moved one boy from that group to the medium-high group and another boy from the medium-high group to the high group. She based her decisions on her observations of the performance of students during the first few reading lessons. These moves resulted in a more even distribution of students across groups with six students in the high group; seven in the medium-high and medium-low groups; and four in the low group.

Thus, due to both time constraints and size-management concerns this teacher decided that she wanted four relatively equal-size groups. Not only were these requirements determined independently of the range of aptitude in the class, they necessitated making further distinctions in aptitude than those which already had been made by the kindergarten teachers. However, the teacher looked for and was able to find additional differences among the students which would justify the moves designed to distribute equally students into more manageable groups.

The effect of time and size constraints on membership stability

Since the teacher's organizational concerns regarding time and management issues are unlikely to change during the year, a group structure of four relatively equal-size groups is expected to remain stable. By influencing group structure, time and size constraints are also expected to restrict the amount and type of movement between groups during the year. For example, if the performance of several students in a medium-ability group improved significantly, one might expect that all of these students would be moved to a higher group. However, this would mean a significant increase in the size of the higher group, making management a potential problem. While some imbalance in group size might be tolerated, there appears to be a limit as to how large a group may be and still be considered manageable. Thus, depending on the initial relative sizes of the groups, only some of the medium-ability-group members are likely to be moved to a higher group. If, however, the teacher wanted to move a student from a large group to a smaller group, this move is likely to occur since it would result in a more even distribution of students across groups. Thus, only those reassignments which would involve moving a student into a group which is viewed by the teacher as already being of maximum size are expected to be inhibited.

One way in which between-group movement can occur, while at the same time maintaining the relative size of the groups, is to exchange students. In an exchange, if a student were to be moved up from a low-ability group to a medium-ability group, another student would be simultaneously moved down from the medium group to the low group so that neither group would increase in size. However, exchanges may not always be feasible. First, in order to make an exchange two candidates for reassignment need to be identified concurrently. Thus, one child might be identified as performing significantly better than his/her group, but there may be, at that time, no one in the next higher group whose performance is significantly worse than other members of that group. Second, by definition, exchanges require a downward move for every upward move, and downward movement may be more problematic than upward movement. To the extent that parents are concerned about their child's progress, they may be more upset about a move to a lower group than to a higher one. Finally, while a child's move to a higher group may be viewed as an indicator of effective teaching, a downward move is not likely to be viewed as such and may even be seen as a failure to motivate the student effectively.

To summarize, while exchanges may be used occasionally to move students while maintaining the relative size of groups, they may not always be a feasible option. Thus, size constraints are expected to limit the amount of mobility which occurs in a classroom, and, in particular, to hinder movement into groups which are already perceived to be of maximum size. Thus, even though a student's aptitude may increase during the year there is no guarantee that there will be an available position in a higher group.

Results

It was expected that time and size constraints would remain relatively constant throughout the year, continuing to influence group membership. Indeed, the number of groups remained the same throughout the year and the relative group sizes were not substantially altered by the moves that did occur (see Figure 7.1). No group size varied by more than two students during the year. High groups tended to gain members, due in part to the teacher's continuing desire to decrease the size of the medium-low group which presented the most management problems. In addition, there was a greater hesitancy to move students to lower groups than to higher groups. In fact, after the downward move in Week twenty the teacher said that the parents were so upset by the move that it was 'almost not worth it'.

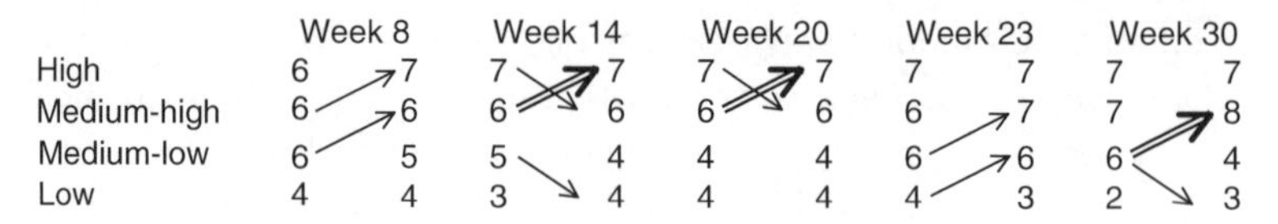

Figure 7.1. Group size prior to and after each set of moves.
Note: Double arrows represent moves into groups which already have seven or more members.

Further evidence that time and size factors were an ongoing concern came from a discussion at the end of the twelfth week of school regarding the possible upward move of a medium-high student. After mentioning that the student was reading very well and could be moved to the high group, she said that the high group already had seven students and she was reluctant to further increase its size. She mentioned the possibility of dividing the high group into two separate groups, but rejected that idea since she did not feel that there was enough time to meet with more than four groups each day. Two weeks later the student was moved to the high group as part of a second set of moves (see Figure 7.1) which also involved an exchange with a high-group member, leaving the size of the high group unchanged. Although there had been no discussion of moving any students out of the high group previously, after the move the teacher said the student who was moved down had been having trouble finishing his work.

Time and size constraints were expected to influence membership stability by inhibiting movement into groups which were already perceived by the teacher to be of maximum size, i.e. those having seven or more students. Of the eleven moves shown in Figure 7.1, only three involved movement into a group that already had seven or more students (shown by double arrows). Furthermore, two of these three moves involved exchanges so that the groups remained stable in size (those occurring in Week 14 and Week 20).

While it could be argued that no further moves would have occurred regardless of time and size constraints, there is some evidence to the contrary. During the year, seven possible moves were mentioned which never occurred, five of which invoked movement into groups with seven or more students. In two of these cases, concerns about group size were explicitly mentioned. Regarding a student in the medium-high group, the teacher said that she was doing very well and could be moved into the high group except that the high group already had seven students. The student remained in the medium-high group throughout the year. In another case, the large size of the medium-high group was mentioned as a reason for not moving a medium-low member into that group.

Another reason for expecting considerable reassignment in this classroom was the fact that the students were assigned to ability groups by the third day of class. Since reading aptitude is difficult to assess at such an early point in students' educational careers, one would expect a need for considerable reassignment as students' actual aptitudes became more apparent. In fact when students' initial assignments were compared with assignments based on their reading-readiness test performance, it was found that twelve students would have been assigned to different groups.[4] At some point during the first nine weeks of the year the teacher mentioned the possibility of moving all six of the students who were initially assigned to lower groups than they would have been assigned to on the basis of their test performance. However, only three of these moves actually occurred, the two moves in Week 8 and the upward move in Week 14. One of the moves which did not occur would have involved increasing the size of the high group to eight. The other two students who were not moved were members of the low group which was already the smallest of the four groups. In fact, none of the students initially assigned to the two lower groups were moved during the entire year. This provides further evidence for the influence of time and size constraints on the stability of group membership.

Discussion

Time and size requirements were found to influence initial assignments to ability groups as well as reassignment decisions during the year. While these requirements might vary somewhat from one classroom to another, all teachers are faced with similar constraints on their time and concerns regarding group management. Indeed, since one of the rationales behind within-classroom grouping is the advantage of smaller instructional groups (Barr 1975), a teacher would be defeating one of the purposes of grouping if she formed groups having, for example, two, two, and nineteen members respectively. Thus it is not surprising that other studies have found within-classroom ability groups to be similar in both number and size to those formed in this classroom. Austin and Morrison (1963), who examined reading instruction in schools with children from a variety of social backgrounds, reported that three equal-size groups were most common. Carew and Lightfoot (1978), whose study also included classrooms from both lower-class and middle-class neighborhoods, found that most teachers had either three or four groups with four to seven members per group.

These organizational constraints on group formation exist independently of the actual distribution of aptitude in a given class. For example, although the range of aptitude in a class might be relatively wide, time constraints are likely to limit the number of groups formed, resulting in groups with considerable within-group diversity (see Figure 7.2). On the other hand, size constraints would require that a certain number of groups be formed even if there was a minimal variance in aptitude. While the formation of groups which were not distinguished in terms of ability level would be an alternative in such a case, this alternative is typically overlooked. Instead, the Harvard Report on Reading found that administrators and supervisors considered ability grouping so essential that 'teachers were expected to group pupils for reading instruction even when the range of ability in their rooms was not a wide one' (Austin and Morrison 1963: 76). What appears to be operating is an assumption that important differences in aptitude exist in any population of students, and, as a result, even small differences between students are often the basis for grouping decisions. However, when differences between students are relatively small, the likelihood of misidentification increases.

Regardless of the amount of variance in a class, the requirement imposed by time and size constraints for nearly equal-size groups is likely to result in greater diversity in some groups than in others. This will occur because aptitude is unlikely to be evenly distributed throughout the class but instead is likely to peak at one or more points. If, for example, aptitude is distributed normally in a class, the range of aptitude would be much greater in the high and low groups than in the middle group(s) (see Figure 7.2).

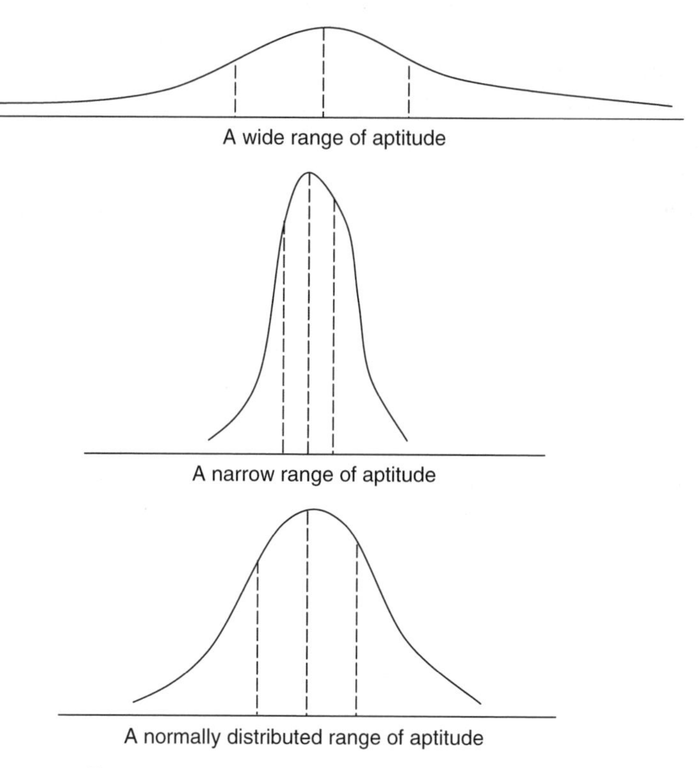

Figure 7.2. Different aptitude distributions divided into four equal-size groups.

It is therefore clear that the basis for assignment decisions is not students' absolute ability or aptitude but their aptitude relative to other class members. Thus, two students with identical ability might be assigned to different group levels depending on the abilities of their classmates. When rankings are used to determine assignment as they were in this classroom, the relative nature of these assessments is obvious. However, even if test scores had been used, a student's assignment to a given group would depend on the distribution of test scores for the entire class.

Thus the initial match between aptitude and assignment is likely to be less than ideal, and the constraints on movement between groups almost guarantees an increasingly poorer fit between student aptitude and group membership. To begin with, it is clear that no matter how many students perform well there will usually be a limited number of 'top' readers in a given classroom. In this classroom, once the high group had seven members it was extremely difficult to move into that group since groups larger than seven were considered to be less manageable. Although another solution would be to increase the number of groups at a given ability level, this teacher considered and rejected the idea of having two high groups because she did not have time to meet with more than four groups on a daily basis. Since increasing the number of groups at a given ability level generally requires at least a temporary increase in the overall number of groups, it is likely to occur infrequently.

Mobility into the top group is not the only form of advancement hindered by these constraints. Since low groups are usually smaller to begin with (Alpert 1974; Weinstein 1976), movement out of a low group would almost always lead to further imbalance in group size. Thus, once assigned to the lowest group, it is likely to be extremely difficult for a student to transfer into a higher group. In this classroom, none of the students who were initially assigned to the two lower groups moved to a higher group even though two of the four students were described at some point as potential candidates for upward mobility.

In general, due to time and size constraints, the initial hierarchy of ability level is likely to be perpetuated. While the flexibility of ability grouping and the continual movement of students between groups is emphasized in theory; time and size requirements clearly constrain the amount of movement which occurs in practice. Rist (1970) found similar results in his study of ability grouping in an inner-city school. Over a three-year period only four moves took place. In the second half of second grade, two students were moved to the medium-high group from the high group. At the same time, two students from the medium-high group were moved up to replace them. It appears that the problem of time and size constraints occurs in schools from all types of socioeconomic areas. However, since initial group assignment is often influenced by students' socioeconomic background (Rist 1970), students from lower- and working-class backgrounds will be most negatively affected by these constraints. Because such constraints restrict movement into higher groups, these students are likely to remain in lower groups even if they improve or are identified as having higher aptitude later in the year.

The impact of organizational constraints on across-classroom grouping

Organizational constraints are likely to be even greater when students of different ability levels are assigned to separate classrooms. Some states have requirements regarding the maximum number of students that can be assigned to one teacher at a given grade level. In addition, most school administrators attempt to distribute students evenly among teachers so that no teacher has an especially heavy or particularly light teaching load. Such organizational requirements would impose fairly rigid size constraints on the formation of across-classroom ability groups.

While these constraints would not automatically limit the number of across-classroom ability groups forming, financial constraints would. Although the ideal teaching arrangement might be a one-to-one teacher : student ratio, schools are faced with limited budgets which restrict the number of classrooms formed at a given grade level. Since there is likely to be little or no flexibility regarding size and financial constraints, they are likely to exert a considerable influence on group formation.

Furthermore, the more rigid organizational requirements of across-classroom grouping are likely to result in little or no movement between groups during or across school years. Movement in an academic year would upset the current balance in teachers' work loads and is thus likely to be resisted. And since budgets, buildings, and faculty resources are rather consistent from year to year, there is also likely to be a limited number of reassignments between academic years.

While size and financial requirements would impose similar constraints on allocation decisions in high schools, larger high schools are likely to have several classes at a given ability level and thus would be better able to match instructional opportunities to a given aptitude distribution than would smaller high schools or elementary schools which have one or at the most two classrooms per ability level. However, even in larger schools, restrictions on certain resources would constrain allocation decisions. For example, a school might have a limited number of foreign-language teachers or science laboratory facilities which would keep the size of the college track relatively constant from year to year despite changes in the aptitude of students. Likewise, if a school has extensive resources for art and craft instruction or clerical training, consistently high enrollment in non-college tracks is likely to be encouraged.

Allocation decisions at the high-school level may also be affected by limited resources at the college level. For example, Rosenbaum (1976) found that high-school administrators and counselors attempted to limit enrollment in college tracks to approximately one third of the students in a given class since many colleges restrict their recruitment to the top-third students in a class. The underlying argument is that it would be a waste of high-school resources to prepare more students than colleges are willing to accept. Because of limitations on the size of college tracks, students who have the aptitude for college would only be assigned to college tracks if there were slots available. The fact that counselors often actively discourage students from changing to college tracks suggests that there are often more students with the aptitude for college than there are available positions in college tracks (Cicourel and Kitsuse 1963; Rosenbaum 1976).

These constraints on track formation exist independently of the distribution of aptitude in a given school, helping to explain why aptitude has accounted for so little variance in curriculum assignment (Alexander, Cook, and McDill 1978; Hauser, Sewell, and Alwin 1976; Heyns 1974). They also suggest that allocation at the school, as well as classroom, level is dependent on the aptitude of others in the school. There is, in fact, some evidence which indicates that the brighter the students in the school, the less likely a student will be assigned to a college preparatory curriculum (Alwin and Otto 1977). Finally, these constraints are likely to restrict movement across curriculum tracks since college tracks could also 'fill up'.

Consequences of a poor fit between individuals and available positions

The problem of matching individuals with available positions occurs at every level of our society. For example, the recent increase in overall educational attainment has not resulted in a comparable rise in overall occupational status (Boudon 1974). This is not surprising since the availability of occupational positions is determined by many economic, political, and technological factors which are unrelated to individual aptitude. Since these factors have remained relatively constant, there has been little change in the occupational structure despite the overall higher levels of educational attainment (Boudon 1974). In fact, as Thurrow (1972) has noted, the current distribution of income is radically different from the current distribution of educational attainment. Thus, at the societal level, the fit between individual aptitude and available positions is relatively poor.

Given that the match between individuals and available positions is usually far from perfect, it is important to consider the consequences of a poor fit. Simmel makes a brief reference to one possible consequence, saying that when a discrepancy exists 'the individual is not sociated' (Simmell 1971: 21). However, this consequence will only occur when the discrepancy is attributed to the lack of an available position. In other words, it is only when individuals are aware that the poor fit results from restricted opportunity and not from personal failure that they are likely to feel uncommitted and alienated from that society.

To avoid such a consequence, poor fits are usually attributed to individuals' lack of aptitude. For example, when high-school students want to change tracks, their counselors do not tell them that the college tracks are full but instead point to their poor performance on examinations or classwork (Rosenbaum 1976). Likewise, parents who question the group placements of their children are told that their children are young for their grade, did not do well on reading-readiness tests, or otherwise show evidence of having low aptitude. By attributing discrepancies to individual deficiencies, the discrepancies no longer appear to exist.

An illusion of harmony can also be established by limiting available positions in one social structure to the number available at the next level of social structure, as when high-school administrators limit the number of college track positions to the number of students which colleges will recruit. This procedure gives the impression of a perfect match between aptitude for college and college enrollment. However, the harmony is only superficial since many students who wished to move into a college track were discouraged from doing so by their counselors (Rosenbaum 1976).

Just as positions in college tracks were limited to correspond with college-recruitment practices, college recruitment is likely to be influenced in turn by available positions in the occupational structure. Again the underlying argument is that it would be a waste of society's resources to prepare more people for professional occupations than there are positions available. And again the fit between college-educated adults and professional positions would imply a harmony that does not really exist.

Although there is no direct evidence, it is also possible that high-school tracking has some influence on ability grouping in elementary grades. If nothing else, it may contribute to the use of hierarchical structures such as ability groups since they would make later allocation decisions easier. This may explain, in part, why ability grouping continues to persist despite lack of empirical support for its effectiveness (Goldberg, Passow and Justman 1966).

Given the use of ability groups, time and size constraints have been shown to further influence assignment decisions. However, because allocation at this level is viewed as being based explicitly and solely on student aptitude, discrepancies are unlikely to be revealed and students in lower groups are likely to be viewed as having low aptitude. Thus an illusion of harmony is also established at this initial level of allocation.

It might be argued that at this and subsequent levels of allocation the comparative nature of allocation decisions is explicit, so that students might be viewed as having lower ability or less maturity but would not be described in more absolute terms. However, references to ability or other indications of aptitude are usually made in absolute rather than comparative terms. For example, high-group members were described by the teacher in this study as having 'a lot of ability' rather than as having 'more ability'. Likewise, low-group members were described as not having 'too much ability' or as being 'immature' rather than as having 'less ability' or as being 'less mature'. Similarly, high-school student handbooks claim that the school seeks to prepare students for college who 'have ability' not who 'have more ability'.

Because attributing poor fits to lack of aptitude is so pervasive and because the comparative nature of allocation decisions is generally not made explicit, it is not surprising that many individuals describe themselves as lacking ability or aptitude. (Rosenbaum

1976) found that most of the non-college track students in his study attributed their placement to either lack of ability or lack of motivation. While elementary students are more or less aware of their group placement depending on the visibility of ability grouping, when visibility is high, low-group members tend to have lower self-concepts (Borg 1966). Sennett and Cobb (1973) also found that many working-class men attributed their positions in the occupational structure to their own lack of ability or motivation rather than to the lack of available positions at higher levels: 'I really didn't have it upstairs to do satisfying work', 'I just wasn't smart enough to avoid hauling garbage', and 'if I'd applied myself, I know I got it in me to be different, can't say any one did it to me' (pp. 95 and 118).

Conclusions and postscript

In summary, because social organizations do not exist solely to provide Simmel's ideal positions for unique individuals, external organizational requirements often directly determine the availability of positions at a given level, making the matching of individuals to available slots an ever present concern. Even the assignment of students to ability groups within a first-grade classroom, which supposedly is based solely on student aptitude, was shown to be affected by time and size constraints. However, here as elsewhere there is an attempt to maintain an illusion of harmony between positions and people by attributing discrepancies to lack of aptitude rather than to lack of opportunity. This attribution, in turn, leads individuals in lower positions to view themselves as failures, while the relative and restricted nature of the competition remains hidden. Recent research on ability groups continues to show that little mobility occurs across reading groups despite the subjective nature of initial ability-group placements. In a study of 756 students in Baltimore City elementary schools, only 19 percent of the first-grade students changed reading groups in the first year and only 1 percent moved to a nonadjacent group (Pallas et. al. 1994). The researchers also found initial reading groups had only a weak correlation with reading comprehension test performance. They go on to report that 'the range of reading-group placements for children whose test scores at the beginning of first grade were fairly similar is remarkable.' Despite their initial similar test scores, students assigned to higher groups benefited by learning more, receiving higher grades, and being perceived by both parents and teachers as more competent than those in lower groups (Pallas et al. 1994).

Given the biases in ability-group assignments, the lack of mobility across groups, and the detrimental effects of low-group placements, more researchers are calling for alternatives to ability grouping and tracking in elementary and secondary schools (Oakes 1985; Wheelock 1992; 1994). One study comparing students in mixed-level classrooms with those in homogeneous classes in the same school found that a higher percentage of students were rated exemplary in the mixed-level classes (33 percent versus 18 percent) and a lower percentage were rated below standard (34 percent versus 56 percent). This suggests that mixed classrooms provide a better learning environment for many students (Wheelock 1992). However, certain conditions are necessary for detracking to succeed, including school-based leadership, professional development and support, a phasing-in process, and parent involvement in change (Wheelock 1992; 1994).

Notes

1. While a form of ability grouping occurs in some kindergarten classrooms, i.e. grouping on the basis of maturity level, there is less information on the frequency of this practice.
2. For a more detailed discussion on the selection of this classroom see Eder 1979.
3. One boy joined the class on that day. The other boy had apparently not been discussed with his kindergarten teacher and was asked to join the medium–low group during their first meeting.
4. These scores were not available when the groups were initially formed. The teacher reported that, had they been available, she would not have relied on them in making assignment decisions, even though test scores provide the main criteria for some teachers' assignment decisions (Austin and Morrison 1963).

8

Developing mathematical literacy in a bilingual classroom

Douglas R. Campbell

Introduction

In this chapter, I would like to address several questions which are not often raised in discussions about literacy, but whose answers may provide important insights into literacy as conventionally conceived – and into the kind of literacy that will increasingly demand attention, that is, the literacy entailed in the rapidly computerized society which appears to be developing worldwide. First, what might be said of the literacy which is implicitly sought through instruction in mathematics at the elementary level? Secondly, how might the role of language in teaching any subject, including mathematics, be revealed, through examining classrooms in which none of the participants are using their native language? Finally, what might an investigation of mathematics instruction in the English language in a Filipino classroom provide as counterevidence to disturbingly long-surviving yet otherwise unsubstantiated propositions

Acknowledgments: The research on which this chapter is based was conducted in a Tagalog-speaking community south of Manila, Philippines, from November 1974 to October 1975. I would like to acknowledge with gratitude the financial support for this work provided by the Philippine-American Educational Foundation and the Institute of International Education under the Fulbright-Hays Act. Among the many who were helpful at various stages in the journey, I am especially grateful to the late Michelle Rosaldo, who first derived from my early and inarticulate mumblings about my data the critical insight that the 'intrusion' of English in the mathematics lessons I had taped might better be seen as an instance of the necessary instruction in modes of discourse which all teaching involves. The results and interpretations reported here, of course, are my responsibility alone.

that children in non-Western settings are constrained by their cultural and linguistic backgrounds from performing in classrooms in the active and creative ways purportedly characteristic of Western children? I propose that the evidence presented here is of crucial importance for furthering efforts to increase the literacy of children everywhere, and particularly in those cases where inequality of achievement is structured along ethnic, linguistic, and social-class lines.

In particular, in presenting here a grade six mathematics lesson taught in a Philippine public school, I will develop the argument that learning and using mathematics is essentially a matter of acquiring patterns of discourse. While this point may seem to be obvious for, and thus restricted to, situations in which the medium of instruction is *not* the native language of the teacher and the students, I propose that such situations provide a 'window' (Merritt 1982) of access to a more general phenomenon not limited to bilingual settings, precisely because the bilingual factor makes the subtle discourse aspects of subject matter teaching more visible for initial investigation. The analysis here, then, represents a starting point toward recognizing how any subject-matter instruction involves talking about concepts and skills, as crucial to their acquisition and use by children.

Looking at classroom questioning in the Philippines

During the 1960s, a 'modern mathematics' curriculum was introduced to the elementary schools of the Philippines. A major goal was to replace traditional 'rote' teaching methods with a child-centered, guided discovery approach. It was hoped that better questioning strategies in particular, both by teachers and among students, would lead to improved conceptual understandings and problem-solving skills seen as necessary for the transformation of Philippine society to 'modernity'. As a Peace Corps Volunteer involved in this effort, I observed that teachers were adopting a question-centered approach. However, they continued to dominate their classrooms by doing most of the talking and virtually all of the questioning. Their questions typically sought cognitively low-level answers ('facts' rather than 'thinking'), and in relatively 'closed' formats (fixed-choice rather than open-ended). Especially troublesome for the discovery/inquiry ideal was the tendency for teachers effectively to 'tell' students the answers, through subtle hints provided in how they evaluated a response and/or followed it up with additional questions, as opposed to directing attention to the lesson's accrued materials so that the children might derive and evaluate answers on their own. I eventually concluded that this pedagogical innovation, formulated as it was in a Western 'scientific' setting, was bound to fail because of conflicts with the authority-based interactional styles of a non-Western, 'traditional' culture. Support for this view was readily available in the literature on Philippine educational problems (Corpuz et al. 1970; Soriano 1969) and culture-and-personality patterns (Guthrie and Azores 1968; Lynch 1964).

My awareness that there was something wrong with this way of thinking developed under the influence of work by Cazden (1970), Cole et al. (1971), Hymes (1971; 1972), Labov (1972a), Leacock (1972), and others, which challenged cultural-deficit explanations for educational problems by emphasizing the situational effects on ways of thinking and speaking, and by proposing that considerable 'communicative competence' is entailed in *producing* the observed behaviors which have formed the basis for falsely dichotomous views about language, culture, and cognition. I also discovered that the conventional view of the 'Filipino personality', as constrained by norms of 'smooth interpersonal relationships' from confronting established authority, was by no means undisputed: Lawless (1969) and Jocano (1975) have argued that a closer look at situational variations in interpersonal behavior belies the broad Philippine/American cultural differences that are often offered as explanations for a variety of national development and educational problems. As for the specific questioning patterns I had observed, it turns out that educational researchers have found similar patterns in the United States and elsewhere (see Dunkin and Biddle 1974; Gage 1978) – which in itself should be enough to recommend caution in too quickly concluding that 'their culture' is the source of these patterns in the Philippines. It is not even clear that the occurrence of low-level teacher questioning is a problem in the first place: there is some evidence in the research on teacher effects and pupil outcomes that, if anything, lower-order questions may be associated with *higher* pupil test scores (Berliner 1976; Gage 1978: 59; Rosenshine 1976).

In 1974 I returned to the Philippines to take a much closer look at the use of questions in teaching elementary mathematics in a Tagalog-speaking community. After several months of informal participant-observation, I tape-recorded seventy-nine formal lessons in one school, in grade one and grades three to six, and including topics in science and social studies as well as mathematics. Under the Bilingual Education Policy in effect at the time, mathematics and science were to be taught in English, and social studies in Pilipino (which is based primarily on Tagalog), beginning in grade one (see Manuel 1974; Pascasio 1977). Under the previous policy, Pilipino had been the medium of instruction for all subjects up to the end of grade four, after which English was used. During the year of my taping, the new policy was being implemented for grades one and two; grades three and four were to begin the following year. In anticipation of that change, the grade four mathematics teacher chose to use English; the grade six social studies teacher preferred not to be taped unless she could teach in Pilipino. Later in this chapter I will consider how central the medium-of-instruction issue became in my grapplings with these data.

Ways of looking at classroom questioning

Initial review of all of the recordings confirmed impressions formed during their taping: the teachers dominated the questioning and often gave away the answers in the process. This did, again, conform to the results of classroom research conducted in the United States, and through the well-established methods of measuring classroom processes. The problem with simply replicating such results through quantitative means, and leaving the matter there – and indeed, with the use of such an approach in the first place – is that, apart from problems of more precise definition of variables and procedures which might conceivably resolve the conflicting results of attempts to correlate process measures with pupil outcomes (see Berliner 1976; Cruickshank 1976; Gage 1978; Rosenshine 1976), there remains the rather more substantial critique that the standard measurement approach to classroom process research misses too much of what is actually involved in teacher–student interaction. Although quantitative/correlational approaches are important for establishing overall profiles of how different behaviors are distributed across classroom participants, settings, and activities, by concentrating on measuring 'objectively' one loses sight of how behaviors are affected by their immediate contexts and of what they mean to participants. One consequence of developing observational instruments from a priori concepts, especially those based on what purports to be good teaching, is that behavior is treated not in its own terms, but as an index of something else, a process of abstraction that can divert attention from the alternative, and often multiple, purposes to which a given behavior might be directed. As Gall (1970) notes, classifying questions in the cognitive terms of Bloom's (1956) taxonomy of educational objectives distracts attention from types which do not contribute directly to the process of information transfer, but which are essential to effective instruction (for example, by creating an *atmosphere* for discussion or creative problem solving).

In the growing 'sociolinguistic' work on classroom language (see Cazden et al. 1972/85; Cherry-Wilkinson 1982; Green and Wallat 1981; Hymes 1974; Stubbs 1976), there has been considerable attention paid to the problematic relation between the *forms* and *functions* of utterances, that is, the fact that syntactic forms and semantic functions do not necessarily stand in a one-to-one relationship with each other. For example, while 'questions' prototypically perform the function of requesting information through interrogative form, they can also issue commands, make statements, and request actions; and information requests can be accomplished by syntactic declaratives as well as imperatives, depending on the context in which the utterance was produced. For children in classrooms, the problem is how to know when an interrogative form is intended to request information, versus issue a command (as in 'Class, you will be quiet?'), or when a statement is meant to elicit whether an answer is known. The coding category 'asks a question' takes this interpretive problem for granted. It relies on the coder's ability to hear utterances as the classroom participants do – something which may be especially troublesome where inter-rater reliabilities, which amount to measures of shared cultural perceptions, are presumed to reflect valid coding of behaviors produced by children from different cultural backgrounds.

Mehan (1977) points to other phenomena of classroom language use which are beyond the scope of a predetermined set of coding categories. Among other things, utterances can perform more than the single function suggested by the codes; talk is not spoken in the isolation that coding systems represent, but in sequences whose achieved coherence over extended stretches is crucial for a full understanding of classroom discourse – including the role which pupils play in influencing the shape of a teacher's extended sequence of questions when an initial exchange proves to be unsuccessful.

The methodological implication here is that classroom interaction analysts must remain as close to the data as possible. For some, this follows from the anthropological tradition of participant-observation, as a way of capturing participants' perspectives on phenomena of interest. For others, this stance insures that locally salient concepts will emerge as the basis for hypotheses that others might wish to test in the light of general educational concerns (see Berliner and Tikunoff 1976; Lutz and Ramsey 1974; Overholt and Stallings 1976). There is also increasing recognition of the importance of having audio or video records of classroom events. Such recordings preserve an event beyond the limits of memory, thus permitting repeated examination that makes possible a demonstration of the grounds of a particular analysis – and thereby the possibility of alternative accounts (Mehan 1978; Erickson 1977).

Across the sociolinguistic and micro-ethnographic literature on classrooms, a number of distinct ways have been identified by which the use of questions in instructional activities can interfere with learning experiences and with wider educational and social opportunities. Those focusing on minority children's difficulties in school have shown the difficulty to reside in culturally organized differences between classroom and home in the situational appropriateness of asking questions in the first place (Boggs 1972; Erickson and Mohatt 1982; Goody 1978; S. Heath 1982a; Levin 1978; Philips 1972; see also Gumperz 1968; Hymes 1974), the results of which can be lowered teacher expectations for student performance and student rejection of academic achievement as an unviable source of personal esteem, all of which feed into a cycle of self-fulfilling prophecy adversely affecting subsequent success in both educational and occupational arenas (Erickson 1976; Labov and Robins 1969; McDermott 1974; Mehan 1978; Rist 1970;

Rosenthal and Jacobson 1968). Those who have addressed the issue of what any child needs to learn about social-interactional norms in order to participate in classroom instruction have shown the difficulties in associating classroom rules for questioning and answering with particular contexts and subcontexts within the daily flow of life in schools, with failure to learn such rules putting a child in jeopardy of having performance mistakes misevaluated as lack of ability (Bremme and Erickson 1977; Erickson 1977; 1982; Erickson and Schultz 1981; Florio 1978). A third line of research has focused on the particular features of verbal and nonverbal behavior which define form/function relationships as intended by speakers versus those understood by hearers – wherein lies the potential for misunderstanding that a classroom interrogative might have been meant as a command rather than an information request, even when cultural differences are not involved (Cook-Gumperz and Gumperz 1982; Gumperz 1982a; 1982b; Gumperz and Herasimchuk 1975; Gumperz and Tannen 1979).

For the Philippine situation represented by my tape-recordings, each of the problematic areas addressed by other investigators proved not to be central to the difficulties my analysis eventually uncovered. The teachers and students shared a common cultural and linguistic background, so that there were no apparent problems with cross-cultural misunderstanding of questions; the home/school discontinuity situation did not seem to put any children at risk within the classrooms observed. As for the inherent problematic of matching speaker intention with listener hearings in achieving consensus that a 'question' of a particular form and function was uttered in the first place, subtle interpretive work was no less involved for these teachers and children than for any other sets of interlocutors. Yet throughout the lessons I taped, in which teachers produced a barrage of questions, overwhelmingly in interrogative form, the children gave every indication of hearing what I heard to be the predominant meaning, the request for lesson-related information. They further had little trouble in hearing non-interrogatives in that way, and in recognizing the use of interrogatives for other purposes. Their problem, I soon realized, was not with *questions* – it was in knowing what the *answers* were, and how to produce them.

Not knowing the answers, of course, is common in classrooms everywhere, for the central purpose of instruction is precisely to impart information not already known by students. However, what is less obvious is how a teacher's questions do the work of producing, with the students' collaboration, an organized set of answers that constitutes a lesson's content and its character as a coherent social event. Sociolinguistic approaches have made important contributions to our understanding of how the transmission of academic knowledge is influenced by continuities and discontinuities in social knowledge about how language is used in various settings. But, in the process, they have neglected the content of those transmissions, and thus another kind of discontinuity which children face in going to school. Furthermore, we will soon see the impact of yet another kind of discontinuity, that entailed in using as a medium of instruction a language which is not native either to the children or to the teachers. Whereas much of the work in sociolinguistics has been concerned with going beyond conventional views of linguistic competence as consisting only of formal grammatical rules at the sentence level, and with referential definitions of lexical items (Gumperz 1982a; Hymes 1974), I will present a case where even those fundamental elements cannot be presumed, given the use of English as the medium of instruction. Here, English itself became a part of the event to be taught – a situation, in turn, which had dramatic consequences for how the mathematical content was handled. While my analysis might therefore seem to deal with matters prior to the insights of sociolinguistics, we will also see how, in its treatment of lesson content as interactional phenomena, the analysis remains at home with an interpretive, sense-making view of language competence (see McDermott 1976).

The emergence of a metaphor: 'Going for the answers'

While I was listening to all of my tapes and rediscovering the pattern of teacher dominated questioning, I was struck with how teachers' tendencies to continue the questioning process, even beyond the point where hints to the answers were unsuccessful in eliciting correct answers, gave the exchanges the overall appearance of a painfully elaborate 'guessing game'. On the advice of R.P. McDermott (personal communication), and in line with his conception of what constitutes the starting point for an adequate ethnographic description of the ways people make sense of their world (McDermott 1976; McDermott, Gospodinoff, and Aron 1978), I decided to address to the recorded data the questions 'What is going on here?' and 'What are they doing here?' – to let the data 'tell' me, as it were, how to characterize the interactions and the key problematic element in them.

These questions were addressed to the recordings of intermediate-grade mathematics lessons, the initial result of which was the formulation of a metaphor consistent with the 'guessing game' characterization: what the classroom participants were doing with their extended question/answer exchanges was 'searching for the answers' that constituted the official lesson content. The central idea here is that answers are elusive entities, at least under the apparent ground rule (possibly a result of taking the guided-discovery method too literally) that answers are not to be revealed if at all possible *except* as the result of a questioning sequence. By their persistent use of questions, the teachers seemed in effect to be searching among their students' varied responses for 'answers' that could stand as evidence that a lesson's content had been successfully conveyed from teacher to learner. The students' continued attempts to respond, even to the point of apparently 'guessing', could be seen as their own 'search' for answers from among the various clues provided in the way the teachers phrased and rephrased their questions. From this angle, I propose, we can look beyond the static and disturbing picture of classroom activity which the 'brute facts' of question/answer behavior often suggest, to the considerable activity which is beneath the surface patterns of questioning and not otherwise apparent at first glance.

In my dissertation (Campbell 1981) I discussed in more detail several reasons why the metaphor 'searching for the answers' had limitations which led me to seek a more satisfying formulation. In brief, these have to do with how classroom situations do not correspond to certain features that we commonly associate with searching activities in everyday life. For example, most searches involve participants who have a nearly equal lack of knowledge about what is being searched for, and where it might be, compared with the rather obvious difference in knowledge and control between teachers and students. Also, less interdependence, and especially face-to-face contact, is prototypically involved in such searches as those in media depictions of detective work, compared with the more tightly intertwined and mutually influential relationship of teachers' questions and students' responses.

I eventually hit upon a more satisfying formulation of the ebb and flow of verbal interaction in my tapes: as a lesson unfolded as a coherent event, the teacher and her students were effectively and jointly 'going for the answers'. This way of talking about the lessons jumped out at me as a result of reading David Sudnow's remarkable *Ways of the Hand* (1978) at just the time when I was again listening to the intermediate-mathematics lessons because of growing skepticism about the 'search' perspective. Sudnow is a sociologist who applied the insights of his ethnomethodological orientation to producing a detailed, elegant account of how he mastered playing improvisational jazz on the piano. He takes the reader through the stages by which his hands gradually embodied the music, first by mastering the basic scales-as-intertwining-pathways, then by accomplishing the 'sounds' that represent a liberation from the routine of drill, finally by reaching out to the free-flowing 'jazz' of the musicians whose special art he had long admired. The key to my recognition of a connection between his work and my tapes was in the book's chapter headings for the stages of his progression: 'Beginnings', 'Going for the Sounds', 'Going for the Jazz'.

My use of 'going for the answers' is more evocative than definitive, as befits what is intended to be a helpful metaphor rather than a formal concept. The image which I drew from Sudnow's use of 'going for' is the situation of having so accomplished the skills of one stage in a developmental sequence that one is prepared for the tasks of a next stage of known but as yet unexperienced behaviors. That next stage is within reach because the prerequisite skills of present and prior stages have now become routine, but it is by no means easily achieved. One must actively *reach* for it beyond present levels, the success of such efforts amounting to 'quantum leaps' rather than gradual progressions. Playing the sounds is dependent on but qualitatively different from putting together melodic runs built from basic scales; likewise, playing the jazz is a distinctly higher accomplishment. How one moves from stage to stage is always a problematic matter, addressed in some ways by instructional rules and the accumulated lore of past journeys. Ultimately, however, there is the individual encounter which is not reducible to exhaustive statements which may be generalized, but only evoked by those like Sudnow whose perceptions of the journey match an inclination and ability to construct a written account.

What does 'going for the answers' capture in the mathematics lessons? For the teacher, the essential task is to organize her questions into sequences in such a way that the children can draw on previous and current experience with the topics in order to produce answers here and now. She must implement this organization moment-by-moment, ever prepared for instituting correctives upon occasions of trouble in the children's productions, and always in the interest of providing just enough information and material that they will be ready to move on to – 'go for' – and *get* that next answer in the overall progression of topics which constitute the lesson's content. Critical here is the teacher's ability to strive for answers which are neither too easy nor too hard for the children's present capacities, but which present just the right amount of change to engage their interest and participation in answering, and thereby, perhaps, in 'learning'. (For a related formulation of learning based on Vygotsky's (1978) interactional theory of cognitive development, see McNamee 1979; Wertsch 1978; Wertsch and Stone 1978.) This requires the teacher to be constantly alert to signs of trouble as they stand out against the backdrop of normal appearances (see Sacks 1972), and to the progress of individual students as 'barometers' for how the class as a whole is doing.

For the children, the immediate task is to figure out what answers the teacher wants for the question currently on the floor. Their sources of answers will ideally be the content of the teacher's question, juxtaposed against illustrations which she presents with concrete materials or on the blackboard. But as the questions become more difficult they will understandably turn to the manner of the teacher's talk for additional clues. In any case, they must do more than merely respond to the question of the moment. They need also to monitor the thrust of a series of questions, as well as to keep track of accumulating answers, in order to be prepared for what might be coming next, and for what the teacher is driving at for the lesson as a whole. If their scanning of previous talk for hints appears to undermine their absorption of substantive mathematical content, I am proposing that it also facilitates their ability to remain engaged in the lesson's progress – a not insignificant prerequisite for learning the content. By 'going for the answers', they are contributing to structuring the lesson as a coherent event, no matter how tied they are to non-mathematical cues, nor how wild their guesses. The 'going for' formulation thus speaks to the children's critical role in the classroom, and as such it points the way toward levels of their interaction competence which are otherwise obscured from view.

At any point in a lesson, either the teacher or the students, or both, may decide the time is right for 'going beyond the information given' (Bruner 1957) by a 'quantum leap' in the answer they are going for. This can happen at points of transition across topical phases of the lesson, or in the effort to drive home the 'punchline' of the lesson. Such efforts require reaching beyond present levels of activity, on the assumption that answers developed so far have taken sufficient hold that the attempt to move on is not premature. Should the attempt fail, further work can be done to reduce the risk of missing on the next try – though the repairs may significantly alter what can be tried next time, or even 'give the game away' by providing so much assistance that the challenge of going beyond is eliminated. There is also the risk that what appears to be a successful movement of the lesson to a higher level is but a temporary gain, with the subsequent crash of what turn out to have been fragile answers, leaving the participants in a worse situation than before the move was attempted.

Essential to what the 'going for' notion captures is precisely this continuing elusiveness and fragility of answers, and the risks in reaching for them too soon – or too late. Under this view, teaching cannot be reduced to rules that can be learned as a way of eliminating risks of trouble in advance, or of remedying problems when they occur. The teacher's task must be recognized for the strenuous work it involves in response to the moment-to-moment contingencies of a particular classroom and lesson. And the children cannot be seen as merely passive recipients of the teacher's efforts, however passive they may appear on the surface. Finely coordinated improvisations from both teacher and students are required to surmount the inevitable risks of using questions to 'go for' answers.

One of the special appeals of the 'going for' idea is that it connects with the ethnomethodological perspective on social interaction which has been applied to classrooms by constitutive/

micro-ethnographers. This is the view that classroom events are the mutually accomplished, emergent, and contingent productions of the joint work of teachers and students who must constantly create and judge behaviors for making sense of and to each other (see Erickson 1977; Griffin and Humphrey 1978; Gumperz 1981; McDermott 1976; Mehan 1978; 1979). Drawing on the work of Garfinkel (1967) and Cicourel (1973) and their colleagues (see Douglas 1970; Handel 1982; Leiter 1980; Mehan and Wood 1975; Sudnow 1972; Turner 1974), these classroom researchers treat such taken-for-granted social facts and roles as 'teacher', 'students', and 'lesson' as phenomena whose sense, coherence, and, ultimately, 'reality' depend on how well teachers and students inform each other that these categories are pertinent to and can be enacted in the immediate situations. The methods by which this is done are unseen by researchers more interested in the measurement than in the production of educational events (Mehan 1974a; 1974b).

What is more typical of classrooms than the production of 'answers'? Classrooms are readily associated with the transmission of knowledge, both the official curriculum of academic subjects and the unofficial, or 'hidden', curriculum of cultural values and social norms (see Dreeben 1968). To the extent that a questioning method is used, the overt subject matter must be reducible to discrete packages which can be expressed as 'answers'. Consistent with Mehan's demonstrations that answers in both testing and classroom exchanges are accomplished *through* interactions between teachers and students (Mehan 1974a; 1978), I see 'going for the answers' as especially compatible with the emergent quality of classroom life, for it is addressed to the work which questions do to assemble the academic content – the 'answers' – of lessons over extended stretches of talk.

Knowing both *that* and *how* this is done is important for filling in gaps left in the assessment of teacher and student competence by conventional systems for measuring and evaluating classroom processes. For example, a number of researchers have noted a recurring feature of classroom interaction across a variety of settings: at one level, classroom talk is organized around a three-part sequence of moves, in which the teacher initiates activity (for example, by asking questions), the children respond (by answering, among other things), and the teacher evaluates the response (see Bellack et al. 1966; Johnson 1979; Mehan 1979; Mishler 1975; Sinclair and Coulthard 1975). This pattern does not exhaustively describe the organization of classroom interaction: students often answer incorrectly, or not at all, which requires the teacher to embed into the basic sequence additional ones which seek to probe, prod, and assist students toward successfully completing the original task; evaluation is often accomplished covertly, that is, not in so many words, and often simultaneously with some other action to remedy whatever occasioned a negative evaluation; there are also higher-order units and hierarchical relations between levels of analysis, necessary for accounting for relationships that obtain *across* successions of the basic three-part sequences (see Griffin and Humphrey 1978).

The contribution which the 'going for the answers' formulation makes to these patterns is its pertinence to the descriptive task called for by Mehan (1978; 1979), that is, that the 'structures' of classroom interaction be complemented by accounts of how participants go about 'structuring' them. In Mehan's own work, this involves an analysis of procedures by which turns at talk are allocated by teacher and taken up by students. The 'going for' idea adds to this a concern with how the *answers* of a lesson are structured. Just as it is possible to extract a content structure for a lesson, so it is important to examine how that structure is assembled. Indeed, in the light of micro-ethnographers' recognition that the pendulum of concern for the *social*, as opposed to the *academic*, dimensions of classroom competence has perhaps swung too far in one direction (see Erickson 1982; Griffin and Mehan 1981), the 'going for' formulation is an especially useful way of bringing the pendulum of concern back toward the *content* of lessons, seen through the 'answers' pursued within them, in a way which maintains a central focus on the *interactional* underpinnings of both academic and social knowledge.

'Going for the answers' in a grade six mathematics lesson

Let us now look at the results of applying these ideas to one lesson from the data set. The lesson is the first in a sequence of three which the grade six mathematics teacher taught to her 'higher-ability' section. The topic of the sequence is 'mathematical sentences'; the purpose of the first lesson is to establish the definitions of 'number sentences', 'set sentences', and 'number phrases', preparatory to subsequent days' work on 'open/closed sentences' and 'equations/inequations/inequalities'. This teacher's style is especially helpful to an analysis of 'going for the answers' in that she records on the blackboard her target 'generalization' (as she calls it) while it is being assembled by the interactional work of her questions and the students' responses. We and the students can thus 'see' as well as hear in example 8.1, the main answers which she goes for, gets, and writes down by the lesson's conclusion:

Example 8.1

Mathematical sentences express complete ideas about numbers and sets.
Kinds of mathematical sentences:

a. Number sentences express complete ideas about numbers.
b. Set sentences express complete ideas about sets.

Number phrases are parts of number sentences that have no complete ideas.

What is involved in going for and getting out these generalizations? Central to my formulation of 'going for the answers' is that 'troubles' of various kinds can be expected to occur during the course of a lesson. It is therefore appropriate to ask at any point, in any lesson, 'What is the trouble *here*?' and to ask of the lesson as a whole, 'What is *the* trouble here?' Answering these questions involves locating within the lesson episodes which can be examined as more or less troubled in their own right, and those epsiodes critical to the overall development of the lesson. For this lesson, I reviewed the transcript and replayed the tape several times, in order to produce a segmentation of major episodes of activity, in terms of which I could determine the current 'question-on-the-floor' and the associated 'answer-established'. These pairs of questions–answers were formulated as summaries of each episode's content – they were only occasionally verbatim quotations of what was actually said. As such, they then served as the basis of a summary chart of the lesson's main phases and subphases – what, in short, the lesson is 'about'.

Accomplishing these segmentations revealed that a recurrent answer to the question 'What is the trouble *here*?' is 'The students' English', as evidenced by the teacher's frequent correction of their responses for specific grammatical errors, her demands for answers in complete sentence form, and her continual request that they repeat corrected answers several times. The sequence in example 8.2 illustrates the types of production problems the children have, as well as the teacher's close attentiveness to them, through what I call 'intra-turn' prompts and corrections (i.e. inserted *within* a child's officially designated turn-at-talk). See Appendix 8.1 for the transcription conventions used.

Example 8.2

342 T How do you compare – the sentences in
343 group A – and in group B?
344 ((pause))
345 S Mam.
346 ((pause))
347 T Ro.
348 Ro The group- the group A
[
349 T The sentences: ↑ ?
350 Ro The: sentences – sentences –
[ ]
351 T in group
352 Ro of group A =
353 T = in –
[
354 Ro in group A
355 is a number sentence =

356 T = (a:re)
357 Ro are – number sentence =
358 T = ses
359 Ro sentences – while the – set B –
360 is – set – set – sentences.
361 T ((chuckles)) Who can say it again?
362-413 ((four more children are called upon to produce the answer, only one of whom does it without error))

The resulting impression from this and similar sequences is that the teacher is going for the *English* as much as – and possibly at the expense of – the mathematics.

When we ask 'What is *the* trouble here?' for the lesson as a whole, the use of English as the medium of instruction is further implicated: the biggest trouble which the teacher encounters seems to be that the children simply do not understand the term 'differentiate'. The lesson proceeds fairly smoothly for the first twelve minutes, during which the teacher's questioning successfully has the students producing answers which effectively identify, define, and label two groups of sentences on the blackboard as, respectively, 'number sentences' and 'set sentences'.

'Number phrases' are then covered briefly. Next the teacher asks them to compare the two groups of sentences, which, as we have seen above, they are eventually able to do with the aid of her well-timed prompts and grammatical corrections. The target answer here amounts to reidentifications of the sentences on the board, produced as a single, compound sentence:

Example 8.3

The sentences in group A are number sentences while the sentences in group B are set sentences.

The teacher now asks them to *differentiate* the number sentences from the set sentences. Five-and-a-half minutes later, after considerable backtracking, remedial work, and drill-like repetitions of answers which had already been established earlier in the lesson, the intended answer is finally elicited and recorded on the board:

Example 8.4

Number sentences express complete ideas about numbers, while set sentences express complete ideas about sets.

Given the difficulty they have in producing this answer, it is tempting to conclude that the use of English per se presents *the* major obstacle to effective mathematics instruction here and, by extension, throughout the Philippines. Yet, true though this may be, it was important to my analysis – and crucial for us now – not to stop with this as our final answer; in the first place, it is too obvious, and secondly it begs the question of just what teachers and children *do* to find their way out of a difficult situation over which they have no control, at least in the short run. As I hope to show below, there is much in this lesson to instruct us on just how – and even whether – to regard 'language' as a 'problem' for mathematics education in the Philippines, and elsewhere, and much to learn from how this teacher is oriented to this problem, as revealing of the close intertwining of the talk about and the doing of mathematics.

Let us look at more of the data. The first answer offered to the 'differentiate' request is shown in example 8.5.

Example 8.5

430 GL In group A – number sentences while –
431 in group B – set sentences.

As the teacher points out, this is in effect an abbreviated version of the answer already established during the 'comparison' segment; she then emphasizes that she wants to know what the *difference* is. The next child's answer is a definite improvement; it goes beyond simply reidentifying the sentences on the blackboard, as shown in example 8.6.

Example 8.6

441 Es The:: –
[
442 T The number sentence =
443 Es = The
444 number sentence like group- –
445 in group A – ( ) uses a
446 number while – while the
447 the examples- in group B uses
448 a set.

This is also not accepted, for reasons to be explored shortly. It is important to note that both of these answers involve some orientation to the teacher's interest in 'differences'; they are thus evidence that the difficulty is not simply that the students do not have any understanding of the English word 'differentiate'. They are nevertheless having difficulty comprehending the teacher's intended contrast between 'compare' and 'differentiate'. However responsible the use of English per se is for this trouble, a context-bound, language-in-use theory of meaning is definitely implicated.

What *does* the teacher intend here? This cannot be established conclusively, but look again at the answer in example 8.6: it is a close structural approximation of what the teacher is after. Apart from minor grammatical and production problems, the 'uses' in example 8.6 needs only to be replaced by 'express complete ideas about' in order to have the final answer as represented in example 8.4. Yet the teacher does not build on Es' answer in this way; instead, she further emphasizes her original question and begins the first of an extended series of repair strategies, as shown in example 8.7.

Example 8.7

452 T I said *di*::fferentiate,
453 ha?
454 Now look at the sentences very well. ((pause))
455 Find the differences. =
456 = What can you say about the number
457 sentences? =
458 = What ideas do they express?
459 ((pause))
460 T Ha? –
461 What ideas: – *do* the number sentences
462 express?

This occasions an obviously wrong answer, drawn apparently from the earlier segment on 'number phrases':

Example 8.8

470 MU = The number
471 sentences are- – complete –
472 while – the (setel)- – set
473 sentences are – incomplete.

In response, the teacher states that both groups of sentences express complete ideas; she asks again *what* complete ideas the number sentences express. She calls on Le, the one child who produced a flawless version of the answer in example 8.4 to the 'comparison' question. When Le now answers with 'The number phrase', apparently following Mu's lead, the teacher moves more dramatically to reestablish the basic components of the answer she wants – components which had already been successfully elicited earlier in the lesson, but which now appear to have been forgotten:

Example 8.9

507 T Now,
508 what do these – number sentences –
509 express?
510 ((pause))
511 T What complete ideas – do they express?
512 ((pause))
513 T What are the sentences about?
514 ((pause))

An answer is finally offered ('mathematical sentences'), but it is wrong. Now the teacher institutes an extended 'simplification sequence' (see Mehan 1979), which begins with a Tagalog rendition and immediate translation of the current question on the floor, and ends with her effectively telling them the answer by providing them with a choice and finally selecting out what she wants when they choose both, as shown in example 8.10.

Example 8.10

531 T Anong buong – kaisipan – ang kanilang –
532 ipinaghahayag? [What complete ideas do they express?]
533 What complete ideas do they express?
534 ((pause))
535 T Complete ideas about: ↑ ?
536 ((pause))
537 T About what? =
538 = Sets or numbers?
539 S Sets.
[
540 Ss Sets.
[
541 Ss Sets.
[
542 S Numbers.
[
543 Ss Numbers.
[
544 Ss Numbers.
545 T Numbers.
546 ((pause)) ((T writes answer on board))
547 T Alright, what do you say now?

The next child called on produces (with prompting) the answer she was originally after:

Example 8.11

Number sentences express complete ideas about numbers.

After she has gotten the students to repeat this several times, it becomes a relatively simple matter to elicit the analogous answer for set sentences. Then, with the sequence shown in example 8.12, the answer originally 'gone for' almost six minutes earlier is finally assembled:

Example 8.12

606 T Class, what are set sentences?
607 Ss Set sentences express complete
608 ideas about sets. =
609 T = What are number sentences?
610 S Mam.
611 T Class.
612 S Number
[
613 Ss Number sentences express complete
614 ideas about numbers. =
615 T = Now what is the difference?
616 ((pause))
617 T Le.
618 ((pause))

619 Le Number sentences –
[
620 T expre-
[
621 Le express
622 complete ideas about numbers,
623 ((pause)) and set sentences ex-express
624 complete ideas about sets.
625-631 ((T repeats the question, and another S
repeats the answer))
632 T There you are.

Elsewhere (Campbell 1981) I have discussed in some detail the evidence available in this lesson to support my claim that the children have significant problems in understanding and producing the English necessary for participating fully in this lesson. In the concluding section, I will discuss further whether the use of English as the medium of instruction per se is the critical issue, overwhelming the significance attached earlier to the 'going for the answers' formulation. For now, and preparatory to that discussion, the question is this: Given that the children are obviously struggling with the medium of instruction, and that the teacher is clearly oriented to that, might the extended sequence of trouble apparently occasioned by her request that they 'differentiate' the sentences have been avoided by a different verbal formulation of the tasks she wanted them to perform, and mitigated, once begun, by having latched onto Es' answer in example 8.6, as the core of what she wanted, the complete version of which might then have been achieved by gradually transforming her 'uses' into 'express complete ideas about'?

The problem with the teacher's approach to the 'differentiation' phase is not so much her use of the term 'differentiate' itself, for the children's responses in 8.5 and 8.6 *do*, as already noted, evidence orientation to the concept 'difference'. The difficulty seems instead to be that the teacher is not progressing from requesting similarities, with her 'compare' question, to seeking *differences*, with her 'differentiate' question. Instead, she effectively wishes them to *identify* the sentences in the 'compare' phase, and *define* them in the 'differentiate' section. This suggests that the trouble would not necessarily have been avoided by not using the term 'differentiate'; the children were more likely confused by the mismatch of the identifying/defining tasks with the 'compare'/ 'differentiate' terms.

Or were they? Es' answer in 8.6, which came after Gl's, indicates that she, at least, followed the teacher's shift upwards in the tasks' cognitive demands: her formulation is not tied to identifying and labeling sets of examples on the board, but is directed to more abstract, defining features. Furthermore, her complete answer is remarkable in its underlying equivalence of sentence structure with the target answer, as shown in Figure 8.1. Given this close equivalence of structures, it does appear that the teacher might have missed an important opportunity here to avoid the extended stretch of trouble that ensued when she instead stepped back to review the constituent concepts of the 'differentiate' answer. Why did the teacher not choose to build on Es' answer with a slot-substitution format for replacing those components in Es' answer which could have been treated as adequate for now but short of the final form she was going for? Had she done the latter, she could have reinforced Es' attentiveness to the shift in task levels, perhaps in the process informing other students what had been wrong with Gl's answer and what she was really after – and teaching, however indirectly, the important structural underpinnings of basic English reflected in Figure 8.1.

Perhaps. But rather than rest with merely suggesting what the teacher should have done, I will offer an alternative account of what she did do, in support of the claim that her response to Es' answer was reasonable, even preferable, under the circumstances that had accrued up to that point in the lesson, and in terms of the troubles that ensued following what was a more crucial lesson turning point than that constituted by Es' answer.

This account is predicated on a number of assumptions about this teacher and her students, the foremost of which is that she is quite aware of the children's difficulties with English. This is hardly surprising, in that she and her colleagues constantly referred to the extra burden of teaching in English. But I am further assuming here, based on her particular care with the English of their answers, that she is so aware of the language dimension of her teaching that she presents the mathematical content in close concert with the language required to express it. She does this in order to prevent disruptions possible because of problems with the English medium, and in order to resolve any language-based troubles that might nevertheless intrude in developing the mathematical ideas. I claim

a	NP-1	VP	NP-2	Conj	NP-3	VP	NP-4
b	The number sentences in group A	use	a number	while	the examples in group B	use	a set.
c	Number sentences	express complete ideas about	numbers	while	set sentences	express complete ideas about	sets.

['target' answer for 'number sentence']

['target answer for 'set sentence']

Figure 8.1. Equivalence of answer structures.

that she is engaged in various types of 'work' toward these ends throughout the lesson, but especially at the outset. The upshot of what follows is that she is indeed teaching English as much as mathematics, but that this is better seen as a necessary process of teaching mathematics *as* language.

Thus, by the time the teacher first poses the 'differentiate' question, she has already given considerable attention to the key mathematical terms, verb phrases, and sentence structures which eventually come together in 8.4, her target generalization. In what I call 'foundation work', she has informally introduced these elements into the public stream of talk quite early in the lesson. For example, the critical frame 'express (complete) ideas about X', which is the basis of the definitions of number and set sentences, as well as essential to the 'differentiate' answer, is introduced with the very first utterances of the lesson: 'Class, what do we say, or write, when we wish to *express* – some *ideas*? ((pause)) You like to say something. You want to *express an idea*. What do we say or write?' (lines 5–11; my emphasis). These 'foundations' form the components which the teacher and students will eventually use to assemble the generalization; they are also in place for the additional work that will later be necessary as more serious troubles emerge.

As the lesson proceeds, the teacher gradually elaborates and juxtaposes the foundation elements into ever closer approximations of their eventual final forms, both by her subsequent questions and in the subtle transformations which she performs on the students' answers. This I call 'shaping work', which is exemplified by how the teacher takes a child's answer 'sets' (to the question 'What - do the other mathematical sentences *deal with*?') and expands it into a complete sentence which both reinforces the use of the phrase 'express ideas about X' and attaches it to the concepts 'mathematical sentences' and 'sets': 'Sets:: =alright. = Other mathematical sentences –express ideas- about-sets:' (lines 140–163). From the vantage point of 'shaping work', the teacher's attention to the lexical forms and syntactic structures of the answers in English is less an *intrusion* of grammatical concerns into the realm of mathematics, and more an essential part of the overall shaping of the concepts to be learned.

'Anticipation work' is a broader way of formulating what the teacher is doing with the mathematics and the English. Most specifically, it covers getting the children to repeat answers in drill fashion, which serves the purpose of determining whether they have absorbed an answer, and of reinforcing their acquisition of it. But the repetitions also serve as preparation for what the teacher anticipates to be possible production problems later. Thus, where drilling might seem to be intrusive upon the smooth flow of instructional talk, I am arguing that it is done to *facilitate* that flow in upcoming phases of greater conceptual difficulty, where insufficiently mastered phrases and sentences from earlier phases might indeed interfere with what the children can learn. Overall, the teacher's efforts anticipate the difficulties the children *might* have with the English, in such a way as either to avoid problems in the first place, or respond to them with the accumulated experience of recently accomplished foundations and shapings.

Amidst all this, the teacher is constantly evaluating the class' progress, in terms of how well they are doing on *this* question *now*, in order to determine how well they are likely to do with what she will ask them next, and how well they are doing on what she is driving at for the lesson as a whole – all of which can be labeled 'monitoring work'. Because she is dealing with children whose abilities differ, she needs to be especially careful in judgments she makes about the class as a whole from answers provided by only one or a few children. To whom she directs her questions, and how she draws on her prior knowledge of individual abilities in treating a given answer as a sign of learning by the class as a whole, all of this entails that aspect of monitoring which I call 'barometer reading': the location of indicators within children's answers of an approaching storm of trouble.

What, then, is the cumulative effect of these types of work by the time they reach the 'differentiate' phase, and how does it condition what happens then? Though the essential elements of the target answer have been laid down and shaped, the children have had various problems with the language and concepts required to produce answers, and they have not in fact been required so far to produce the full definitions of 'number sentences' and 'set sentences' which will eventually be conjoined into the 'differentiate' answer. The teacher, therefore, through her monitoring work, is likely to have but modest expectations for what she is about to ask, if not more serious reservations about troubles yet to come. It is accordingly in her best interests to move on cautiously, and to be on the lookout for further signs of trouble, in order to draw on what has already transpired for remedies, if necessary.

And what happens? Right away there are indications of trouble. No one responds when she puts the 'differentiate' question to the class as a whole; the first child nominated is unable to answer; and the teacher is already beginning 'elaboration work', by providing a reformulation and specification of the basic question: 'How do you differentiate? = What is the difference? Between the two?' (lines 420–422). Gl then produces her truncated version of the 'comparison' answer (see 8.5), which is the first overt sign that perhaps they do not understand her question. Es now offers her answer, in 8.6, which can be seen as the lesson's key turning point. But from the perspective which I have attributed to the teacher, this point now has a history behind it; it is no longer quite so clear that the children need only to be led through a substitution procedure applied to Es' answer. As barometers, perhaps Gl's response is a better sign of what the rest of the children understand than is Es'? We cannot be sure, but certainly the children's troubles with the language so far suggest so. But perhaps the teacher is not sure yet either. Consistent with this interpretation, she responds to Es' answer with one more attempt to highlight the core of her question (in 8.7, lines 452–455).

The teacher's next move (in 8.7, lines 456–462) represents the beginning of 'probing work' into the strength of foundations she may otherwise have been taking for granted. The first wrong answer, in 8.8, foreshadows deeper problems; Mu appears to be guessing by grasping at an earlier contrast made between 'number sentences' and 'number phrases'. The teacher then calls on Le, at what is a more important lesson turning point and barometer reading than that represented by Es' answer in 8.6. Le was the only child who could produce a virtually flawless version of the answer to the 'comparison' question in the previous phase; later, she will be the child called on to produce the 'differentiate answer (see 8.12). Thus, the teacher might reason, 'If even she can't answer the review question about number sentences, which we already covered fairly thoroughly, then the rest must really be lost!' The question is posed – and the result? Le hesitantly offers 'The: -number phrase', thus following Mu's wrong turn. They *are* in trouble.

My proposal for how the teacher read Le as a barometer is that she now realizes more is at stake than just their comprehension of the 'differentiate' question; the foundations which were laid down in the 'presenting concepts and terms' phase at the beginning of the lesson have not set well enough. After repeating one more time that she wants them to 'differentiate' the groups of sentences, she moves unequivocally to remedy the more fundamental problem of how well the target answer's foundation elements have been absorbed, beginning an extended sequence of 'repair work' with 8.9.

At its outset, the teacher's repair work can also be construed as 'recourse work', in that her strategy is to reach back to foundations from earlier parts of the lesson. In 8.9, she is effectively directing their attention to the specific sentences on the board, which amounts to repeating a question they had been able to answer in an earlier phase. But when they cannot answer it now, the teacher begins the first of a series of steps that constitute 'simplification work', which initially does not produce correct answers either. The teacher's response to this is the more dramatic simplification moves represented in 8.10, in which she translates the recourse question into Tagalog (lines 531–532); repeats it in English (line 533); truncates it into 'sentence completion' form (line 535); further reduces its demands by the 'slot-*wh*' form (line 537); begins to give up, for all practical purposes, by providing a multiple choice/guess opportunity (line 538); and finally, when even this amount of telling results only in their cascaded production of *both* answers (lines 539–544), concludes that 'all else has failed' by virtue of snatching from the stream of talk the answer 'numbers' which her 'snatching work' and blackboard record reify as correct (lines 545–546). This leaves them at a different type of turning point for the lesson. In effect, they have reached the pit of their troubles and can now begin the gradual climb back to the original question, through what I call 'recovery work', a process which is not without its own stumbles and delays, but which nonetheless in fairly short order sets the stage for Le's formulation of an answer so persistently pursued (see 8.12, lines 617–624).

Was Es' answer in 8.6 a lost opportunity, a way to have avoided the troubles encountered during the 'differentiating' phase of the lesson? I think not. My interpretation is that the teacher did a remarkable job in assessing the difficulty as more than their comprehension of the term 'differentiate'. I claim that she sensed the fragility of foundations developed for the 'number sentence' and 'set sentence' components, and that for her, Le's answer was more revealing of what she had to do than was Es'. I have tried to show that the various types of work which were done in the early phases of the lesson had as their purpose the prevention and remedy of just the types of trouble that occurred later. And, lest we be tempted to suggest what the teacher might have done differently at various other points in the lesson, let us remember that in 'going for the answers' in teaching there is always the element of risk, of reaching for an answer too soon or too late. Let us therefore assume that she took a chance that enough about 'number sentences' and 'set sentences' had been established earlier to permit their taking a shot at defining the terms in contrast to each other. That she misjudged their readiness should not detract from the reasonableness of taking that chance, given the supportive work she was simultaneously conducting, the fact that they had succeeded in the 'comparing' task, and her own readiness from prior foundation, shaping, anticipation, and monitoring work to meet the 'differentiate' problem head-on. And especially since teaching can never be a problem-free, foolproof matter in every case, let us regard Es' answer as wisely foregone in the light of the further instruction and reinforcement of basic ideas that was accomplished through the repair work. Furthermore, had this teacher not attended to the children's English in 'going for the answers', they might have failed to reestablish the foundations for contrasting the mathematical ideas encapsulated as linguistic terms, and for summarizing the lesson's work as a 'generalization' to be written down and, perhaps, remembered.

Conclusion

Whether or not anyone actually *did* learn anything in this lesson cannot, of course, be conclusively determined from the tape-recording nor from my interpretation of it. Yet for anything to be learned, it must first be made publicly visible, or audible, and thus available for whatever the learning process is. It is this task to which the 'going for' formulation is addressed, and it has been my purpose in this chapter to illustrate through a close look at a single lesson how the formulation can focus attention on the intense interactional work in which both teacher and students must engage in order to accomplish lessons as contexts for teaching and learning.

But this lesson reveals more than this. The use of English as the medium of instruction obviously presents a serious obstacle to the learning of mathematics here. In any setting where a non-native language is used as the medium of instruction, however, it is important to go beyond the obvious, by examining in detail just how that language interferes with the transmission of lesson content, and in what ways the classroom participants are able to deal effectively with the intrusion. In the process of developing my account of how the language obstacle was managed in this lesson, I discovered in this teacher's close attention to the children's English that she was systematically preparing them in the language necessary for producing the mathematical answers required in this lesson. Out of this came my realization that language is not merely the 'medium' of instruction but also its essential *point*, even in officially non-language subject areas such as mathematics. The bilingual situation makes this point painfully obvious, even trivial; one might argue that of course it is necessary to teach English along with mathematics in situations like that of the Philippines. Indeed, as has been widely observed, English itself is best learned when used in other subject areas such as mathematics (see Tucker and d'Anglejan 1976). In my analysis, however, I tried to show how one grade six teacher was positively oriented to teaching language as a crucial part of teaching mathematical ideas. Her task was more than just teaching English as a means to the mathematics, in that she was engaged in teaching them what they needed to know to do the *talking* of mathematics.

This was especially salient in the lesson analyzed here, given the metalanguage nature of its subject matter. This feature of the lesson became a fortuitous circumstance for orienting me to the proposition that any subject matter, even in the most monolingual classroom, involves instruction in a domain of *discourse*. To a large extent, learning subject-matter content for maximally effective use outside the classroom necessarily entails learning to talk about it, or with it. I propose that this is especially important – and difficult – to acknowledge for mathematics, given the common image of that area as a domain of context-free rules and concepts, unsullied by the imprecisions and ambiguities of everyday, 'natural' language. Even mathematicians must occasionally use their native language as a resource for talking about and conducting their work. How much more prepared for and comfortable with the mathematical (and, increasingly, computerized) dimensions of contemporary life might children be if more concerted attention were paid to situations and strategies for *speaking* about, as well as computing with, numbers and such? In such directions lie potentially fruitful and detailed answers to questions about improving the quality of literacy instruction in general, and about the practice and pedagogy of mathematical literacy in particular.

As for the recurring allegation that non-Western children are predisposed by their cultural and linguistic backgrounds toward classroom behaviors that handicap their efforts to acquire the fullest, most creative aspects of literacy, I offer my analysis of 'going for' the mathematics and the English as counterevidence, especially in those policy contexts in which such allegations are offered preemptively as 'proof' that inequalities in access to educational and socioeconomic opportunities are the natural outcome of factors intrinsic to a people's way of life and manner of speaking. Whether schooling is a means to overcome such putative barriers to social and national development, or merely the means by which such barriers are perpetuated; whether or not 'further research' may eventually clarify in what ways teachers can realistically expect to prepare children for development, personal or national, I conclude from my plunge into the details of classroom interaction that there is no basis for claiming that Filipinos are, by culturally conditioned nature, too passive to participate in whatever levels of questioning may be required to use educational institutions for the acquisition of literacy and for socioeconomic transformation toward equality.

Postscript

The lesson described in this article was taped in July of 1975; by the time ten years later that I prepared this article for the 1986 publication of this book, I had begun to move away from classroom interaction research, in part because like many dissertation writers, I'd simply had enough of that topic, and of course (as many of my students have worried), I was more concerned about all that was wrong with the work rather than what it might contribute in its substantive areas and themes. But I was also moving away as new opportunities presented themselves to me at Michigan State, first into a collaborative research, reflection-based professional development project with my colleagues Fred Erickson, Richard Navarro, Becky Kirschner, and four outstanding elementary-school teachers and principals, and eventually on to our College's Professional Development School program.

Now, in the spring of 2005, some thirty years after the taping, and almost twenty since the original publication of this book, I have been gratified in going back to my dissertation work to reflect on what it represents. This is not to say that I turned my back on it completely, for in my classes I have regularly presented it, but mostly in terms of its methodology and its lessons for students about to undertake their own research. These lessons include arguments for qualitative approaches in general and small sample sizes in particular; encouragement to follow the lead of one's interests and of the situation at hand once in the field and while writing rather than feeling inextricably bound to one's original research questions and design (let the 'findings' emerge, so to speak, from the data); and cautionary tales about not taking the 'emergent' point too far, as I unfortunately did (and as glossed over in this article in my recounting of how my original plan was based on models in the literature that did not end up fitting my field situation), with adverse consequences that even now I am reluctant to put to writing but find much easier to share in oral-teaching contexts. Overall, my 'methodological' presentations have had the deliberate quality of a 'warts-and-all' demystification of a process that over the years I have found can be quite paralyzing to many students, not just to me.

More substantively, I now see that my 'going for' metaphor resonates with Vygotsky's 'zone of proximal development' (ZPD) even more than I realized at the time – but also less. As I was finishing my dissertation in the late 1970s, Vygotsky's *Mind in Society* (1978) had only recently appeared in English, but the ZPD did look very close to what I was arguing for: how the teacher and her students were closely attending to each other so as to adjust their talk in the direction of a 'zone' in which the answers she was seeking could be articulated by the students, if not grasped by all of them, or learned by any of them. And so, as I now tell students who encounter helpful 'literature' late in the game, I made a 'nodding' reference to Vygotsky at the end of my 'literature review' chapter ('on the way out', so to speak; see Campbell 1981: 107–8). Five years later, in writing this article, I made but passing reference to Vygotsky, with no direct mention of ZPD, and I wondered while preparing this postscript why I had missed that opportunity to make more of it rather than less. But with the help of Gordon Wells' excellent overview of ZPD (Wells 1999), I now see that this backing off was just as well, in light of the explosion in uses and diversification in definitions of ZPD since it was first introduced in *Mind in Society* – particularly in light of my long realization that I could make no claims from my data about whether or what students actually learned during that lesson, either inter- or intra-psychically.

More compelling to me now is the argument that evolved as I analyzed and wrote up my data, about the lesson demonstrating the necessity of teaching the discourse of mathematics, not just the manifest mathematical content, versus seeing the use of English as a second-language medium of instruction as just an obstacle to be overcome in teaching the mathematics. I cannot be sure where this point stood amidst 'the literature' at the time, nor even now – but what I hear around me from colleagues and students suggests that this argument fits within the 'communities of discourse' realm of contemporary educational research.

But most important to me now, as in the beginning some thirty years ago when I finished the Peace Corps work which led to my dissertation research, is the case I find must still be made in these days of high-stakes testing and the continued disproportionate blaming of teachers for our educational problems: it is possible to belie, counter, or at least complement what may look so terrible (read, 'passive', 'deficient', 'incompetent', etc.), with an alternative, more positive (read, 'active', 'dynamic', 'competent') characterization that can help direct attention to the circumstances and larger contexts that create the surface appearances and their no doubt problematic consequences – while also avoiding stereotypical attribution of problem sources to 'their culture' (here I am especially indebted to Charles Frake, member of my dissertation committee and exemplar in his own work of finding people 'smart' where others seem so compelled to render them 'stupid'). Although this may strike you, as it has me, as 'romanticization', and although, like me, you may also have been bogged down in the detail and density of my presentation, as is often said in other contexts 'the devil is in the details', and my details do provide the reader with an evidentiary basis for evaluating my claims for what was going on that day and what it all could mean.

For now, I conclude with my gratitude to those whose published work, and in several cases direct counsel, originally inspired me to set aside the 'cultural-deficit' thinking I brought with me from the Philippines as I began graduate work (C. Cazden, J. Cook-Gumperz, F. Erickson, S. Florio-Ruane, C. Frake, H. Garfinkel, P. Griffin, J. Gumperz, D. Hymes, W. Labov, E. Leacock, R. McDermott, H. Mehan, M. Rosaldo, S. Philips, H. Sacks, D. Sudnow), even if in most cases their specific work did not directly apply to the situation in which I conducted the research reported here. On balance, while I set out to 'look elsewhere' for competence in question-and-answer sequences, along the lines of the 'situational variation' theme of sociolinguistic theories, I found that competence could also be discerned by 'looking through' the surface appearances that so many others so quickly see as problematic. I hope that you can trudge your way through the dense details of my argument to see what I mean in these data, and even apply it to your own situation!

Appendix 8.1: Transcription conventions

The following are explanations for the conventions used in the presentation of transcribed data in this chapter (line numbers refer to those used in the complete lesson transcript). These conventions were adopted from the system worked out by Gail Jefferson and her colleagues (see Schenkein 1978: xi–xvi).

[ ]	T: Set sentence [ ] S: Set sentence [S: Set-	*Square brackets* are used to indicate overlapping talk across speakers.
=	S: Set. = S: = Number = T: = Number.	The *equal sign* is placed between utterances which are so precisely timed that there seems to be no pause between them, both within and between speaker turns.
-	S: The:- [T: The set.	A *hyphen* indicates an abrupt break in the stream of talk, as when someone is uncertain of an answer, or is interrupted.
–	S: The – phrase.	*Long dashes* are used to indicate brief pauses, too short to time.
,	T: Set, or set.	The *comma* also designates a brief pause, used when the pause occurs at the end of a syntactic phrase or clause, as in written discourse.
	((pause))	Longer pauses are shown this way, both within and between speaker turns.
::	T: Sets::. al:right	*Colons* are used proportionately to show elongations of syllables.
Italics	T: *Di*fferentiate	Syllables or words which are italicized are spoken with noticeable emphasis.
↑ ?	T: Complete ideas about ↑ ? S: Sets.	This combination of symbols marks the 'sentence completion', or 'fill in the blank' question.
( )	T: It is (there). S: The ( ).	*Parentheses* are placed around transcribed material about which there is some doubt about what was said. If empty, the parentheses indicate sound which could be heard but not deciphered.
(( ))	T: ((chuckles))	*Double parentheses* enclose comments, contextual information, non-verbal activity, etc.
[ ]	*[*What is it?*]*	*Slanted brackets* enclose English translations of Tagalog utterances.

9

Spoken language strategies and reading acquisition

Herbert D. Simons and Sandra Murphy

Example 9.1

CHILD 1 It looks like a music note . . . but it has points and it sort of looks like a saucer.

CHILD 2 This one just looks like a . . . something right here, like this part right here, look like a key. And this right here . . . looks like a planet . . . like a ship.

Both of these children are describing an abstract figure in the presence of an adult. They have been told that their description, which is being tape-recorded, will be heard by one of their classmates, who will have to pick out the figure they are describing from an array of nine abstract figures. Although these descriptions were equally successful in accomplishing the task, they have a number of differences. One of these differences concerns the degree to which they are tied to the temporal and physical situation in which they are produced. The first description is appropriate for written communication, but the other is not.

Communication in oral and written language is different in multiple ways (Rubin 1978; Schallert, Kleiman and Rubin 1977). Speech tends to be multi-channeled, including lexical–semantic–syntactic, interactional, paralinguistic and nonverbal modes of transmission, while writing is most often unimodal, depending heavily on the lexical–semantic–syntactic channel. Early formulations of oral and written language characterized oral language as having a high degree of interaction and involvement of participants who share the same temporal and spatial context, often in face-to-face encounters. Written language, on the other hand, was seen as having little or no interaction and less involvement (Olson 1977; Ong 1982). Literate language, particularly expository prose, was characterized as decontextualized, explicit, and self-referential, with few of the interpersonal devices that are common in conversation. In turn, the process of becoming literate was characterized as learning to encode and decode print and to make meaning out of decontextualized language, i.e. language-on-its-own (see for example, the work of Olsen 1977; Olsen and Torrence 1981; Snow 1983). More recent theorizing challenges the characterization of written text as autonomous and decontextualized as well as theoretical frameworks that dichotomize orality and literacy along the lines of context-versus-message or text versus situational context. For example, Brandt argues that social involvement is 'not merely a cultural impetus for literacy but its interpretive underpinning as well'. (1990 p. 103). From Brandt's perspective, becoming literate is not learning how to encode and decode decontextualized text. Instead, it is learning how to draw on knowledge of both language and context to create and maintain involvement and to guide and interpret meaning. In other words – to communicate. But from either theoretical perspective, writing and reading put new demands on children whose previous experiences have largely been confined to face-to-face encounters and ordinary oral language. Because the reader and writer do not necessarily share the same temporal and spatial context, the production of the written message is separated from the decoding of the message. In example 9.1, the first child compares the stimulus item to other contexts of culturally shared knowledge (e.g. a music note, a saucer). The second child employs the same strategy (e.g. a key, a planet, a ship), but also refers to the context of the situation itself (e.g. something right *here,* like *this* part right *here*). The second child is relying on strategies that are appropriate for oral language, where reference can be directly made to entities in the immediate physical context, and is less sensitive to pragmatic differences in the frames of reference that are appropriate for written language. Children's sensitivity to this difference in the circumstances of the communicative contexts of speech and writing, and their awareness of the characteristics of written language, may influence their acquisition of reading skill. It is to this theme that this chapter is addressed.

Example 9.2

TEACHER Say the word 'sand' without the 's'
CHILD 1 and
CHILD 2 sand

In example 9.2, the teacher is attempting to guide the children's transition from oral to written language strategies in a reading lesson. Example 9.2 illustrates one of the complex adult notions underlying the transition to literacy which may not be easily acquired by children. In order to perform this task successfully, children must be aware of the segmental nature of English words, and they must be able to focus on the phonological properties of the words apart from their meanings. In example 9.2, the first child is successful, but the second is not. The first child exhibits what has been called phonological awareness. Such awareness is important in learning to read, because early reading acquisition involves learning to map sequences of sound segments onto sequences of graphic units. This chapter will focus on the relationship among (1) sensitivity to pragmatic differences between the frames of reference that are appropriate for oral and written language, (2) metalinguistic awareness of the segmental nature of language, and (3) reading acquisition.

The language demands of school

The entry into school marks major social, linguistic, and cognitive transitions for children. Children coming to school must learn to communicate and cooperate with adults and peers outside of the children's home network who do not share their communicative background. They must develop new language-use skills in order to participate in classroom activities, to gain access to learning opportunities, and to demonstrate what they have learned (Simons and Gumperz 1980). Children also face the demands of becoming literate, which is the major focus of much of schooling. The sophisticated language skills that children develop in the course of their early oral language acquisition are not sufficient for an effortless transition to literacy. Their encounters with written text require them to become aware of their spoken language and its units, and to develop different discourse strategies. These new discourse strategies are needed because of the differences between spoken and written language.

As noted above, written language is sometimes said to be more decontextualized, or autonomous, than spoken language, because it 'is minimally dependent upon simultaneous transmission over other channels, such as the paralinguistic, postural or gestural' (Kay 1977). In most written language activities, the audience is generalized and the communication is not anchored to a specific time and place. Thus written language is typically less dependent on the spatial and temporal situation in which it is produced than spoken language. Spoken language, in contrast, is often characterized as contextualized, or dependent upon the context for its interpretation. This terminology may be misleading, however, since it suggests that written language does not need a context for interpretation while spoken language does. Pragmatic knowledge of how language is used in different communicative contexts is required of both listeners and readers in the interpretation of language. Although written language may be 'decontextualized' to the extent that it depends less on cues from the immediate physical context, both spoken and written language require that a context exist or be envisioned for interpretation. As Deborah Brandt explains,

> Even in oral exchanges context is always an accomplishment of the participants, not a given. Meaning is not already there to be relied upon but must be made and remade, minute by accomplished minute, through people's particular interchanges and interpretations. 1990: 30

While they may require somewhat different referential strategies, both spoken and written communication require that participants construct a context for interpretation. For these reasons, and because the term 'context' can be used to refer to both the verbal and the situational context of an utterance, we adopted the term 'situation-dependent' to refer to language strategies that rely on reference to the immediate situational context, and the term 'text-based' to refer to language strategies that support interpretation without reference to the immediate physical context. Situation-dependent strategies and text-based strategies are often associated with spoken and written language respectively. However, either may appear in written or spoken form. For example, a transcript of a conversation may be a written record of exchanges in which situation-dependent language strategies are employed. Spoken forms of language are situation-dependent only to the extent that they rely on cues in the immediate physical context, while written messages are text-based to the extent that they do not.

The 'textual' character of language takes on new salience when it appears in written form. Because information can be exchanged over more than one channel in oral language communication, gesture, intonation and posture, etc. can be used redundantly and sometimes even substitute for elements of the lexical–semantic–syntactic channel. Because the burden of the transmission of information must be carried by the lexical–semantic–syntactic channel in written language, one of the tasks for children acquiring literacy skills is learning to shift from multi-channel signaling to single-channel signaling. This task may be difficult for children, because children tend to foreground the intonational channel and background the lexical–semantic–syntactic channel (Cook-Gumperz and Gumperz 1978).

Evidence that this shift presents a problem for children in reading comes from a study by Kleinman, Winograd, and Humphey (1979). These authors used a task that required fourth-grade children to parse written text into meaningful units with and without intonational support. Intonational support was provided by having the text read to the children. Poorer readers were better at parsing sentences when they had such support than when they did not. Better readers did equally well with and without intonational support. Other evidence is provided by Clay and Imlach (1971), who found that poor readers in first grade use a word-by-word intonation pattern that is not sensitive to the chunking cues provided by syntax, while better readers produce intonation that is sensitive to these cues. Both of these studies provide some support for the claim that the shift from dependence upon intonation to the use of the lexical–semantic–syntactic channel may be problematical for children acquiring reading skills.

As children develop literacy skills, they learn many new things about language and strategies for its use in different communicative contexts. Young children encountering written text for the first time must learn to understand the distinction between given and new as it is expressed lexically and syntactically rather than through prosody (Cook-Gumperz and Gumperz 1981). Given information is what the listener/reader is expected to know already while new information is what the listener/reader is not expected to know (Chafe 1972; Clark and Haviland 1974a; 1974b; Vande Kopple 1986). If their learning is successful, what children eventually learn in school and from reading are the language structures and strategies of 'academic language'.

In contrast to the highly personal everyday language of homes and communities, academic language has more complex syntax, more specialized vocabulary and more sophisticated reference strategies that allow children to express complex ideas in logical and coherent structures and enable them to comprehend such texts. As children develop literacy skills, they gain control over new syntactic structures encountered frequently in reading, but more rarely in ordinary, everyday language, for example, structures such as center-embedded relatives (e.g., 'The legislation which the senator proposed gave women the right to vote' instead of 'The senator proposed legislation and it gave women the right to vote.'), and nominalization (e.g., 'Establishment of a system of government was their first task,' instead of 'First they had to establish a system of government').

As they become more familiar with written language, they learn the 'metadiscourse' or 'signaling devices' that writers use to help readers navigate written text (Lorch 1989; Vande Kopple 1985). Such features include, among other things, phrases or words that mark topics or convey information about the function of sentences they introduce (*for example, for instance, in summary, briefly*), that establish the relationships between ideas and events (*moreover, subsequently, however, in contrast*) that remind readers of material presented earlier (*Again. . ., As I explained before*), that mark the organization of the text (*first, second, finally*), that explain or interpret (parenthetical expressions, definitions), and that signal such glossing (in other words, that is to say), that mark attitudes (happily, unfortunately), as well as features that directly index segments of written text (*see below, Chapter one introduces, In this section*). Readers use the cues present in the text if they have knowledge of the structures of texts and how to use the cues in the comprehension process (Goldman 1997; Goldman and Murray 1992).

One very early step for children in the very long process of learning how to use such cues is coming to understand how reference strategies in face-to-face situations differ from those used when the message is separated from the time and place of its production. In face-to-face oral communication, words may be used to refer directly to elements present in the situation, and to its participants, because the physical and temporal situations are shared by the speaker and the listener. This type of reference, where a word refers to an element in the context of the situation, is exophoric (Halliday and Hasan 1976).

In general, reference specifies the information that is to be retrieved by a listener or reader. Exophoric reference signals to the listener or reader that the information is to be retrieved from the context of the situation, while endophoric reference signals that the item is co-referential with another item in the text itself. For example, if in a conversation the speaker says: 'Will you please put the cheese over there', the interpretations of 'you' and 'there' depend upon being present in the situation in which the utterance occurs, 'You' and 'there' are used exophorically. In the sentence 'Johnny walked over to the table and he put the cheese on it', the words 'he' and 'it' are used endophorically, when 'he' is co-referential with 'Johnny', and 'it' is co-referential with the table[1].

Exophoric reference is more characteristic of spoken language than of written language, with the exception of texts in which the author refers to himself, or to the reader, as in first-person narratives, or letters, etc. In fictional narrative, however, all reference is ultimately endophoric, because in narrative fiction the situational context provides a context of reference that is itself a fiction constructed in the text (Halliday and Hasan 1976). One problem for children when they are initially learning to read is learning when to interpret forms endophorically, and when to interpret them exophorically, without the disambiguating cue provided by stress, intonation, and gesture that are available in oral-language situations.

Linguistic forms are deictic if they point to the context of the situation. Deictic categories are relevant to the exophoric–endophoric distinction and to the question of the acquisition of literacy skills, because deictic categories relate an utterance to a particular time, location, speaker, or discourse context. Categories of deixis include:[2]

Person-deixis:
pronouns

May I ride your bike?
You have my pencil.

Temporal-deixis:
temporal adverbs; tense

I saw the game yesterday.
Give it to me now.

Place-deixis:
adverbs: here; there

Put it there.
Put it here.

demonstrative adjectives and pronouns: this; that

I want this little toy.
Give me that.

motion verbs: come, go; bring, take

May I come in?
Do you want to go in?

Forms that are typically deictic in character may be used non-deictically. The word 'here', for example, when used in represented thought in a third-person narrative, does not require knowledge of a speaker's location, because it refers to the location of the character whose thought is being represented. In other words, if I write 'He liked it here' in represented speech or thought, 'here' refers to the location of 'He', rather than to my own location as I write (or say) the sentence. In most oral-language situations, and many written situations, such forms are used deictically, i.e. they incorporate information about the speaker's perspective. Represented thought appears in some early reading texts, although it is an infrequent phenomenon. It is likely that most children will have had little experience with this narrative mode, especially if they have not had such stories read to them in the home.

More commonly, forms that are typically deictic are used endophorically in direct quoted speech in early reading texts. In indirect speech, the word 'here' would refer to the location of the speaker of a sentence, e.g. 'She said (that) "he likes it here".' In direct quoted speech, the word 'here' would refer to the location of the quoted speaker of the sentence. In other words, in hearing or reading the sentence, 'She said, "He likes it here",' the child must interpret 'here' as referring to the location of 'She', rather than to the location of 'He' or the speaker (or writer) of the sentence. The comprehension of indexical and referring expressions requires an understanding of how these elements function in different communicative contexts. Although all of the sentences above could occur in either speech or writing, they require a shift in context from the child's own temporal and spatial context for interpretation. The use of deictic terms in written text requires different language processing strategies of children, whose language experiences are mainly oral, and who are accustomed to using the physical and temporal situation to interpret and anchor deictic terms. When learning to read, the child must learn to anchor deictic terms in imaginary contexts and/or to interpret them endophorically (an exception, of course, would be instances of direct address to the reader). Some examples from primary-grade (grades 1–3) reading texts follow, in which deictic terms, as well as other lexical items, must be interpreted from the perspective of the text and the situation described.

Example 9.3

But wait! Someone was *there*! 'That's just the old baby,' thought Nicky. But no! It was not just the baby. Butch was there, too. Macmillan 1975

In Example 9.3, the proximal–distal contrast which underlies the distinction between 'here' and 'there' must be interpreted in relation to Nicky, the main character of the story. 'There' refers not only to the location of the baby, but to a place other than where Nicky is at that moment in the narrative.

Example 9.4

'See that thing in the bush!' Dad and Paul went near it. A fawn! (Bloomfield and Barnhart 1961)

In example 9.4 'that thing' is co-referential with 'A fawn', and must be interpreted endophorically, while 'that' implies a distal location in relation to 'Dad and Paul'.

Example 9.5

Sally said to Jill, 'Come to my house tomorrow.' Rubin 1978

When reading example 9.5, the child must realize that 'my' refers to Sally, that 'tomorrow' refers to the day after the utterance is produced, that 'come' indicates that Sally will be at home the next day, and that Jill will come from some location other than Sally's house. 'Come', 'my', and 'tomorrow' must be interpreted in relation to Sally, and to the hypothetical moment when she utters the invitation in the context of the narrative. While quoted discourse provides an indirect kind of anchorage for deictic expressions, in that one can interpret them from the perspective of a character in the context of the narrative, some first-grade texts use deictic forms without introducing a speaker. Some examples follow; we could refer to these as voiceless statements in contrast to those which establish a speaker's perspective or narrative voice.

Example 9.6

Such a load to bring into the house. Bloomfield and Barnhart 1961

In example 9.6, the deictic form 'bring' indicates that the speaker is in the house, but it is left to the child to create a context for its interpretation. There is no explicitly named person who can be identified as the speaker.

Example 9.7

Jack may play with this train, and Dick may play with that train.
Bloomfield and Barnhart 1961

In example 9.7, the proximal–distal contrast implicit in the meaning of 'this' and 'that' indicates that the train that Jack will play with is closer to the speaker of the sentence than the one that Dick will play with. Because the sentence is not part of a larger text, however, the creation of a context for interpretation is left entirely to the child. The speaker is never explicitly identified.

Example 9.8

Nick and Frank cannot lift the big bench. Gus and Dan will help them bring it out on the lawn. Gus will help Nick and Dan will help Frank. Gus will help lift Nick's end, and Dan will help lift Frank's end. Gus will help at this end and Dan will help at that end. Bloomfield and Barnhart 1961

In example 9.8 the deictic term 'bring' suggests that the speaker is out on the lawn. The proximal–distal contrast between 'this' and 'that' indicates that Nick's end is closer to the speaker than is Dan's.

Examples 9.6, 9.7 and 9.8 would be easily interpreted in appropriate oral, face-to-face situations, because the location and identity of the speaker would be given information which could be easily retrieved from the immediate physical context, providing an obvious reference point for interpreting 'bring', 'this', and 'that'. As written texts, they are peculiar, because the deictic uses of the terms 'bring', 'this', and 'that', in examples 9.6, 9.7 and 9.8 are unanchored. Charles Fillmore's (1975) classic example of unanchored text is a note found by a man in a bottle in a stream, the note saying, 'Meet me here tomorrow with a stick about this big.' Deictic terms such as 'me', 'tomorrow', and 'this' are difficult, if not impossible, to interpret when they are unanchored, because information about the situation is not available. All of the texts above may be difficult for children to interpret, because interpretation depends solely on the information that is presented within the text itself, upon the relationships among its internal elements, and upon children's knowledge of the different ways language may be used in pragmatically different kinds of situations.

The examples above illustrate a variety of ways in which deictic categories may be used in some early reading texts. Successful interpretation of such texts requires that a child have an intuitive grasp of some rather complex and abstract notions, including knowledge of when indexical and referring expressions are to be contextualized externally, and when they are to be contextualized internally. When learning to read, children must learn to imagine a context for reference when one is not provided in the narrative, and to interpret the text in terms of it. When a verbal context is provided, as in quoted dialogue, children must learn to interpret deictic terms endophorically, from the perspective of the speaker of the quoted sentence. There is some evidence in the literature that children find it easier to interpret deictic terms in face-to-face oral language tasks than in written language tasks (Murphy 1986).

But precisely how deictic terms in text may create reading problems for children is not clear. In some cases, children may misinterpret deictic terms and actually misunderstand the text, or, the shifting of perspective may add more processing time and demand more attention to reading, and thus add to its difficulty. One would also expect that there would be individual differences in the ability to adapt to interpreting deictic terms endophorically. These individual differences should be related to children's ability to detach themselves from the immediate situational context and to imagine a different perspective from which to interpret deictic terms. They may also be related to children's familiarity with the referential strategies that are employed in written text. One of the purposes of this study was to examine the relationship between the use of situation-dependent language and reading achievement. An association would be predicted, given the assumption that the use of situation-dependent language reflects a lack of sensitivity to pragmatic differences in the ways indexical and referential expressions are appropriately employed in pragmatically different situations, and the further assumption that sensitivity to such differences translates into improved reading performance.

Metalinguistic awareness, discourse awareness, and reading acquisition

Another demand that reading makes on children's language use is that they be conscious or aware of their primary linguistic activities – listening and speaking. This awareness has been called metalinguistic awareness (Mattingly 1972). Metalinguistic awareness is the ability to focus on the language itself as an object rather than on the meaning or the intention of the communication. It allows language users to focus attention on the phonological, lexical, syntactic, semantic, and pragmatic levels of language, to notice anomalies at these different linguistic levels, and to comment on them. It allows them to segment spoken sentences into words, and words into phonemes (see Ehri 1979). In their informal conversations, speakers and listeners focus on the meaning and the intention of the participants rather than the form of the communication. The phonological and syntactic rules and units used are out of their focal awareness.

While all normal children develop into linguistically competent users of spoken language, there are great individual differences in metalinguistic skills, and these individual differences vary depending upon the linguistic level. As Rosin and Gleitman (1977: 99) put it:

> The lower the level of the language feature that must be attended to and accessed for any language like activity beyond comprehension, the more individual differences we find in adults; further, the lower the level of

language feature, the later its accessibility to the language learning child, Semantics is easier to access than syntax, and syntax easier than phonology. With phonology, again, global syllables are easier to access than phonemes and phonetic features.

It is believed by Rosin and Gleitman and other researchers that metalinguistic awareness in general, and phonological awareness in particular, are important factors in, and possibly necessary prerequisites for learning to read. This belief is based on

1. the existence of individual differences in metalinguistic awareness
2. the fact that learning to read is often difficult while learning to talk is apparently effortless,
3. the findings of positive correlations between reading achievement and metalinguistic skills such as the ability to segment words into phonemes and sentences into words
4. the fact that phonological-segmentation skill, which has strong relationships with reading achievement, appears to be closely related to understanding the alphabetic nature of English orthography and learning sound–spelling correspondence.

Understanding the alphabetic nature of English orthography and learning sound–spelling correspondences are important in learning to read because they are important in learning to decode. It has been argued that metalinguistic awareness at the phonological level is an important skill in learning to read because it appears to be a prerequisite to learning to decode, and because large individual differences exist which show high correlations with learning to read. This argument has some problems, however. The empirical evidence is mainly correlational; thus it is consistent with several other possible versions of the relationship, including the possibility that metalinguistic awareness develops as a consequence of learning to read.

Ehri (1979) has reviewed the evidence and has argued that it facilitates but is not a prerequisite to learning to read, However, whether or not metalinguistic awareness is a cause or a facilitator of learning to read, it is an important language skill that is associated with it, and it is not very well developed before reading is encountered. The teaching of metalinguistic skills in school asks children to use language in a different manner than in their normal communication.

Instead of focusing on the content or meaning of the language, they must focus on its form at the phonological level, in order to acquire decoding skills, and since most beginning-reading programs focus on decoding to some degree, almost all children need to develop phonological awareness.

At the level of discourse, children must learn how language is crafted to fit the situation or context in which messages are communicated, and at the same time, how language is used to create that very situation or context, e.g. to project a certain identity, to accomplish a certain purpose, etc. (Gee 1996). As James Gee explains, discourses 'exist as the work we do to get people and things recognized in certain ways and not others, and they exist as maps that constitute our understandings' (1996: 23). From Gee's perspective, utterances, whether spoken or written, are made up of 'cues or clues' about how to 'move back and forth between language and context (situations), not signals of fixed and decontextualized meanings' (p. 85).

Among other things, to acquire discourse skill children need to gain control over the cohesive devices that link sentences and sentence-sized units to one another across whole texts. They need to learn how more than one perspective is represented in a text and how perspectives and shifts in perspective are marked (e.g., by verbs such as *assert, contend, deny, claim* and phrases such as *in my/his opinion, although plausible*). They also need to gain control over the various possible macro-structures which organize different genres. There are of course great individual differences in the possession of these skills among children entering school. These differences may in part be due to exposure to literacy and literate-like activities; thus some children may have previous experiences that make meeting these new demands easier.

Phonological and discourse awareness

The relationship between phonological awareness and discourse awareness is unexplored. However, we expected that they would be significantly correlated because they both reflect the ability to manipulate language outside of its everyday use. To some degree, phonological awareness requires that language be treated as an object of attention. At the phonological level, phonological awareness requires attention to the segmental nature of the sound system. Discourse awareness, on the other hand, requires an awareness of the different ways that language is used in pragmatically different situations. We expected that the use of situation-dependent language in a situation in which its use is inappropriate would be negatively correlated with phonological awareness.

These skills differ in that they obtain at different linguistic levels, and they may require different degrees and types of cognitive skills. We expected that phonological awareness, because it is so far removed from the focus of normal discourse, would be more difficult to develop and would exhibit greater individual differences, as Rosin and Gleitman (1977) claim, than would sensitivity to the need for text-based language use, which is a discourse skill. This assumes that discourse skills would be more available to subjects' awareness. We also expected that phonological awareness would show a higher correlation with reading skill than discourse awareness, because greater individual differences appear at lower levels of language features.To summarize, we had the following expectations in our investigation. First, we expected that children who used situation-dependent language in inappropriate situations would exhibit poor reading skills; second, that children who exhibited phonological awareness would be better readers; third, that children who exhibited phonological awareness would use less situation-dependent language in such situations.

Our hypotheses were tested through a correlational analysis of the relationships among phonological awareness, situation-dependent language use and reading achievement. The data for our investigation came from the School–Home Ethnography Project (Simons and Gumperz 1980). The subjects in the study were second-grade students in a classroom in a school in northern California. The classroom contained 29 children. Two children were excluded from the study because they failed to complete several of the tasks. The class was ethnically mixed with 13 lower-class black children (7M and 6F) and 14 middle- and upper-middle-class white children (7M and 7F). Race and socioeconomic status were almost totally confounded in this study, so that it was impossible to distinguish separate effects.

Spoken language strategies and reading acquisition

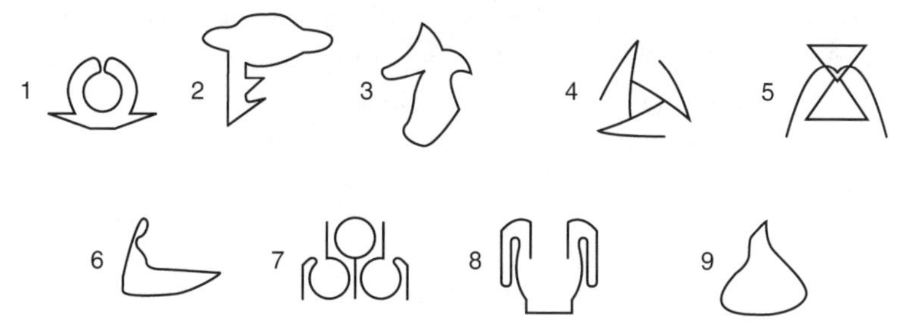

Figure 9.1. Spoken language strategies and reading acquisition.

Discourse awareness

The children's use of inappropriate situation-dependent language was measured by a modified version of the referential communication task developed by Krauss and Glucksberg (1969). The task requires subjects to describe a series of nine abstract figures so that they could be identified by another person. For this study, the figures were drawn in black ink mounted on separate 3 × 5 inch cards, and assembled into a fixed array, as shown in Figure 9.1. The task has frequently been used as an index of communicative effectiveness. Previous research has demonstrated that older children produce more effective descriptions in the task than younger children (Glucksberg, Krauss, and Weisberg 1966; Krauss and Glucksberg 1969). In addition, investigations of variability in the use of language by middle-class and lower-class speakers have demonstrated that lower-class children adopt different verbal styles and perform less effectively than middle-class children (Heider and Cazden 1971; Krauss, Glucksberg, and Rotter 1968). Initially, such findings were interpreted as indicating differences in ability between lower-class and middle-class speakers. Other research, however, indicates that such verbal style differences are due to differential application of speech styles in particular stimulus situations (Jewson, Sachs, and Rohner 1981).

In previous studies where this task has been used to investigate variability in speech styles, two dimensions have been employed in classifying descriptive styles. First, the descriptions could refer to whole units, or, the units could be descriptively analyzed into parts. Second, the figures could be described in terms of other contexts, or, they could be described literally, within the given context. The two dimensions, (1) the part/whole distinction and (2) the inferential/analytic distinction were not employed for coding descriptive units in the present study. Instead, a single dimension was employed, the distinction between situation-dependent and text-based language use.

The modifications in coding were adopted so that we could evaluate the children's performance of the task in terms of what is required when one communicates in writing. When writing, both analytic and inferential styles are appropriate, regardless of the question of their effectiveness. Similarly, one could adopt a style that describes the object as a whole, or in parts, and produce language that is appropriate for writing. However, the use of situation-dependent language is generally inappropriate for written text because it relies on a restricted frame of reference within the immediate physical context of the utterance.

The task requirements differed from those employed in several other studies of referential communication. The referential communication task has typically been administered with the 'listener' present, but behind a screen. In this study, subjects were asked to describe each of the nine abstract figures into a tape recorder, for the purpose of enabling a 'future' peer listener to select the stimulus item from the array.

This modification was adopted in order to make the language requirements of the task as similar as possible to a written language task. The task, as used in this study, requires the use of text-based language because the sender and the receiver are separated in space and time. Both written language and this task require a subject to use language that is not dependent upon reference to the immediate situation in which the utterance is produced. Our procedure in this respect was similar to that adopted by Jewson, Sachs, and Rohner (1981). Assuming that for very young children part of what it takes to learn to read written language involves learning to give up a dependence upon the immediate physical and temporal context, we expected that the use of situation-dependent language would be negatively correlated with reading achievement.

The task was individually administered and each child received the following instructions:

> Do you see all these pictures? I'm going to point to one, and I'd like you to look at it and describe it . . . tell what you think makes it special from the others . . . mention anything you'd like to say about it. But the description is not for me. You're doing it for someone else who's not here right now. You are talking to this person in a way that, if I were to bring him here later, show him the pictures all mixed up, and play him the tape, he could pick out the one you're talking about just from your description, without you present here.

The experimenter drew the attention of the child to each figure in a systematic order, although some subjects spontaneously varied this order slightly. The subjects were permitted to take the target stimulus card and turn the figure around or upside down in examining it. If a child stopped after a minimal encoding, the experimenter prompted the child to say more. When the children produced descriptions with excessive situation-dependent language, they were reminded that the person who would hear the tape was not present.

The descriptions produced by each subject were transcribed, and the written texts were used for scoring. The number of restricted exophoric uses of deictic categories divided by the number of clauses was the measure used. A clause was defined as any single word or group of words operating in conjunction with a verb to convey an idea. The T unit, which has been used in many language studies, was not used as a measure in this study because the ratio reflecting the subject's communicative strategy would have been distorted by such a measure, having the effect of penalizing those students who exhibited greater control over syntactic subordination. If one subject tends to produce single-clause T units, and another produces more complex structures, the ratios would not be strictly comparable. (A single T unit is an independent clause with any number of attached dependent clauses. However, coordinated clauses are counted as separate T units.)

Items were counted as separate clauses if all or part of a verb construction was present. In the following sentence, for example, three separate clauses would be counted: 'Sort of looks like a moustache. . .going like that and. . .c. . .curls.' This type of construction presented something of a problem in that curls in the example cited could be either a noun or a verb with the subject deleted. Only two such incidents occurred, however, and they were counted as clauses. Items were not counted as clauses if they were lists of attributes, e.g. 'and looks like a . . .turtle, *and a tail.*' Only clauses that represented the children's attempts to actually describe an object were counted. Responses were omitted if they were conversational digressions. Incidents of situation-dependent language use were counted if it could be determined that the reference was to one (or part of one) or, in a few cases, more than one of the objects, e.g. 'These look like those.' These incidents of restricted exophoric use of deictic categories consisted almost entirely of items that could be clarified by gesture: *this*, *that*, *here* and *there*. Less frequent was the occurrence of plural deictic pronouns, e.g. *these, those*, and *them* (a form used interchangeably in some dialects with *those*). 'That' was not counted if it was used endophorically, to introduce a relative clause, or to signal the end of a sequence. All three conditions apply in the following example: '*That*'s all *that* I can say about *that*.' Repetitions were not counted. Only the first item in such a series was coded, e.g. 'um. . .*this* one, this one is shaped like a triangle.' However, sequences such as 'this one got lines and *this* one got lines', were counted as having two incidents of situation-dependent language use when it was clear that the child was contrasting separate items or parts of items.

The following examples from the protocols are representative of the types of restricted exophoric reference that occurred. The asterisk indicates a word not counted because it is a repetition.

Examples of restricted exophoric reference

'*This* looks like . . . **that* looks like a flyin' saucer . . . but . . . *that* looks like a big, giant hook!'

'*This* one just looks like a . . . uh . . . somethin' right *here*, like *this* part right *here*, looks like a key.'

'. . . it looks like . . . um . . . it's a monster . . . *here*'s his lip and *here*'s his paw.'

'*This* one is shaped down, and . . . it's . . . it goes around and *these* little points.'

'It kinda like a key, 'cause it have two of *these* things . . . two of **these* ri- . . . and it's round an' got *these* little things stickin' out.'

'*These* . . . **them* two is down . . . '

'*That* one looks like a square . . . it's like *that*.'

'That's-, **that* looks like a square . . . it's like *that*.'

'That s-, **that* looks like the gun shooter like, when you hold it like . . . *this*n' . . .that's look like that.'

'*That* look like . . . um . . . part . . . of a . . . right *here* . . . *these* look like . . . um two fingers . . . look like two fingers . . . um that look like . . . um . . . a vase, like you put water in *there*.'

'. . . *that's* a triangle . . . right *there* . . . and *this* look like . . . a thing you cut grass with, right *there* . . . and you put *here* a little . . . it got *here* a little hook.'

'Oh . . . and *these*, n' **these* don't have no holes like *this*, don't have nothin' like *this* go around like *that*, go straight like . . . '

'And *this* one, **this* one look like *this* . . . '

' . . . and *these* look like some fingers go-goin' around '*em*, and it gots two and it gots two corners, no, no it got four corners right *there*.'

'And-, and *that* one, like, and **that* one, um down there, it kinda it look like, um the one that, that um, I'm talkin' about.'

'Well, there's sort of a . . . triangle in *here*, and there's sort of . . . almost a triang- . . . um . . . a- . . . triangle in *here*, on *these* things that don't go all the way down yet.'

'See- . . . *this* one . . . *these* two is the same, but *this* one is not.'

Phonological awareness

Phonological awareness was measured by a phonemic segmentation task in which subjects are required to listen to a word, repeat it, and then say the word with the initial or final segment missing. For example, the children in the study were asked to produce the word 'tall' without the /t/. When they failed to produce the correct response, they were given a second trial. There were 22 words included in the task, 11 real and 11 nonsense monosyllables. The nonsense words were parallel to the real words, e.g. pray – [p] and [pra] – [p]; ship – [s] and [sæp] – [s]; soap – [p] and [foop] – [p]. When the specified segment was deleted all of the real words produced real but different words; the nonsense words all produced nonsense words.

Prior to testing, the children were given two practice words to illustrate the nature of the segmentation task. Compound words were chosen for practice because the segmentation of compound words has been shown to be easier than phonemic segmentation. The units are more salient in spoken language than are phonemes. The practice words were 'toothbrush', in which 'brush' was to be deleted, and 'cowboy' in which 'boy' was to be deleted. All of the children appeared to understand the nature of the task. The total number of each child's correct responses was used in the correlational analysis. The major assumption underlying the use of this task was that the ability to accomplish it indicates an awareness of the segmental nature of English pronunciation.

The phonemic segmentation task and the discourse awareness task were administered during the first half of the year by members of the research team who were familiar with the children. They were administered in a private room, separate from the classroom. Reading achievement was measured by the Comprehension Subtest of the California Test of Basic Skills (CTBS) Level I Form S (McGraw Hill 1973). The CTBS was administered at the end of the school year by the teacher as part of the regular school district testing program. The children's percentile scores on the Comprehension Subtest indicated that the group as a whole was well above average. Several of the children were at the 90th percentile or above (37.5%) and the majority (62.5%) were above the 50th percentile.

Results and discussion

The analysis of the data provides support for our predictions about the relationships among phonological awareness, use of situation-dependent language and reading acquisition. It also supports the notion that the ability to manipulate language underlies these relationships.

First, it was found that phonological awareness was substantially related to reading achievement ($r = 0.74$; $p < 0.01$). Subjects who exhibited phonological awareness tended to be better readers than subjects who lacked such awareness. Awareness of the segmental nature of spoken language thus appears to be an important factor in learning to read.

Second, the prediction that children who used situation-dependent language would exhibit poor reading skills was also confirmed. The relative frequency of inappropriate situation-dependent language use as measured by the number of restricted exophoric uses of deictic categories divided by the number of clauses was negatively related to reading achievement ($r = -0.39$; $p < 0.05$). The number of clauses produced was not related to reading achievement. This suggests that it is not mere verbosity that is responsible for the relationship but the amount of situation-dependent language per unit of language. Those subjects who used more situation-dependent language per clause were poorer readers than those who used less per clause. The ability to use communicative strategies that are appropriate for written language appears to be related to the development of reading skill.

Third, as predicted, the inappropriate use of situation-dependent language was negatively correlated with phonological awareness ($r = -0.46$; $p < 0.05$). The children who exhibited less situation-dependent language also exhibited more phonological awareness. This suggests that the two tasks used in the study reflect, on different linguistic levels, the same underlying ability to manipulate language outside of its normal context of conversational use. This, together with the other findings mentioned above, suggests that the ability to manipulate language is important in reading acquisition.

An important question to be dealt with in this discussion is how are these abilities acquired? In the case of phonological awareness the child, either before or during the process of learning to read, must become aware of the segmental nature of the phonological system. He or she needs this awareness in order to learn to decode and it can be gained through language activities which focus on linguistic segments below the word level. Before formal reading instruction, this can be accomplished through language activities that focus on phonological segments; word games and rhyming activities such as pig latin, etc. and working with letters and sounds can contribute to the development of this awareness (Cazden 1970; Savin 1972). However, one would expect that it is during the course of reading instruction in decoding that much of children's phonological awareness develops, since it appears to be the implicit purpose of this instruction. In the classroom under study the low reading group (all black and lower class) received much more decoding instruction than did the high group (all white and middle class, with the exception of one black child). The high group received mostly an emphasis on 'meaning'. The middle group, which was racially mixed, received a mixture of decoding and meaning emphases. This situation is not untypical. Low-group readers tend to receive more decoding instruction than better readers, because it is believed that they lack phonological skills.

If this decoding instruction had been successful in the classroom under study, then one would expect a lower correlation between phonological awareness and reading achievement than the one found (r = 0.74). Decoding instruction should have closed the gap between those in the high group, who had a high degree of phonological awareness to begin with, and those in the low group, who did not. The high correlation found between phonological awareness and reading achievement (r = 0.74) suggests that this did not happen. It is not possible to be definite about this interpretation because there was no post test on phonological awareness. However, assuming that the low group did not profit from decoding instruction, the question is why not? Collins (this volume) shows that the low group's decoding instruction was not placed in a meaningful context and argues that it interfered with reading acquisition. The high group who possessed considerable phonological awareness to begin with may have profited considerably from an emphasis on meaning. While the low group who exhibited little phonological awareness to begin with, paradoxically may have failed to profit from decoding instruction. If children lack phonological awareness and if instruction is not successful in helping them acquire this awareness, then it is not surprising that they lag behind in reading. This line of argument is meant to be suggestive rather than definitive because it is based on correlational rather than experimental evidence.

Turning to the use of situation-dependent language in inappropriate situations, it is much less clear how children learn to suppress their use of situation-dependent language and adopt the kind of text-based communicative strategies that allow them to communicate more effectively in writing. There do not seem to be any obvious explicit instructional practices that are directed at helping children who have difficulties in this area to make this particular transition. However, it is reasonable to assume that as children are increasingly exposed to written texts, they will become familiar with and knowledgeable about the strategies for reference that are typically used in them. That this knowledge is important is clear. The ability to connect individual ideas into a coherent whole is central to reading comprehension (Kintsch and van Dijk 1978).

Early research on sentence connectives indicates that children's understanding of connectives develops during the school years. Research conducted after this study was complete indicates that knowledge of cohesion separates good readers from poor readers as early as third grade (Cox, Shanahan and Sulzby 1990). Cox et al. found that good readers achieved more complex cohesive harmony than did poor readers, regardless of genre (narrative or expository) and grade. One classroom activity which may serve as a vehicle for the transition to literacy in the early grades is the activity known as sharing time or 'show and tell'. Michaels and Cook-Gumperz (1979) suggest that this activity is implicitly designed to bridge the gap between situation-dependent oral discourse and the acquisition of literacy skills. In an analysis of the teacher's questioning strategies in sharing-time episodes in the classroom under study, Michaels has demonstrated (chapter 5, this volume) that the teacher's notion of adequate sharing follows a literate model. The teacher's strategies are designed to elicit tightly structured discourse which highlights particular topics with lexicalized thematic ties. In addition, the teacher's strategies elicit discourse which is explicitly grounded temporally and physically. Thus, the teacher's strategies encourage the shift from situation-dependent language use to text-based language use. Text-based language use requires that the children lexicalize information that may be 'given' in the situation in typical 'oral' language activities. Examples 9.9–9.12 from the sharing-time protocols illustrate the teacher's strategies.

Example 9.9

C Yesterday, when I came home my mother took me to a store and I bought these.
T What are they?
C Bells.
T Little jingle bells.

Example 9.10

C Saturday I got a Tom and Jerry game.
T How do you play it?
(Child starts to open game.)
T Pretend I can't see it.

Example 9.11

C1 I went to the beach and I found this little thing in the water.
T For goodness sake, what is it?

C2 A block.
CS A block, a block.
T A block. When did you go to the beach?

Example 9.12

C When I went to the . . . when I went to the doctors and I thought I was gonna get a shot but I didn't and, I had to put this thing in my mouth for a long time.
T What was it?

In examples 9.9–9.12, the teacher intervenes when the children fail to ground their talk temporally and physically with explicit lexical information. In examples 9.9–9.11 the objects are present in the temporal and physical situation. The teacher's strategy elicits an explicit name or description. In example 9.11 the child is encouraged to anchor his narrative temporally. In example 9.12, the child describes an object that is not present in the situation, and again, the teacher attempts to elicit an explicit name or description. The teacher's comments are designed to help the child detach him or herself from the immediate context (e.g. 'Pretend I can't see it') and to encourage the use of names as opposed to pronominal or deictic reference (e.g. 'What is it?').

The teacher in Michaels' study attempted to shape the children's oral-sharing discourse through her questions and comments so that it would conform to her notion of adequate sharing. In doing so, she may have helped the students to become familiar with the requirements of written text at the discourse level. However, Michaels and Cook-Gumperz (1979) have shown that there was wide variation in the degree to which 'sharing' was successful in the teacher's terms, and that the variations were associated with verbal style. The white middle-class children in this study produced more successful sharing discourse, while the black lower-class children were less successful. Many of the black children exhibited a 'topic-associating' style in which thematic ties were not explicitly lexicalized. Because the discourse style of the black children differed from that of the teacher, her questions may have had the effect of fragmenting narratives which would have been considered stylistically and culturally appropriate in other contexts. Thus, her strategies may have been ineffective and the sharing activity may have been less successful as a vehicle for the transition to literacy for the black children in the study than for the white children.

This possibility was supported by the finding that race/class correlated with reading achievement ($r = 0.79$; $p < 0.001$) and situation-dependent language use ($I = -0.37$; $p < 0.05$). The black/lower-class children were poorer readers and used more situation-dependent language than the white/middle-class children. However, in all probability, other factors may have contributed to this finding. In addition to the considerable access middle-class children often have to books in the home before they come to school, research suggests that parents in middle-class homes prepare children for written forms of literacy by providing literate features in oral discourse.

We now know from a large body of research that certain home-based literacy practices, such as storybook reading, take place more often in middle-class, school-influenced homes, and that these literacy practices relate significantly to school success (Dickinson 1994; Goelman, Oberg, and Smith 1984; Heath 1982b; Smith 1997; Wells 1986b). We also know that the talk around texts in print-reliant households helps children learn the early lessons of literacy (Cochran-Smith 1984; Gundlach, McLane, Stott and McNamee 1985). This early socialization of mainstream children to the language of school and written text appears quite powerful as a predictor for later success in school. For example, the school success of children in Well's long-term study of language development of children from the Bristol area was found to relate most strongly to how well children had been prepared for literacy at the time they entered school, even at the age of 10. In turn, the children's preparedness was related to their social class.

Similarly, Smith's long-term study of fifty-seven children suggests that parents' early literacy practices play a substantial role in the children's subsequent reading development and further, that disproportionate numbers of children from low-income homes enter school lacking experiences with print that promote successful literacy development. Thus, while the instruction received by the black/lower-class children in this study may have been ineffective, it is also true that they may have been less well prepared for making the transition to literacy in school than the white/middle-class children.

Further research is needed with larger numbers of subjects and a greater variety of measures of situation-dependent language use and discourse awareness skills to add a firmer empirical base for some of the speculations presented here. We also need more detailed descriptive studies of the development of children's discourse skills to get a clearer picture of the role of instruction in supporting or hindering such development. Although reading instruction provides some systematic instruction that is explicitly designed to help children bridge the gap between their oral language experiences and the requirements of written text at the lower linguistic levels (through phonics instruction), reading instruction pays relatively little attention to the new principles for constructing and monitoring meaning that children must learn when they make the change from the multi-modality of speech to the lexicalized discursive sequences of written language.

Notes

1. It is possible to use the same words exophorically, however, if 'he' and/ or 'it' bear heavy stress and are accompanied by a gesture, etc., indicating that their referents are present in the context of the situation, in which case 'he' would refer to someone other than 'Johnny', and 'it' to something other than the table.
2. Social deixis (forms of address determined by social status) has also been discussed in the literature. Features which signal new, and given or 'old' information are sometimes referred to as 'discourse deixis'. Textual deixis occurs when reference is made to a linguistic entity, e.g. *this example, see above,* etc. and is distinguished from endophoric reference, where an item in a text is co-referential with another (Lyons 1977).

10

Speaking and writing: discourse strategies and the acquisition of literacy

James Collins and Sarah Michaels

The writer is a lonely figure cut off from the stimulus and corrective of listeners. He must be a predictor of reactions and act on his predictions. He writes with one hand tied behind his back being robbed of gesture. He is robbed too of his tone of voice and the aid of clues the environment provides, he is condemned to monologue; there is no one to help out, to fill the silence, put words in his mouth or make encouraging noises.

(Rosen 1971:142)

This heartfelt comment comes from a well-known researcher on children's writing, in his study of the language of primary-school children. Rosen's comment identifies a central problem for all writers: the need to create an imaginary audience. This task is often difficult for any writer, but is perhaps especially so for children, since it requires of the writer the special effort of distancing oneself from the present context into a non-existent yet imagined time and place. Such a transposition of self in time and space requires the writer to make an inferential leap between placing the words on the page and their ultimate reception thereafter at some unspecified time and place. Work with children's writing in the early grades suggests that the more that can be done to reduce this leap by providing specific cues to audience reception for children, the easier the task of placing words on the page might be.

The literature on discourse analysis over the past thirty years suggests that in conversation, inference is a matter of multi-level linguistic signaling whereby speakers process intonational and

Acknowledgment: An earlier version of this paper appeared in *Coherence in Spoken and Written Discourse*, edited by D. Tannen. Norwood, NJ: Ablex (1984).

rhythmic cues along with lexical and syntactic options. There is evidence that this inferential process is subject to developmental constraints as well as subcultural differences (Cook-Gumperz and Gumperz 1978; Gee 1996; Goodwin 1990; Gumperz 1982a, 1990; Hanks 1996; Heath 1983; Michaels, O'Connor and Richards 1994; Ochs and Schieffelin 1983; Ochs 1995; Scollon and Scollon 1982). In learning to become literate in school the child has to learn to shift from his or her home-based conversational discourse strategies, which depend on multi-level linguistic inference, to the more discursive strategies preparatory to written expository prose. To the extent that the home-based discourse strategies differ from those of the school, the transition between speech and school-based writing is made more complex (Barton and Hamilton 1998; Cazden, John, and Hymes 1972/85; Ivanic 1997; Kress 1993). Researchers concerned with linguistic differences between speaking and writing have often overlooked this difficulty, because they have focused largely on the formal differences between spoken and written language. Their work, based on counts of lexical items and syntactic constructions, has argued that written language is more studied, complex and consciously planned, while spoken language is more improvisational, simple and direct.

More recent research, however, has suggested that distinctions between spoken and written languages are to be found at the level of discourse. This can be shown by the fact that the communicative tasks of speakers and writers, and the communicative events within which the spoken or written language occurs, have more telling consequences for language form than does actual modality. So, for example, a spoken technical discussion between two academics is likely to have more formal complexity than a casual letter exchanged between old friends; while a formal petition compared with a casual chat will show the stereotyped relation between linguistic form (complex or simple) and modality (written or spoken). In fact, evidence shows that perhaps one of the key distinctions that exists is not between formal and informal characteristics; it is between what can be assumed to be the audience's private background knowledge of the communicative intent and what is estimated to be the audience's ability to make particular inferences which depend on knowledge of both language and the audience's real-world situation (Chafe and Danielewicz 1987;

Green and Morgan 1981; Halliday 1989; Tannen 1982). We can suggest therefore that differences between spoken and written language are not as absolute as had been previously assumed; these differences are not of the same order, for example, as in the comparison of the structure of two languages, or even as in the comparison of two literary genres.

However, in the case of written versus spoken communication there are channel constraints, that is, conditions on communicative form which are derivable from the nature of the medium. If we consider for a moment what is involved in a speaker or writer estimating an audience's ability to make inferences, we regain an appreciation of the basic communicative differences in spoken and written language. For one, in written language there is little information about intonation (Chafe 1988). For another, there is no gestural or kinesic information. Last, there is no immediate feedback – no way of telling if the audience agrees or disagrees, follows the arguments, or has lost the point. Although there are recognizable signaling differences between speaking and writing, we suggest that there are other features or conventions shared by both modes, whatever the task, in that speakers and writers have a common problem in recognizing the coherence or linkage of a piece of discourse. In order to comprehend a discourse a listener or reader must be able to perceive how one utterance or stretch of text relates to what came before. Speakers and writers must somehow signal the relation, and when ways of signaling connections are not shared, the perception of a discourse as coherent and comprehensible usually breaks down. But little research comparing spoken and written language has focused on the ways in which connective ties between parts of a discourse are signaled.

One approach to the question of coherence in discourse is expressed in the construct of thematic cohesion (Gumperz, Kaltman, and O'Connor 1984). The concept refers to the processes by which a spoken utterance or written text is tied together, including the linguistic devices used to signal speech activity, to chunk information so as to highlight certain parts and background others, to signal topic shifts, and to establish and maintain perspective within a topic. In determining what makes a discourse cohere, there are many syntactic and semantic categories which must be taken into account, for example definiteness and co-reference (cf. Chafe 1979;

Halliday and Hasan 1976). However, it has become increasingly clear to discourse analysts that participants' prior knowledge (loosely, their knowledge of the world) powerfully influences their interpretation of a discourse and hence the connections which they perceive, and impose, on a stretch of speech or a piece of writing (Hanks 1996; Rumelhart 1982). In written language, knowledge of genre and of communicative intentions forms an important framework for an audience's expectations and inferences. In spoken language, it is in the context of face-to-face communication – with all the resources of intonation, gesture, and immediate feedback – that semantic connections, prior knowledge, and genre expectations are signaled and evoked. By suggesting that at various discourse levels spoken and written language use different signaling conventions to transmit the same kinds of information, the notion of thematic cohesion points to an important problem for comparative research: the need to constrain the communicative task so that it is possible to compare conventions across the two language modalities.

Design of the study

In our study we investigated how thematic cohesion was signaled by young children in both spoken and written discourse. We compared the spoken and written narratives of a group of first and fourth graders who participated in a year-long ethnographic study of literacy at school and home in Berkeley, CA.[1] The classrooms in our study were made up of approximately half black children from working-class backgrounds (hereafter BWC) and half white children from upper-middle-class backgrounds (hereafter WMC).[2] For the purposes of this study, eight oral and four written narratives were analyzed.

Our primary purpose in examining how thematic cohesion was achieved in the narratives was to gain insight into the linguistic problems resulting from the quite different linguistic and discourse skills which are required in shifting from spoken to written modes. These problems are frequently identified by teachers but are usually attributed to problems of basic reasoning ability and not defined as discourse problems at all. An additional set of questions arose because, after a cursory examination of all the narratives, the

WMC narratives 'sounded' or 'seemed' more sophisticated to us (as well as to the teacher and other university colleagues). This initial, intuitive, judgment raised several additional questions. One question was whether there were particular stylistic characteristics of the WMC narratives which might make them sound intuitively more 'sophisticated' to a casual adult listener; that is, we wished to examine as precisely as possible the basis for the assumption of university-educated adults (the researchers, the teacher, our university colleagues) that one group of narratives sounded more literate or written-like than the other. A second question was whether aspects of the BWC children's oral discourse styles might relate to their acquisition of literacy skills, making the shift from oral to written modes more difficult; that is, we wished to examine whether there were characteristic ways of signaling thematic connections used by these narrators which would not carry over into written styles of communication. A third question was whether ways of signaling cohesive ties in oral discourse also influenced teacher–student interaction, so that the very children who needed the most practice in transferring their oral skills into writing were in fact receiving the least.

In designing our study we were concerned that it allow us to go beyond frequency counts, that it be ethnographically situated, and that it provide us with material to analyze the role of prosody in oral-discourse style. In our analysis of the narratives we were particularly interested in differing uses of prosody and in the relationship between intonation and syntax. By this we mean variations in pitch, loudness, duration, and rhythm. We were interested, for example, in the use of intonation and pausing, together with various types of syntactic structures, to establish and maintain topic-connections within the complex multi-clause units found in some forms of spoken language. We were interested in the prosodic features of speech, first, because these features are not available in written discourse, except for the limited set represented by punctuation and italicization; second, because studies of social dialects and inter-ethnic communication have shown that conventional ways of combining prosody with syntactic and lexical forms are frequently specific to ethnic and social groups (Gumperz 1982a).

In our study the interviewer who elicited the narratives had served as a teacher's aide in the children's classroom throughout the entire school year. As a participant observer, she was very much a familiar figure to the children, working with them individually and in small groups in and out of the classroom and even visiting them in their homes on occasion. Moreover, in her role as ethnographer, she had observed and catalogued the various recurring speech events that the children encountered on a daily basis, in and out of school. Many hours of conversation in various contexts, both formal and informal, had been recorded and indexed. On the basis of detailed linguistic analysis of selected episodes of this naturally occurring talk, a number of hypotheses were generated relating to the children's use of intonation and various discourse strategies in school-related discourse tasks. To test out some of these preliminary hypotheses, we needed a more controlled setting and stimulus, whereby we could channel the topic of discourse and minimize complicating interactive elements. Having the children tell us about a single, specific topic would provide us with comparable data from a large number of children and would also allow for replication by others.

As the experimental task, we showed the children a six-minute silent film about a man picking pears, the stealing of the pears by some passing children, and the man's discovery of the theft (Chafe 1980). The film, often referred to as 'the pear story', was open to ambiguous interpretations about motive and posed problems with respect to referential clarity (as there were a number of male characters). We asked the children to tell the researcher about the film as she had not been present at the screening and explained that she had not seen it. Our purpose in asking the children to organize a monologue recounting the events in the film was to pose an exercise which would place few restrictions on narrative strategy, but would give us some control over what was being reported. Since the first-graders were not yet fluent writers, we also included fourth-graders in the study, from whom we could get both oral and written narratives on the same topic. The design permitted us to compare different children performing the same task – producing oral narratives on the same topic – and the same children performing different tasks – giving oral and written narrative accounts of the pear story.

In selecting the narratives for intensive analysis, we chose those which were well-formed narratives, that is, episodically complex, attentive to detail, and fluently delivered, with little hesitation and no major omissions of story plot. In analyzing the four first-grade narratives we found that the WMC narrators used a variety of lexical and syntactic devices to signal agent-focus and co-reference relations. BWC narrators used some of the same devices but were more likely to rely on prosodic cues to signal similar relations and distinctions. The fourth-graders' narratives (both WMC and BWC) were more fluent and accomplished, but reflected the style contrast seen in the younger children's narratives. More interesting, the same stylistic dichotomy showed up in their written versions of the same narrative.

Analysis of oral narratives

Before going into the differences in detail we should say something about a level of analysis, that is, a way of looking at the narratives, which told us very little about the stylistic differences of the groups of children.

Frequency counts

When we compared the narratives simply for number and variety of nominal and verbal complements, no conclusive pattern emerged. While one of the BWC children's narratives had the fewest nouns and verbs and the fewest intraclausal complements, and one of the WMC children's narratives had the greatest number and variety of these constructions, the other narratives overlapped on these measures. It was revealing that raw counts of lexical items and grammatical constructions gave us little insight into narrative style and strategy. Although studies of construction types comparing the spoken and written language of adults have shown consistent differences between modalities (Chafe 1980; and below), these findings have always been circumscribed by the fact, discussed above, that communicative task and speech situation are powerful influences on the kind and quality of discourse produced. We were interested in how thematic cohesion was achieved and maintained in narratives, not only in the distribution of formal elements. Simple counts of lexical items and construction types gave little purchase on the question of how the narrative styles differed.

Use of complements to signal thematic cohesion

However, when we looked at the deployment of complements within and across clause boundaries, with regard to the work they did to provide ties between events in the narratives, we did find clear differences. These differences had to do with two related aspects of narrative structure: (a) whether the syntactic complements typically used were verbal or nominal; and (b) whether syntactic complements or prosodic cues were used to distinguish reference to major characters in the narratives.

In the BWC children's narratives, complements tended to be verbal complements, that is, they added information about actions, states, and events, as in example 10.1.[3]

Example 10.1

a. and then he dro-ve off *with 'em*
b. and he had a wreck *on his bike*
c. and the peaches fell out *on the ground*

The italicized prepositional phrases in example 10.1 add information about the verbal activity. The phrase 'on his bike' clarifies what is meant by 'had a wreck'; 'on the ground' adds to the verb 'fell out'.

In the WMC children's narratives, in contrast, complements tended to be nominal complements, that is, they added content about characters in the narrative. For example:

Example 10.2

a. he em . . . saw 'em *with the pears*
b. a man . . . *that was pickin' some . . . pears*
c. this boy *on this bike* came along

The *that*-compound and the italicized prepositional phrases in example 10.2 specify the actors referred to by the nouns and pronoun. The that-complement 'that was pickin' some pears' qualifies the noun phrase 'a man'; and the phrase 'on this bike' gives additional detail about the character referred to as 'this boy'; 'with the pears' modifies the previous 'em' (referring to the boys).

These patterns of using complements were part of more inclusive strategies for maintaining thematic cohesion. It turned out on closer analysis that the two groups differed in the way in which they identified a character in the film and later reintroduced that character into the narrative. The WMC narrators used complex nominal syntax when introducing a new character. Then, at a later stage, referring back to this character, after other events or characters had been talked about, the children used embedded complements, as well as lexical and grammatical parallelism, to reestablish reference. The BWC narrators were more likely to use paratactic appositional structures when introducing a character. Then later, to refer back and reestablish the character in the narrative, they employed a special prosodic cue – vowel elongation with a high rise-fall intonation. Let us contrast two examples. A WMC child begins:

Example 10.3
there was a man
that was pickin' some. . .pears

Twenty-four lines later she mentions the character again, saying:

Example 10.4
they walked by the man
who gave . . . *wh-who was pickin' the pears*

Note the use of relative clauses in examples 10.3 and 10.4 to establish and maintain reference to 'the man'. A black child begins:

Example 10.5
it was about . . . this man
he was um . . . um . . . *takes some* . . . Peach
some . . . *pea-rs off the tree*

Twenty-five lines later he mentions the character again, saying:

Example 10.6
. . . when he pâ-ssed/ by that mâ-n
. . . the man . . . the mâ-n came out the tree

Vowel elongation which in example 10.6 occurs with a high rise-fall intonation contour serves to indicate definiteness and to suggest that a previously introduced character is being reestablished in the narrative. The strategic use of this elongated high rise-fall intonation contour in example 10.6 serves as an implicit cue meaning 'the man – you know what man I'm talking about, the man I already told you about – that man came out the tree'.

One style of narration uses relative clauses to pack information around a nominal indicating a major character, using that information when reintroducing the character. The other style introduces characters with appositional constructions, relying on a specialized prosodic cue to signal 'definiteness' in later mentions. Both styles, while communicatively effective, make different interpretational demands on the listener. The first strategy requires general knowledge of English lexicon and syntax. The second requires the subculturally specific knowledge that vowel elongation and contoured intonation can signal definiteness. In other words it seems that the BWC children here are relying on home-based strategies which may not be familiar to the audience.

What the different use of intra-clausal complements reveals is a delicate but systematic divergence among young speakers. Both groups of first-grade children used nominal complements in their narratives but in different places and for different discursive purposes. The WMC narrators were far more likely to use them to introduce key characters and refer back to them later in the narrative. They thus used nominal complements strategically to signal reference relations between parts of the narrative. The BWC narrators were more likely to rely on prosodic cues to accomplish the particular discursive task of introducing a character and signaling co-reference later in the narrative. In an important sense the WMC discourse style could be said to be more literate, not because of the occurrence of nominal structures per se, but because of the way in which those structures were used.

Comparing oral and written narratives

A similar stylistic difference was also found in the fourth-grade narratives. We will examine the difference by contrasting the spoken and written narratives of two fourth-graders on this particular measure of how characters are introduced and reestablished in the narrative. Then we will briefly discuss some other features of prosodic style found when the spoken and written narratives of a larger sample of eight fourth-graders were analyzed.

The BWC fourth-graders relied more on prosodic cues than their WMC counterparts. One student, Geoffry, was a good reader and oral narrator, but had difficulty in his written narrative just at those points where he used prosodic cues to distinguish major characters in his oral narrative. It was when the man picking pears was reintroduced into the story that he failed to make the necessary lexical/syntactic distinctions. Consequently, his written text at this particular point was ambiguous. A corresponding WMC fourth-grader, Paul, used nominal complements to distinguish major characters in both his oral and written narratives; his written version was unambiguous. In short, when we compare the relative transferability of signaling devices from spoken to written discourse we find that the fourth-grader who has an oral-discourse style that relies heavily on prosodic cueing has more difficulty expressing himself, in writing, than does the fourth-grader who uses more lexicalized and grammaticalized cohesive ties in his oral discourse.

Use of complements

In the oral narrative of Paul, the WMC fourth-grader, thematic cohesion is achieved through a variety of devices, ranging from lexical and grammatical ties to prosodic cues and the use of the temporal connective 'then'. Anaphora and lexical ties are used to maintain referential cohesion and agent-perspective throughout the narrative. An example of cohesion and perspective maintenance can be seen in the introduction of the major characters and in the subsequent mention of one of them later in the narrative. 'This man' is introduced in the first few lines of the narrative:

Example 10.7
well there was this um . . . ma-n
and he was . . . um . . . collecting
um . . . some . . . kind of fruit

The man in example 10.7 is then referred to as 'he' in the following lines. Nine lines later, in example 10.8, a new character is introduced. The shift in perspective is signaled both grammatically, by use of the indefinite article, and prosodically, by means of a stressed falling pitch on 'boy' (a contour that Paul frequently uses to highlight new information):

Example 10.8
and then um . . . a bóy came along on a bicycle

Paul refers to the new character as 'he' until another perspective shift occurs later in the narrative. Thus there are overlapping cues – lexical and grammatical, as well as prosodic – which indicate a shift in perspective from the man to the boy. Lastly, in example 10.9, when the man is reintroduced at the end of the narrative, Paul uses a noun plus *that*-clause to explicitly identify the character.

Example 10.9
the man that was um
that was collecting the fruits

This, of course, is the same strategy used by the WMC first-graders.

In his written version, Paul relies on paragraphing, lexicalization, use of the indefinite article and subordinate clauses to indicate new information and shift in perspective. In example 10.10 he begins his narrative with a complex nominal describing the man.

Example 10.10
There was a *man collecting fruit* from a tree

In example 10.11, several lines later, having described the man's activities, he shifts perspective by opening a new paragraph:

Example 10.11
After the man had returned to the tree, a boy came riding along on a bicycle. He saw the man in the tree and the baskets of fruit

The paragraph indentation by itself indicates a shift in perspective. In the first sentence, however, Paul also uses a subordinate/main clause construction and introduces the boy as a new character by the use of the indefinite article. Relegating 'the man' to the subordinate clause leaves 'a boy' as the subject and agent of the main clause, thus anticipating a shift in perspective. The final sentence completes the transition. If the sentence had read simply 'He saw him', it would have been ambiguous as to who saw whom. In the actual sentence, however, 'the man in the tree' is identified as the one who was seen; 'He', the one who does the seeing, must be the boy. With the shift in perspective completed, the new character is referred to simply as 'he' until another shift occurs. Paul later begins a new paragraph when the man is reintroduced. As in his oral version, he uses a complex nominal construction to identify the character:

Example 10.12

The *man collecting fruits* noticed that one basket was empty and that three boys were eating fruits

It is clear that Paul uses many of the same devices found in his oral narratives to indicate shifts in perspective in his written narrative. The devices include use of indefinite articles and lexical items, as well as use of complex nominal syntax for denoting a major character. In his written version, perhaps to compensate for the loss of prosodic cues, he also uses subordinate/main clause sentences and paragraphing to clearly signal shifts in perspective.

Let us now look at the same events in Geoffry's oral and written narratives. We will see that the BWC fourth-grader has a different way of introducing the man, shifting perspective to the boy, and later returning to the man. In Geoffry's oral narrative he introduces the man in the first few lines, saying:

Example 10.13

this guy . . . this man was picking pears
from . . . his tree

He then introduces the boy in the following line, saying:

Example 10.14

and so . . . th- this guy-y
he was riding around . . . he was riding on his bike

The first and second mentions of 'this guy' (examples 10.13 and 10.14) are distinguished prosodically. The fall-rise-fall contour on the latter mention ('guy-y') is an implicit cue, signaling a new character and a shift in perspective. Additionally, his intonation on the first mention ('guy') is a high level tone, followed by a high stressed syllable on 'man'. The combination indicates that a correction has been made and that 'man' is the more apt descriptor. The second mention of 'this guy-y' therefore contrasts with 'man', not 'this guy', but the clues to this opposition lie in the prosodic alternations. From this point on, Geoffry refers to the second character as 'he'. At the end of the narrative in example 10.15, when the man is reintroduced, this is done with a special rise-fall contour and vowel elongation:

Example 10.15

and so the mâ-n had seen that he had three baskets

This, of course, is the same strategy used by the BWC first-graders when they are reestablishing this character in the narrative.

In Geoffry's written version he does not use paragraphing, nor constructions such as subordinate/main clause sentences, to signal changes in perspective. He begins by writing the following:

Example 10.16

This man was picking pears and this boy was riding by on his bike and he saw the pears

The use of different lexical items denotes a change of characters (man and boy), but without the various grammatical devices used by Paul (indefinite article, subordination, and change of 'the man' from agent to patient). Given this state of affairs, the use of 'he' in example 10.16 is potentially ambiguous: the only cue guiding the reader to interpret 'he' as referring to the boy rather than to the man, is that it directly follows a clause in which the boy is mentioned. Additional reading does make the perspective shift and reference to 'he' more clear, but the point is that the transition, the perspective shift, is not clearly marked by lexical and syntactic devices. It has to be retrospectively inferred from further reading (or, of course, from prosody in the oral narrative). Finally, when Geoffry reintroduces the man at the end of his narrative, he simply writes:

Examples 10.17

and when the man came down he saw a basket was missing

In contrast to his WMC counterpart, Geoffry does not use noun complements to explicitly identify the character, but rather simply mentions him and proceeds to describe his actions.

Overall, Paul used more varied sentence structures, more lexically overt cues, and greater redundancy in signaling thematic cohesion in his oral narrative. Many of these conventions carried over into the written mode. For Paul, learning to write involved enriching a system he already knew. Geoffry, on the other hand, tended to rely more on prosodic cues. They were often the sole indicators of information-chunking and perspective-shifting in his oral narrative; and these of course do not have an equivalent in the written mode. Geoffry's written narrative was characterized by weakly signaled transitions between major perspective shifts. For him, with the prosodic options lost, learning to write means learning new strategies for signaling thematic cohesion.

Other features of the transition from speaking to writing

A later analysis of a larger corpus of fourth-grade narratives, focusing on more general aspects of rhetorical organization, supported the finding that culture-specific differences in use of prosody correlate with different styles of writing. The later analysis was done on the oral and written narratives of eight fourth-graders – four BWC children and four WMC children – including Paul and Geoffry. As noted above, in examining the transition from oral to written discourse, we were particularly interested in the functions served by prosody because, to a great extent, these signaling devices are not representable orthographically in standard written language. In the later study the focus was on whether the prosody and syntax of oral discourse somehow matched the typical sentence patterns of written prose, rather than on how topics were established and maintained in a narrative. The following briefly summarizes the set of findings dealing with the stress patterns found in the children's oral and written narratives.

We found that the WMC children used rising or falling intonation on the last word of a 'tone group' (i.e. a connected intonational phrase) in 85 per cent of all cases, and in 90 per cent of the cases this intonational marking fell on the last word of a syntactic clause. This prosodic pattern (with emphasis on the last content word of a tone group) is reflected in their writing, with key content nouns occurring close to clause boundaries. These facts have implications for the readability of these children's written texts. The linguist Bolinger noted that there is an 'unmarked accent pattern' of standard written prose whereby 'we tend to put a major accent on the last content word before a major syntactic break' (Bolinger 1972:

603). For this reason, the transition to writing would not entail a radical loss of prosodically signaled information. To a large extent, the child's own prosodic patterns are reimposed by a reader, or more importantly for our purposes here, the child's teacher, in interpreting and evaluating the child's written work.

In the BWC children's narratives, the occurrence of rising and falling tones on the last word of a tone group is far less frequent, a fact we have also noted in sharing-time narratives. One of the reasons for this is that sustained level tones (tones which neither rise nor fall), while rarely used by the WMC children, account for nearly 30 per cent of all occurrences of primary intonational tones in the BWC children's narratives. Secondly, these children appear to be using rising or falling tones early in the tone group to organize the discourse into larger rhetorical units (episodes or action sequences). For example, when introducing and describing *characters*, they used sustained level tones on the last word of a tone group. When describing a series of actions, carried out by a single agent, there is a perceptible shift, with emphasis on the pronoun or verb *early* in the tone group. While the unmarked accent pattern of standard prose does match these children's character-focused discourse, it does not match these children's stress pattern in signaling action progression (where stress falls early in the phrase). The BWC children's use of shifting stress contrasts with the WMC children's regular pattern of clause-final emphasis throughout the narrative.

With regard to writing, the WMC children are more likely to write in syntactically isolable, multi-clause units, thus approximating the literate standard at the level of sentence organization. In contrast, the BWC children have far more difficulty segmenting their texts into sentential units; sentence fragments and 'and' conjoined run-on sentences abound. Some of these difficulties are apparent in the following excerpt from Geoffry's written narrative (partially repeating example 10.16):

Example 10.18

This man was picking pears and this boy was riding by on his bike and he saw the pears so he stole a basket of pears and he started riding away and this girl bumped into him

The child uses no punctuation whatsoever to mark off clausal boundaries; his entire one-and-a-half page written narrative is one long, run-on sentence. Moreover, if the last word before a major syntactic break receives primary stress, as in the unmarked stress pattern, the passage sounds dysfluent and difficult to follow. If instead, the text is read with shifting stress (the rhythmic pattern used by the child in his oral narrative), emphasizing 'man' and 'pears', 'boy' and 'bike', and then shifting to verb emphasis on 'saw', 'stole', and 'riding', the passage is systematically judged to be more coherent by both black and white adult informants. No empirical work that we are familiar with has addressed this issue of a reader's reimposition of prosody on written text. But whether there is a match or mismatch between teacher and child's stress patterns would seem to have important implications for the accurate reading and assessment of children's written texts.

Conclusion

It is now worthwhile to look at several specific questions in the light of this analysis: (1) what features of the narratives of WMC children gave those narratives their apparent literate quality; (2) what features of the BWC children's oral discourse were not transferable into written discourse; and (3) could those features have affected interaction during other classroom speech events?

The first two questions are best dealt with together. In analyzing the narratives we found a differing pattern of use of nominal as opposed to verbal complements. That pattern agrees with general analyses of the communicative efficiency of differing grammatical constructions in written discourse (Halliday 1967), as well as with recent findings regarding typical differences in spoken versus written language (Chafe 1980; Chafe and Danielewicz 1987). We also found a use of prosodic cues to signal definiteness, a signaling convention which would not transfer into written discourse.

Concerning the effect of the prosodic conventions on other classroom events, Michaels (chapter 5, this volume) has analyzed the role of identical prosodic cues in sharing-time sessions and has shown the disharmonious teacher–student interaction which seems to occur when cues are not shared. Collins (chapter 6, this volume) has analyzed an analogous situation in reading groups. In his study it is not specific prosodic cues that are at issue, but rather general differences in the placement of tonal contours.

What several papers in this volume argue at length is that children in school settings are evaluated, from the very beginning of their school career, with reference to a narrow standard for what constitutes literate behavior in speech and writing (a point made also by Bloomfield (1933) and Fowler et al. (1979)). Where children use an oral discourse style that departs from both the teacher's expectation and this narrow literate standard, there is a decline in the quality and quantity of interaction during those very classroom activities that should provide the practice for the acquisition and mastery of literate discourse strategies. This differential access to practice and instruction cannot be attributed to individual teachers or students. What occurs in classrooms is influenced by many things, including standardized testing and tracking policies, cutbacks in support staff, and the overcrowding of classrooms. What differences in discourse style do is introduce an additional factor into an already complex classroom setting. Moreover, cumulatively, this kind of disharmonious interaction results in a pattern of differential treatment and negative evaluation. These, in turn, diminish the students' access to the kind of instruction and practice necessary for the acquisition of literacy.

Notes

1. At the time of the study (1977–79), Berkeley's hills and 'flatlands' neighborhoods were largely segregated by class and ethnicity (white professional families tended to live in the hills and black working-class families in the flatlands). And because of the city's voluntary bussing policy, all schools were integrated. The first and fourth grade classrooms in our study were representative of Berkeley as a whole, with approximately half black children from working-class backgrounds and half white children from upper-middle-class backgrounds.
2. As indicated in note 1, in this study ethnicity and social class were intertwined, as they are so often in social life. At the time of the original study, we were not analyzing class per se, though we realized, and realize, its significance (see especially Lareau 2003, for a recent

ethnographic demonstration of the significance of class-and-race for language use). Accordingly, we use the more cumbersome but accurate BWC (black working class) and WMC (white middle class) in place of purely ethnoracial labels.

3. In the examples in this chapter the '-' following a vowel indicates vowel elongation; a '∧' over a syllable indicates a high rise-fall tonal contour; a pause is indicated by '. .' and a longer pause by '. . .'.

11

The implicit discourse genres of standardized testing: what verbal analogy items require of test takers

Mary Catherine O'Connor

A decade ago, the publication of *The Bell Curve* (Hernstein and Murray 1994) provoked a wide range of responses. Among them was the establishment of a task force by the Board of Scientific Affairs of the American Psychological Association. Their charge was to create a report clarifying what the community of experts on intelligence agree is and is not known about intelligence. At the heart of their work (Neisser et al. 1996) was the question of causes behind group differences in performance on standardized tests of achievement and aptitude, sometimes referred to as 'the achievement gap' (Jencks et al. 1998). The report was framed within the most influential conceptualization of intelligence and achievement, the psychometric approach. With respect to the gap of about one standard deviation between scores of black and white Americans on tests of intelligence and aptitude, the panel concluded that

> [it] does not result from any obvious biases in test construction and administration, nor does it simply reflect differences in socioeconomic status. Explanations based on factors of caste and culture [as explicated in, e.g.: Ogbu and Matute-Bianchi 1986] may be appropriate, but so far have little direct empirical support. There is certainly no such support for a genetic interpretation. Neisser et al. 1996: 97

The same inconclusiveness attends the achievement gap between other groups, including males and females. In the absence of a

Acknowledgments: Many thanks to Jenny Cook-Gumperz and John Gumperz, Sarah Michaels, Marj Hogan, Alissa Shethar, and to the individuals who agreed to be interviewed. All errors and infelicities are my responsibility.

consensus from the scientific community (which is perhaps most invested in an answer), should we assume that the public has refrained from drawing conclusions about the source of this gap? Probably not. Discovering the full range of explanatory factors, along with their various weightings, so that these can be addressed, is a task that is far from done.

Nevertheless, the reissue of this volume calls us, as it did twenty years ago, to consider more carefully the ways that ideas, institutions, and practices concerning 'literacy' which come to seem natural and unquestionable are in fact conventional, collectively accomplished decisions. As Berger and Luckmann originally laid out the task of the sociology of knowledge, it

> must concern itself with whatever passes for 'knowledge' in a society, regardless of the ultimate validity or invalidity (by whatever criteria) of such 'knowledge.' And insofar as all human knowledge is developed, transmitted and maintained in social situations, the sociology of knowledge must seek to understand the processes by which this is done in such a way that a taken-for-granted 'reality' congeals for the man in the street. Berger and Luckmann 1967: 3

This task is particularly urgent in the case of educational assessment. As Cook-Gumperz stated in her 1986 introduction to this book, 'From the interactional sociolinguistic perspective we see that the selection–reproduction cycle is not automatic but arises as a function of a series of activities and decisions which involve evaluations and judgments of children's learning potential' (1986: 3). Cook-Gumperz's exploration of the socially constructed categories of literacy encourages us to consider the many ways in which taken-for-granted reality is constructed in a domain as multifaceted and diffuse as intelligence and aptitude.

My task here is to point to ways that issues in the social construction of literacy as identified by the authors in this volume may figure in the test-score gap introduced above. Although the genetic and biological environmental explanations (nutrition, lead and alcohol exposure etc.) are difficult to demonstrate, and have not yet been definitively demonstrated, as Neisser et al. unambiguously state, nevertheless these factors are attractively simple materialist explanations for differential performance. In contrast, explanations of differential performance in terms of sociolinguistic or sociocultural practices are not persuasive for many people. In the past, broad assertions of 'cultural bias' in the concepts and language of standardized tests were common; test items containing concepts such as 'coxswain' and 'rugby' took on the status of urban legends. In fact, testing companies long ago filtered out such easy targets, and have long since appointed panels to identify and delete items that even hint of differentially available or 'biased' cultural information. After these easy-to-understand examples were rooted out, the possibility of sociocultural or linguistic bias became more difficult to see. Pervasive sociocultural or sociolinguistic factors are difficult to trace and difficult to explain. References to these are often attacked as the poorly specified apologia of liberals; 'that's just glorifying non-standard language (or reasoning)'.

This still leaves room, nonetheless, for items that are differentially difficult for different groups.[1] There are unanswered questions in this realm, just as there are in the biological realm. The idea of language use and linguistic practices as cultural capital is explored by Bourdieu (1991), Eckert (2000), Gee (1996), Hanks (1996), Heath (1983), and many others. Yet tracing the origins of specific practices and tracking their consequences through the arena of schooling is not a trivial task. In order to make a convincing case, we are called to examine closely the socioculturally and sociolinguistically specific nature of the tasks contained in actual tests of intelligence and aptitude, to see if we can identify anything in the way of systematically different responses by different groups.

An approach to this used by large testing companies such as ETS (Educational Testing Service) has been to examine the answer patterns of thousands of test takers, categorized by gender, ethnicity, language background, and so on. Studies of answer choices, however, do not offer evidence about the reasoning used by test takers to get those answers. For this, we need a more labor-intensive, qualitative approach, one that makes use of think-aloud protocols or other such devices. Such studies are not common, but examples include work over many years by Clifford Hill (Hill and Larsen 2000). An example I will use here is Lardiere (1992), which is not precisely a study of test items per se, but which demonstrates the possibilities.

Lardiere addresses previous claims by Alfred Bloom, who linked the absence of a morphological marker of counterfactuality in Chinese to what he claimed to be a lack of ability by Chinese speakers to correctly answer the question 'If all circles were large, and this small triangle 'Δ' were a circle, would it be large?' This question was part of a study of counterfactual reasoning; it is not taken from an intelligence test. Nevertheless, as Lardiere points out, similar questions have traditionally been used on intelligence tests and continue to be so used, e.g. in Sternberg's CAT (College Aptitude Test, Sternberg 1992).

Lardiere sought to test Bloom's (1981) claim that Chinese subjects' unwillingness to answer the circles and triangles question with a 'yes', as Western test-taking logic required, was due to their lack of a counterfactual marker and thus was support for Whorf's linguistic relativity hypothesis. It was countered by others that his subjects' answers were due to low levels of schooling. Scribner and Cole's (1981) well-known work on literacy and syllogistic reasoning among the Vai would support the hypothesis that Western schooling might be the source of access to a valued practice of counterfactual reasoning. Lardiere had found in pilot work that a few subjects who were native speakers of Arabic, a language which displays a counterfactual morpheme, nevertheless rejected or answered 'no' to Bloom's question. Moreover, these pilot subjects were US college graduates. Therefore, their answers could not be attributed either to lack of a counterfactual marker or to lack of education. Lardiere followed up this observation with more systematic study of eighteen native speakers of Arabic, all of whom were attending elite colleges or graduate schools in the Boston area. Most were in the sciences, and clearly had excelled in taking standardized tests in English.

Lardiere presented them with the question in Arabic and in English: 'If all circles were large, and this small triangle "Δ" were a circle, would it be large?' Given their linguistic and educational backgrounds, neither the absence of counterfactual markers nor lack of Western schooling could be a factor in these subjects' responses. Nonetheless, about three fourths of her interviewees rejected the question as unanswerable, or said that the answer was no. She concluded that aspects of their Arabic cultural background were the reason, and gained support for this from subjects' remarks, unprompted, about why this was just not a good question. The subject below makes explicit reference to the cultural meaning of *lau*, the counterfactual marker in Arabic.

For example, if I leave now and go and drive my car, for example I didn't push the brakes, I got into an accident, and I say '*lau, lau . . .*' –'*lau*' which means *if* I took another route, I wouldn't have went into the accident, and that's considered to be forbidden, because it was meant to be from God . . . it's like you're doubting the existence [of God], and that's one of the top forbidden things in the Koran. Lardiere 1992: 244

Lardiere's investigation featured a question with no confusing linguistic constructions, and no unfamiliar content. The reader above can obviously reason counterfactually, and can talk about that reasoning explicitly. The item nevertheless presents a culturally problematic activity and the reader, a very articulate graduate student in the sciences, does not want to engage with the text in the ways he knows the item is requiring.

As sociolinguists and linguistic anthropologists have pointed out in other contexts (e.g. Hanks 1996; Heath 1983; Ochs 1996), this is not an uncommon phenomenon: linguistically and textually mediated activities and events are usually laden with social and cultural presuppositions and limitations. Discourse genres of various types can be usefully conceptualized as distinct communicative activities that are embedded within more encompassing social practices. Even written genres constitute communicative activities with rules for participation: the writer and reader are displaced interlocutors; successful interpretation depends upon the reader and writer understanding and anticipating one another's assumptions about how text interpretation is to proceed.

The cultural specificity of these conditions poses a potential problem for paper-and-pencil (or computer-based) tests of aptitude and achievement. If the activity in which the reasoning is embedded is unfamiliar or culturally off-limits in some fashion, then a student's failing results are uninterpretable. If a student succeeds in answering an item, we at least can infer that the student can do the task, and can work with the practices within which the task is embedded. If the student cannot answer an item correctly, we have no idea whether the problem is a lack of knowledge of vocabulary or concepts, a lack of ability to reason in the way the problem requires, or a response to an unfamiliar or uncomfortable speech activity.

This social-interactional micro-analytic perspective is notably absent from research on assessment of ability, aptitude and achievement in the two fields that dominate the development of standardized tests, psychometrics and cognitive science. These fields differ in their approach to operationalizing an ability or aptitude construct such as 'mathematics computation' or 'vocabulary knowledge', but neither one has a clearly articulated understanding of the kinds of socioculturally rooted linguistic practices that make up the discourse genre of standardized tests and how these differ from the everyday practices of the test takers themselves.

Oversimplifying for current purposes (see O'Connor 1992 for a longer discussion) psychometric progress in the theory and practice of assessing aptitude and achievement results from careful and inventive application of the methods of correlation and multiple regression, built around the comparison of an individual within a group. Within this tradition, a score on a test is transformed in a number of ways into a measure of the test taker's position relative to other test takers. Some see this as a pointless and pernicious allegiance to ranking individuals. Others see it as an ingenious way to gain information about how intelligence, aptitude, and achievement are distributed in various populations, and how these properties are correlated with one another and with other criteria external to the particular test. They see the enterprise as helpful in predicting how resources may best be allocated to meet the needs of various populations. Whatever the actual theory of intelligence concurrently viewed as plausibly underlying the psychometric enterprise (and there have been many different ones), this use of correlation as a discovery tool is a hallmark of the research and practice of the psychometric community. In this tradition, modeling of the actual on-line processes of cognition does not receive the emphasis found in recent cognitive psychology and cognitive science.

Within cognitive science, in contrast, many researchers value an accurate and detailed modeling of relevant behavior of an individual. The goal is to understand and eventually replicate the interplay of knowledge structures and processing strategies and routines. The focus in education-oriented cognitive science research is to better understand the learner (and the variety of learners), and thus to improve the ability of schools to foster learning and development. In this tradition, analysis of intelligent behavior for its own sake generally precedes the development of assessment tools. First, the knowledge or action domain must be understood; only then will there be time for development of diagnostic tools. Because the domain of behavior must be understood first in terms of a small number of intensely analyzed individual performances, the correlational approach is not as important. Thus, the characterization of ability or achievement is usually not in static and quantitative terms. Rather, there is a concern with characterizing skill and knowledge developmentally, and there is a deep concern with the *context-specificity* of thinking and learning. To what extent do the subject matter, the context of performance and the context of learning itself determine the outcome, over and above the learner's individual characteristics? Cognitive studies of ability take seriously the problem contexts within which the thinking is embedded. This leads to very careful and detailed accounts of the problem context, and what the subject does in solving the problem.

However, while both the psychometric and cognitive perspectives on the study of ability and its measurement have resulted in deep insights and expanded understandings, neither has consistently provided a place to consider the implications of the social and linguistic practices that make up the discourse genres of standardized test items. Neither tradition has considered how these might differ from the everyday practices of the test takers themselves.[2] As other contributors to this volume have asserted in their own work on educational settings, it is crucial not to neglect study of interactional aspects of the 'selection–reproduction cycle' – it is here that discriminatory practices can be obscured as 'natural' or 'merely technical' aspects of assessment and the subsequent justification of resource allocation. In the brief exposition that follows, I present some evidence that in fact these hidden interactional demands are of potential importance in understanding the literacy-related requirements of some standardized test items, and the concomitant performance patterns associated with them.

Analogy items and their interpretation[3]

For many years, the SAT has been used as an entrance requirement at colleges and universities in the United States, and as a criterion in decisions to allocate scholarship funds after students matriculate. It has long been observed that students of Latino, African-American, and Native-American backgrounds perform below their Asian and White counterparts on this test, and depending upon the weight given to the test it has played a major gate-keeping function on university entrance. Recently a few elite public universities have dropped the SAT as an entrance requirement (e.g. University of California, Berkeley). Some see this action as coming partially in response to efforts by federal and state government to curtail affirmative action, particularly the use of admissions criteria that might favor minority students.

Within mainstream education, as many of the contributors to this volume have demonstrated, interpretive practices are often non-transparent. They may require experience with isomorphic practices based in the home or community discourse, and are not the direct indicators of 'pure' ability they are thought to be, but rather are mediated through tacit understandings that are socioculturally provided and therefore, as argued by Cook-Gumperz, socially constructed.

Verbal analogy problems present an interesting case in the study of discourse genres viewed as social activities. Other than in standardized tests of 'scholastic aptitude' (and in programs and curricular materials intended to help students prepare for such tests), verbal analogy problems are a rarely encountered discourse genre. Yet performance on verbal analogy problems is widely considered to be an excellent index of the ability to use analogical reasoning (Zwick 2002). In traditional studies of this topic, the main requirements for successful solution of verbal analogy problems are thought to be vocabulary knowledge and analogical reasoning, as laid out in the work of Sternberg and others. However, explorations within an interactional sociolinguistic framework suggest that the picture is more complex than that.

As I will attempt to demonstrate below, there is another type of knowledge that must be brought to bear in solving such problems. This knowledge involves awareness of a particular kind of restriction on the role of language use in at least some of these problems. Specifically, the words in a verbal analogy problem are to be understood metalinguistically, as entities in a lexicon, not as expressions used in communication in everyday life. Success in solving an item can depend on this. Although it is seemingly straightforward, I will attempt to show that it baffles some otherwise very competent students. A successful 'reading' of one of these problems requires that the test taker understand, if not endorse, the precise nature of the test maker's expectations. It requires that the test taker recognize that the textual format and contents of the analogy test item (even encountered outside the context of an actual test) are indexing a special type of communicative practice, as discussed further below.

In the most general sense, what is an analogy? Simply, it is a way of understanding situations and entities in one domain in terms of situations and entities in a different domain. On this view, an analogy 'is an assertion that a relational structure that normally applies in one domain can be applied in another domain' (Gentner 1977: 156). In an analogy like the following, we understand the domain of lawyers and clients *in terms of* the relations between doctors and patients.

DOCTOR : PATIENT : : LAWYER : CLIENT

Typically, this is read formulaically, as 'Doctor is to patient, as lawyer is to client.' To solve an analogy problem, it is generally assumed that the problem solver discovers the important relations and attributes in the first 'base' domain (say the relations between doctor and patient), maps these into another 'target' domain (say the world of lawyers and their clients), and then checks to see to what extent the relations and attributes in the base domain apply in the target domain. In much of the cognitive literature on analogical thinking, the base domain and target domain are complex structures or situations in the everyday world or in science. In the problems I'm considering here, the test item stem (the base domain) consists of two words in relation to each other. The possible answer choices (target domain) are also pairs of words. But what are the objects and attributes in the base and target domains, and what is the nature of the important relations between the two? I will argue that there are two relevant possibilities.

Words as referring or predicating expressions

As is well known, words can function as instruments in human communication. They can be used to refer (to identify entities who will then be incorporated into the recipient's ongoing model of the discourse, e.g. *Jan, my niece, the Pope*). They can be used to predicate (roughly, to attribute properties or acts or states to an entity, e.g. *Jan left*, or *Jan is a doctor*). Considered as a communicative element in an ongoing discourse, a word can call up, or index, a situation or entity in some world. For the recipient, the word 'rain' may call up memories of the entity known as rain, or instances of situations in which that word was used in a referential way. Linguists sometimes refer to words in action as referring or predicating *expressions* (cf. Lyons 1977: 23).

If we construe the words in an analogy problem as communicative expressions, or words used to refer to situations or events in the world, then the test taker is being asked to reason about the objects or situations those expressions are indexing. The task is to think about the objects referred to by these expressions, and to figure out the mapping from the base domain to the target domain. As such, the systematic relationship between the base domain and the target domain will involve relations between objects or situations in the world or similarities and differences among their various features and properties.

For example, consider the stem and answer pair

DOCTOR : PATIENT : : LAWYER : CLIENT

If we take these words as referring expressions, then they simply point to the entities in the world they refer to. It's a generic pointing out, to be sure – there is no specific reference to 'Dr. Maguire' or her patient 'Mr. Kaplan'. It is as though the item is using the words *doctor* and *patient* to *refer* to participants in the generic situation of a medical encounter, and thus prompting the reader to envision a representative scenario. So a reader taking this route into meaning would begin to consider the worlds of doctors and lawyers, their patients and clients, and would begin to look for similarities and differences in those worlds: both patients and clients have problems that doctors and lawyers are expected to solve. Both are paying relationships, and so on.

Words as linguistic objects

On the other hand, words can be seen as objects in themselves, outside of the actual situations of use, as lexemes. Lexemes are words considered as objects in the mental lexicon, or, more practically, as objects in the dictionary. They have properties that limit what they can be used to refer to, but they also have grammatical and lexical properties, such as belonging to the class of mass nouns, or intransitive verbs, and numerous other properties as well. If the objects in the base and target domains of an analogy are lexemes, then we will see quite different relationships emerge as important in the solving of an analogy problem.

If we return to the stem-and-answer pair above, we note that DOCTOR and LAWYER are words that name professions, and PATIENT and CLIENT are words that name the roles of individuals who go to them for services. If we assume that this sort of item indexes an activity of pondering the relations between words, i.e., a metalinguistic activity, then a reader should begin to look for similarities and differences in those *words*, for example in the kinds of features that characterize them, in the ways they can be used, in their category, and so on.

At this point, some will raise objections. First, it's obvious that no matter how one 'reads' the item, one will see a strong parallelism between the stem DOCTOR : PATIENT and the answer pair LAWYER : CLIENT. Either way, whether one is thinking about situations or about the words themselves, there is a clear basis for the analogy. So what is the point of the distinction? As I will demonstrate below, it is not always the case that both 'readings' converge on the same answer.

Second, one might reasonably point out, the situation of reading a test item is not a conversation. There is no discourse connecting these terms; why should anyone see the item in terms of actual referring expressions? Isn't it obvious that the only sensible reading of these terms is as lexemes that are set up in parallel for the purpose of comparing their features? Those who raise this objection generally cannot imagine how anyone could read the typographically and situationally marked pair DOCTOR : PATIENT as anything other than 'The *word* DOCTOR is to the *word* PATIENT as. . .'

My preliminary investigation of this topic indicates that this 'sensible' reading is not obvious to some test takers, and furthermore that some items can be solved using either construal. Therefore, such items have an unrecognized complexity that is introduced by the unusual social-interactional nature of the task. Effectively, the test maker expects the successful test taker to intuit or recognize that the communicative practice (Hanks 1996) at issue is metalinguistic, about language, not about the world. The test maker sees the set of objects that are being mapped and the basis for the higher-order relations as relative to the lexeme. The test taker, on the other hand, may understand the analogy to be about the set of real-world entities and situations.[4] While the test taker will not always fail with this understanding, over the long run, I suggest, performance will be affected.

If this is so, then the test taker must perform in three different dimensions in order to succeed with this complex 'interlocutor,' the test and its maker. The test taker must display analogical thinking, as discussed above. The test taker must display word knowledge, and finally the test taker must display an ability to reason about words as objects. This is different from thinking analogically about events and situations with words functioning only as an index to the situation and its properties. If the reader fails in the third area, he or she will likely be labeled as not being able to think analogically, as being deficient in vocabulary knowledge, or both. My claim is that in fact the reader may be deficient in neither, but rather may have a different understanding about the activity itself.

The illustrative examples are taken from interviews with undergraduate and graduate students at an elite public university and with a few people who were no longer in school. This group of about twelve individuals included people of African-American, Latino, Chinese, and Anglo ethnicity. Several were bilingual. It's important to note that in the examples used here I do not identify their ethnicity or gender (gender has been randomly changed in some cases). My purpose in this is twofold: first, the topic of explanations for differential group performance has become, if anything, more contentious in the years since the data were collected. It would be irresponsible with such a small sample even to suggest a correlation between a particular stance toward analogy-item text interpretation and ethnolinguistic background; even if such a claim is disavowed, one cannot control how examples are used out of context. Second, this small study can only legitimately be used, in my view, as an existence proof of sorts. It can support a claim that there are test items that require the particular lexeme-based reading introduced above, and that there are test takers who do construe those items as though they involved only generic referring expressions that were directing the reader to consider aspects of the world as fodder for their analogizing. Once we know that this kind of distinction exists in some test takers, we can conduct more systematic research on its possible role in overall performance.[5]

Words as expressions: evoking and considering a situation

In the following example, Danielle, an adult in her mid-thirties, a former college student who was no longer enrolled, was asked to read through verbal analogies taken from an actual SAT, and 'think aloud' as she solved them. The item is given first, followed by the transcript of her problem solution.

Example 11.1

PATTER : RAIN :
RAINBOW : STORM, CALL : TELEPHONE, CLANK : CHAIN, VOLUME : RADIO, ERUPTION : VOLCANO

DANIELLE [reads aloud] Patter – rain, rainbow – storm, call – telephone, clank – chain, volume – radio, eruption – volcano. . . Patter – rain . . . eruption – volcano.

RESEARCHER Why?

DANIELLE [sighs] patter.. is the sound. . . of . . . is a type of rain. In. . . in. . . in this analogy, patter is to rain as eruption is to a volcano, because the patter of the rain, is something that you hear. . .

RESEARCHER mm-hmm

DANIELLE Aaand the eruption of a volcano is something that most people hear, very few of us are close enough to see it. You could also get away with volume – radio. As patter. . . patter is to rain, volume is to radio. Aaand, maybe. . . volume to radio, call – telephone? No, I don't like call – telephone. Clank – chain. . . these-this-this series is a little bit better because. . . because clank is a sound of a chain. Call is [coughs] telephone. . .not relevant, Rainbow – storm, not relevant 'cause they're not sounds. Patter to rain. So we have the three sound choices. Volume to radio is something you can control.

Patter [rain] is not. . . is not controllable. Forces are controlling that. Clank – chain is also controllable, because you're the one doing

	the clanking on the chain, And the only- the only two natural functions here are eruption and volcano, as patter to rain.
RESEARCHER	So which one do you pick.
DANIELLE	Eruption to volcano.

The correct answer is CLANK : CHAIN. Yet Danielle has followed a chain of analogical inference that evidences both adequate word knowledge and the appropriate process of mapping objects from the base domain into the target domain. What are the different assumptions and actual practices that distinguish her interaction with the test item from that intended by the test makers? First consider the fact that Danielle correctly identified the situation/ semantic field indexed by the stem: that of sounds and their sources. She narrowed down the field of correct answers to the three that could be used to refer to situations in which a sound emanated from a source. She then proceeded to compare, not the words, but the situations themselves. She compared the situations with respect to the dimension of agency in the relation between source and sound (‘*Volume is something you can control. . .clank–chain is also controllable*’ and ‘*patter [rain] is not controllable*’). When Danielle notes that the stem words, PATTER : RAIN, are being controlled by ‘forces’ she shifts to a focus on another higher-order set of features that might allow an analogical mapping, that of ‘natural’ v. man-made. Thinking analogically involves searching for the most systematic higher-order set of relations between the two domains (cf. Gentner 1977), and this is what Danielle is doing.

What would the test maker, or a test taker more attuned to the interpretive practices of standardized tests, have made of this item? First, such a reader would have considered the words themselves, as lexemes, to be the objects of the analogy. As such, the relations would not have been between situations involving sounds and their sources, but between words that denote sounds, and words that denote sources of sounds. Thus, VOLUME : RADIO could have been eliminated, since the word *volume* does not denote a sound, but rather the degree or intensity of a sound. Similarly, ERUPTION : VOLCANO could have been eliminated, since the lexeme *eruption* does not denote a sound, but a process or instance of violent explosion. CLANK : CHAIN would be the only item in which the first term has as its central semantic function the designation of a sound.

A sceptical reader may object that the word *eruption* does not denote a sound; Danielle has simply made an error, this is a vocabulary deficiency. I would counter that the error lies at a higher level, the level of assumptions about appropriate language-use conventions. Danielle's protocol provides evidence that she is thinking about these words as expressions communicating to her about situations, as they would in ordinary language use. In ordinary language use, her assumption that *eruption* can be used to refer to a sound would have been perfectly acceptable as an instance of *metonymy*, the process whereby a speaker refers to an entity by using, instead of its usual label, a word that refers to another entity that subsumes or is associated with the first entity.

There are many conventional expressions, such as 'the pen is mightier than the sword' that rely on this figurative use of language. However, less striking instances permeate everyday language use. Every time we say something like 'Chomsky takes up two feet on my bookshelf', or 'Without the emergency brake on, the car rolled down the driveway' we are using this 'figurative' means to refer. It is books authored by Chomsky and the wheels of the car to which we intend to refer. The most noticeable examples are those in which the association between the referred-to entity and the metonymic label is unusual, as in the hapless waiter's 'The ham sandwich walked out without paying' (Nunberg 1995). Such examples are ubiquitous and are often completely unnoticed in the course of everyday language use. The ordinariness of such devices in conversational discourse does not, however, sanction their use in the particular discourse genre of test taking. Although they may be the default mode that speakers assume when approaching a text, successful test takers have been socialized into applying a different set of linguistic norms for this particular kind of textual interaction.

Danielle's protocol can be viewed as a case of 'indexical breakdown' (Ochs 1996: 414). The intended social activity is the analogical comparison of words as lexemes, not the analogical comparison of situations that might be described by these words. For those who correctly assign the situational meaning here, the textual properties of an analogy test item index the social activity of considering closely the properties of word meaning. The task is metalinguistic, it does not call for consideration of the characteristic or contingent properties of the situations that can be denoted by the words. Does this transcript reveal that Danielle could not think analogically? Because of her misconstrual of the task, in fact we cannot infer much about Danielle's analogical abilities.

The next examples provide explicit evidence that a test-taker can fail to construe an analogy test item in the required fashion, and yet can still successfully reason analogically in other intellectual contexts that in some ways are more demanding. These examples involve a freshman, Gloria. She agreed to participate in a study of analogy test items, in which she would read through verbal analogies taken from the SAT, and 'think aloud' as she solved them. She, like the other subjects, was told that the researcher was interested in studying 'how people think' while they take standardized tests, and was paid ten dollars for the hour-long session. Later, the researcher examined her written work on a midterm in an introductory course in cultural anthropology. The comparison of her 'analogical reasoning' in these two discourse genres reveals how the social context within which a text is situated shapes the ways that people make sense of that text.

SPOUSE : WIFE ::
HUSBAND : UNCLE, SON : MOTHER, CHILD : DAUGHTER, BROTHER : SISTER, GRANDPARENT : PARENT

The correct pathway to the solution for this item involves an analogy between lexemes, not situations in the world. It is trading on a property of the lexeme *spouse*, namely that it is unspecified as to gender of the potential referent. The word it's paired with, on the other hand, *wife*, is semantically specified for gender. It is restricted in reference to picking out the female half of a married couple. In other words, the terms *spouse* and *wife* can both be used to refer to the female partner in a married couple, but the word *spouse* can also be used to refer to the male partner. The crucial relationship that determines the correct analogical mapping is this fact about the semantic specifications of the first word in relation to the second word. The only other pair where the same lexical relationship holds is CHILD : DAUGHTER.

Gloria does not construe this task as one about relationships between lexical items. Rather, she seems to be searching for an analogical mapping between real-world referents of those lexical items.

Example 11.2

GLORIA	Yeah. . . Spouse is to wife. . .. . say male and female,
RESEARCHER	Sorry?
GLORIA	Male and female? I guess relationship. I don't. . . cause they're all related, all those things are related to each other. Husband and uncle, and . . . that's the only thing I would think of . . ..and then I would say brother and sister.
RESEARCHER	OK. OK, so you would pick brother and sister.
GLORIA	Yeah

Gloria starts out by considering the two stem lexemes as a pair of terms referring to a male and female, as we can infer by her utterance 'Spouse is to wife. . .. . say male and female'. She seems to be thinking about a use of these two terms together, in actual reference to a pair of individuals. If these two terms were used together to refer to the relationship between a pair of individuals, as the other terms in this item do, they would only be referring to that of a husband and wife. Her mention of the attributes 'male' and 'female' indicate that she is not thinking about the lexical features of *spouse*, but rather what it would refer to in tandem with *wife*. Given that she is dealing with entities in the world, we can assume that she has isolated the dimension of opposite sexes as potentially holding across the two domains of analogy.

So in this problem we can hypothesize that she sees the domain as being family relationships, between a male and female. Furthermore, the relationship may crucially be reciprocal: given an A and a B, if X is Y's A, then Y is X's B. With these facts in mind, only one or two of the five answer pairs fits her schema. In one of the pairs, CHILD : DAUGHTER, only the second term explicitly denotes a kinship relation. Two others, GRANDPARENT : PARENT and HUSBAND: UNCLE, do not denote reciprocal relationships. Moreover, they do not specifically involve male and female relatives. The others, BROTHER : SISTER and SON : MOTHER, do denote reciprocal relationships involving males and females. Though we have no evidence for this, we might guess that Gloria chose BROTHER : SISTER because those relations are on the same generational level, as are husbands and wives, by definition. Sons and mothers involve another dimension, that of lineal descent.

To summarize, if a reader construes this problem as being about relationships between people, rather than relationships between words, a very different picture of thc answer options emerges. What is clear is that Gloria is seeking, as did Danielle, the appropriate analogy. She is searching for higher-order relations, she appears to know the meaning of the words, and she seeks to find corresponding pairs that preserve the crucial meaning links within each pair. However, the objects she is manipulating are situations in the world, not properties of lexical items. If this analysis is correct, then Gloria is misreading the intent of the test makers – this is again an 'indexical breakdown'. She has not understood the constraints on this particular discourse genre. Yet it is also clear from her protocol that she is very uncomfortable with the whole procedure. She repeatedly mentions that she hates taking these tests, doesn't do well on them, and finds them very troubling. The reason she doesn't like them comes up again and again. Gloria claims that she doesn't understand what the test makers want from her. This is the source of her discomfort. In the following brief excerpt, she has just chosen an answer for one question, and spontaneously begins to display these feelings.

Example 11.3

GLORIA It's that same feeling, I was like. . .I couldn't think and I was like. . .and that's why none. . . none! not even one I would feel positive about. None! So I'd come out of there like–I don't know what I did! I just-pbbbh! you know, crossed out whatever.

RESEARCHER Yeah.

GLORIA [sighs] Ok, paragraph is to prose. . . .mmm. Well, I guess prose has paragraphs? I don't know. [laughs] Uh, ...[sighs] see that's- oh God, those feelings. . .

A bit later Gloria stops and says 'You just read 'em and you don't really know what ch-what they want from you.'

This desire to know the rules of the discourse game is consonant with a larger picture of Gloria's life as a freshman. She and other subjects in the study were observed during a semester-long study-skills class given as an adjunct to their large, introductory cultural anthropology lecture course at the university. In this study-skills class she was one of the top two or three students. She clearly enjoyed learning, applying and displaying her knowledge of new study techniques. Similarly, her work in the introductory anthropology class, for which she usually received As, showed interest, diligence and a desire to discover and meet the standards of this new field. Gloria's vivid displays of frustration during the verbal analogy test contrast with her enthusiastic analogical reasoning in the assignment described below.

An introductory anthropology class requires that students learn to think analogically about cultural practices and institutions found in their own and other cultures. Two of the guiding questions in introductions to cultural anthropology concern the status of cultural differences and cultural universals. In order to consider cultural universals, students must begin to distinguish between cultural practices that are only superficially similar, and those that are deeply similar, that serve a similar function or have a similar positioning in the cultures being compared.

In Gloria's anthropology class, one of her in-class exam questions required her to construct just such an analogy. In many ways it is a paradigmatic example of analogical thinking and vocabulary knowledge. And in this discourse genre, whose rules are clear to Gloria, she is able to enter into the textually mediated interaction without fear, eager to display her analogical thinking. In this particular exam, students have been asked to identify and discuss several cultural universals. In order to do this most successfully, a student must display not just analogical reasoning, but sophisticated analogical reasoning. The best examples of cultural universals will be those practices or processes that may not look the same from culture to culture, but that can be argued to be underlyingly similar in important ways. In the academic game this interaction is embedded within, she must discuss superficially different cultural practices, creating a level of description at which the particulars of these practices serve as objects that can be mapped analogically from culture to culture.

Gloria chooses the concept of *reciprocity*: the incurring of obligation in the exchange of gifts. She compares the systems of exchange whereby people incur obligations in Becedas, Spain, the Trobriand Islands, the Punjab, the Kalahari Desert, and the United States. In all examples, she lays out what is exchanged, the nature of the obligation, and the reciprocity of the obligation. The text given below is transcribed directly from her handwritten midterm, though for ease of reading we have corrected superficial errors in spelling or punctuation.

Example 11.4

Cultural universals are those occurrences of culture – aspects, custom – that seem to appear in every culture. Many studies have been done to question the existence of these universals. The idea of reciprocity has been set to see if every cultural group has this sense of obligation in the exchange of gift-giving, – if in every culture there exist total prestations. Those systems of exchange by which people make contracts and are bound by obligations have been shown in the Trobriand Islands with the system of Kula – by which all the islands engage in an intertribal and island exchange of shells, necklaces, and arm shells. There is an obligation to take part in this system, for it is a part of the economy. Reciprocity exists in many forms as has also been shown in Becedas, with the ofrecijo and hay stacking customs. The donors at one time are the recipients the next time around. There is definite obligation in both customs whereby some member of the family must repay gifts or services the next time around. Reciprocity thus involves an obligation to give, receive and repay – as is seen in both examples. Many other societies in the world have customs of reciprocity. The !Kung share their meat – as a refrigeration method – but there is the obligation to give meat to those who give to you – failing to receive and repay in these cultures is not accepting the culture – it is like declaring war. The !Kung also have their system of gift-giving which is called Hxaso. Reciprocity is also seen in the Punjab – with their system of gift-giving within the castes. Even in our own culture we see reciprocity – during Christmas we feel the obligation to give to family and friends or any others we know are giving a gift to us. It is the exchange of gift for gift, and the obligation to return if someone has given you a gift and you have not returned the favor. These are all examples of reciprocity – and it does seem to be a universal phenomenon. It is just a question of the degree it partakes in the culture.

In this example, Gloria maps objects from one cultural domain into another. Her answer lays out an analogy between Becedas and its customs of hay stacking and ofrecijo, with the Trobriand Islands and its custom of Kula. She shows that the higher-order relations of gift-giving and reciprocal obligation through cycles of gift-giving are maintained in the mappings. This excerpt is only part of her answer; Gloria continues on to draw analogies between cultures in order to derive the cultural universal of the incest taboo. She then shows the reader that not all cultural practices are universal, by laying out a failed analogy: cultural practices that might seem to reflect a universal notion of 'life crisis', but in fact do not. She received thirty points, the highest possible total, for her answer.

The assignment of situational meanings may involve multiple indexical links, and is interactionally accomplished (Ochs 1996). What are the differences between this midterm, which Gloria participated in quite successfully, and the verbal analogy test that gave Gloria so much trouble? Both are 'tests', and both require adherence to a fairly narrow and technical use of language. Both require analogical thinking. The difference lies partly within the way the test taker acquires knowledge of the acceptable objects and relations that constitute the analogy. In effect, the class lectures, interactions with the instructor and students, and the class text provide the workshop within which the student can forge that knowledge. The rules of the discourse are part of the learning enterprise, whether or not these are explicitly labeled. The verbal-analogy test, on the other hand, requires that the student already know the appropriate objects and relations that constitute the targeted analogies. They must recognize and be able to engage the intended communicative practice with no prompting.

Conclusion

In the discourse of standardized tests, whatever dialogic interaction exists is sharply limited by the differences in power and control between the two 'interlocutors'. This difference in power and control stems from the larger activity system of which a particular testing incident is a part. The individual activity of taking the SAT and the roles participants play within it can only be fully understood in terms of their relations to the whole activity system, and the wider sociocultural setting. Although I will not be able here to specify fully the ways that standardized test results shape attitudes toward schooling, aptitude, life chances and matriculation at college, the existing literature documents amply the profoundly important role played by tests like the SAT (e.g. Zwick 2002).

In viewing the test item as a site for complex interpretive interactions, we must keep in mind this power differential. There is good reason to think that test takers do subjectively experience their lack of control over the pertinent discourse norms as anxiety. This may contribute to what Claude Steele (Steele and Aronson 1995) has identified as a source of differential performance: the anxiety that one's performance will be interpreted in light of expectations due to the fact that one is a member of a group which has historically performed below the norm. Steele's experimental results (that members of minority groups do worse on tests when asked to identify their ethnic background) are compelling. We can augment these with examples like the ones below, a protocol of a graduate student at a major research university, which provides an unprompted glimpse into this subjective experience. (Like the students described above, this student was not involved in taking an actual test, but had agreed to think aloud as she solved the problems in my office.)

Example 11.5:

YAWN : BOREDOM : :

DREAM: SLEEP, ANGER : MADNESS, SMILE : AMUSEMENT, FACE : EXPRESSION, IMPATIENT : REBELLION

STUDENT So yawn, boredom. So I'm thinking about myself that I'm yawning. And I'm trying to figure out how that goes with bored. Well, I yawn when I'm bored. So I dream when I sleep. . . . Go through the other ones, anger – madness, no, smile – amusement, could be, face – expression, no for some reason, impatient – rebellion, no cause those are like opposites.
For some reason I'll say smile – amusement. Because it's something to do with the face. And the reason I say dream – sleep is because it could be either A or C. The reason I think it's C is more like it is that with smile you're showing a feeling, and yawn is also a feeling.

Now wait a minute though, it's not really a feeling, it's an action. This is crazy. Dream when you're asleep, well, if you're bored sometimes you yawn, if you're sleepin' sometimes you dream. If you're amused, sometimes you smile.

Well, now I'm thinking it's A. If you're sleeping, sometimes you dream, but not necessarily. Well, if you're bored, you could sometimes yawn.

My first thing is well, I want to go look at the answers, to see how close I am to normal. And that's another stress that I'm feeling. That's another stress that I'm feeling, it's like, ya know, it's because I've been given these things a lot and I'm not real good with these and I'm real nervous thinking 'I know she's not gonna test.. this is not a test, 'cause I don't score good on tests, but, I'm still nervous because this is gonna put me again in the remedial level again, and I'm really aware of this because I've been through the university, and I know these things tend to be used for . . .'

On a later item this student finds the answer and feels certain it's correct. She continues:

And I think oh good, I didn't spend as much time on this one, see that's always in the back of my mind, they're testing me. What are they testing for, how am I gonna rate? See, that's something testing does to us. If you're not a person who scores high on these tests you're really subconsciously aware of that all the time.

As Steele has remarked, the presence of such anxiety in members of minority groups detracts from valid inferences about their abilities. The same can be said about the distinction I propose between two ways of construing the domain of verbal analogies. I have claimed that in these few examples it is possible to see test takers failing to use the distinction I identified above. In my view the examples demonstrate the failed interaction between test taker and the textual offering of the test maker. They do not speak decisively to the question of Danielle's and Gloria's abilities to think analogically. The psychometric approach to the process of construct validation relies, as stated above, on correlations within groups and across different criteria. This gives short shrift to the reasons behind performance on particular items. And this is where I think detailed work on the sociocultural and linguistic nature of interaction with test items may reveal systematic intergroup differences.

Is a significant portion of the 'achievement gap' due to differential access to linguistic practices privileged by standardized tests? The answer is unknown. It is likely that ultimately explanations of group differences will be complex functions of numerous factors. Exploration of these will require divergent methods as well as a commitment to rejecting simple and monolithic answers, no matter how convenient. It is interesting to note that in the past year or so the College Board has announced plans to end the practice of using analogy test items on the SAT, while at the same time the use of high-stakes tests at the K-12 level has skyrocketed. There is much research to be done in this area. In keeping with the theme of this volume, I will close with a sociological injunction from four decades ago:

Because they are the historical products of human activity, all socially constructed universes change, and the change is brought about by the concrete actions of human beings. . . Reality is socially defined. But the definitions are always embodied, that is, concrete individuals and groups of individuals serve as definers of reality. To understand the state of the socially constructed universe at any given time. . .one must understand the social organization that permits the definers to do their defining. Put a little crudely, it is essential to keep pushing questions about the historically available conceptualizations of reality from the abstract 'What?' to the sociologically concrete 'Says who?'. Berger and Luckmann 1967: 116

Notes

1. The largest testing companies have the resources to conduct tests of 'differential item functioning' (DIF). This effort identifies items that are statistically divergent for different groups – items that one group does better or worse on than its overall mean would predict it should do. This still does not ensure that there are not effects of language or culture. Individual items can be affected by different factors, but as long they do not depart significantly from the predicted value, given the group statistics, these items will not be culled by a DIF sweep. Refined statistical methods for detecting DIF have proliferated (see e.g. Berk (1982) for earlier foundations) but the conceptual problems of explanation for DIF persist.
2. For an extended discussion of various hypotheses about the sources of differential performance on standardized tests see O'Connor (1989) and the reviews cited there.
3. The examples and discussion in this section rely in many places on my portion of a previously published, co-authored chapter on discourse analysis. In that chapter (Gee, Michaels and O'Connor 1992), I used the data included below to exemplify one kind of discourse analysis, not primarily to make a point about differential performance on tests. Several paragraphs are taken almost verbatim from that text and Danielle's and Gloria's transcripts are unchanged.
4. In both cases, test maker and test taker, it is likely that this distinction will remain inchoate and unexamined at best.
5. It may be that the real-world significance of this particular type of test item has peaked: Freedle (2002) reports that as the analogy (and antonym) items were among the most difficult for minority test takers, in the absence of a solid account of the reasons for their difficulty, they will be dropped in future SATs.

References

Akinnaso, N. F. (1982). The Consequences of Literacy in Pragmatic and Theoretical Perspectives. *Anthropology and Education Quarterly.* 12: 163–200.

(1992). Schooling, Language and Knowledge in Literate and Non-Literate Societies. *Comparative Studies in Society and History.* 34 (1): 68–109.

Alexander, K., Cook, M. and McDill, E. (1978). Curriculum Tracking and Educational Stratification: Some Further Evidence. *American Sociological Review.* 43: 47–68.

Alexander, K. and McDill, E. (1976). Selection and Allocation within Schools: Some Causes and Consequences of Curriculum Placement. *American Sociological Review.* 41: 969–980.

Allington, R. (1980). Teacher Interruption Behavior during Primary-Grade Oral Reading. *Journal of Educational Psychology.* 72(3): 371–377.

Alpert, J. (1974). Teacher Behavior Across Ability Groups: A Consideration of the Mediation of Pygmalion Effects. *Journal of Educational Psychology.* 66: 348–353.

Altick, R. (1957). *The English Common Reader: A Social History of the Mass Reading Public 1800–1900.* Chicago: University of Chicago Press.

Alwin, D. F. and Otto, L. B. (1977). High School Context Effects on Aspirations. *Sociology of Education.* 53: 259–273.

Apple, M. (1979). *Ideology and Curriculum.* London: Routledge & Kegan Paul.

Applebee, A. (1976). *The Child's Concept of Story.* Chicago: University of Chicago Press.

Austin, J. L. (1962). *How to do Things with Words.* Oxford: Clarendon Press.

Austin, M. and Morrison, C. (1963). *The First R: The Harvard Report on Reading in Elementary School.* New York: Macmillan.

Barnes, D. (1976). *From Communication to Curriculum.* Harmondsworth, Middlesex: Penguin.

Barnes, S. B., Gutfreund, M., Satterly D., and Wells, C. G. (1983). Characteristics of Adult Speech which Predict Children's Language Development. *Journal of Child Language*. 10.

Barr, R., (1975). Grouping and Pacing. *School Review*. 83: 479–498.

Barton, D., and Hamilton, M. (1998). *Local Literacies*. London: Routledge.

Baugh, J. (2000). *Beyond Ebonics: Linguistic Pride and Racial Prejudice*. London and New York: Oxford University Press.

Bellack, A. (1966). *The Language of the Classroom*. New York: Teachers College Press.

Bereiter, C., and Engleman, S. (1966). *Teaching Disadvantaged Children in the Pre-School*. Englewood Cliffs, NJ: Prentice Hall.

Berger, P.l., and Luckmann, T. (1967). *The Social Construction of Reality: Treatise in the Sociology of Knowledge*. New York: Anchor.

Berk, R.A. (ed.) (1982). *Handbook of Methods for Detecting Test Bias*. Baltimore, MD: The Johns Hopkins University Press.

Berliner, D. C. (1976). Impediments to the Study of Teacher Effectiveness. *Journal of Teacher Education*. 27(1): 5–13.

Berliner, D. C., and Tikunoff, W. (1976). The California Beginning Teacher Evaluation Study: Overview of the Ethnographic Study. *Journal of Teacher Education*. 27(1): 24–30.

Bernstein, B. (1971). *Class, Codes and Control*. Vol. I: *Theoretical Studies towards a Sociology of Language*. London: Routledge and Kegan Paul.
(1973). *Class Codes and Control*. Vol. II. London: Routledge and Kegan Paul.

Bex, T., and Watts, R. J. (1999). *Standard English: the Widening Debate*. London, New York: Routledge.

Bigler, E. (1998). *American Conversations: Puerto Ricans, White Ethnics, and Multicultural Education*. Philadelphia: Temple University Press.

Blommaert, J. (2005). *Discourse*. Cambridge: Cambridge University Press.

Bloom, A. (1981). *The Linguistic Shaping of Thought*. Hillsdale NJ: Lawrence Erlbaum.

Bloom, B. S., ed. (1956). *Taxonomy of Educational Objectives. Handbook 1: Cognitive Domain*. New York: David McKay.

Bloomfield, L. (1933). *Language*. New York: Henry Holt.

Bloomfield, L., and Barnhart, C. (1961). *Let's Read, a Linguistic Approach*. Detroit: Wayne State University Press.

Boggs, S. T. (1972). The Meaning of Questions and Narratives to Hawaiian Children. In *Functions of Language in the Classroom*. C. Cazden, V. John, and D. Hymes, eds., pp. 299–327. New York: Teachers College Press.

Bolinger, D. L., ed. (1972). *Intonation*. Harmondsworth, Middlesex: Penguin.

Borg, W. R. (1966). *Ability Grouping in the Public Schools*. Madison, WI: Dembar Educational Research Services.

Boudon, R. (1974). *Education, Opportunity, and Social Inequality*. New York: John Wiley.

Bourdieu, P. (1977). Cultural Reproduction and Social Reproduction. In *Power and Ideology in Education*. J. Karabel and A. H. Hasley, eds., pp. 487–510. Oxford: Oxford University Press.

(1991). *Language and Symbolic Power.* Trans. G. Raymond and M. Adamson. Cambridge, Malden MA: Polity Press.

Bourdieu, P., and Passeron, J-C. (1977). Reproduction. In *Education, Society, Culture*. Trans. R. Nice. London and Beverley Hills: Sage.

Bowles, S. (1977). Unequal Education and the Reproduction of Social Division of Labour. Reprinted in *Power and Ideology in Education*. J. Karabel and A. H. Hasley, eds., pp. 137–152. Oxford: Oxford University Press.

Brandt, D. (1990). *Literacy as Involvement: The Acts of Writers, Readers, and Texts*. Carbondale and Edwardsville: Southern Illinois University Press.

Bremme, D. W., and Erickson, F. (1977). Relationships Among Verbal and Nonverbal Classroom Behaviors. *Theory into Practice*. 16(3): 153–161.

Brophy, J., and Good, T. (1974). *Teacher–Student Relationships. Causes and Consequences*. New York: Holt, Rinehart and Winston.

Bruner, J. (1957). Going Beyond the Information Given. In *Contemporary Approaches to Cognition*. J. Bruner, et al., pp. 41–69. Cambridge, MA: Harvard University Press.

Burton, W. (1956). *Reading in Child Development*. New York: Bobbs-Merrill.

Calhoun, D. (1973). *The Intelligence of a People*. Princeton, NJ: Princeton University Press.

Campbell, D. R. (1981). 'Going for the Answers' with Questions in a Philippine Elementary Mathematics Classroom. Unpublished Doctoral Dissertation, School of Education, Stanford University.

Carew, J., and Lightfoot, S. (1978). *First Grade: A Multifaceted View of Teachers and Children*. Final Report Grant No. 90-C-256. Office of Child Development.

Carney, G. and Winograd, P. (1979). Schemata for Reading Comprehension Performance. Technical Report #120, Center for the Study of Reading, Champain, Illinois.

Cazden, C. (1970). The Neglected Situation of Child Language Research and Education. In *Language and Poverty: Perspectives on a Theme*. F. Williams, ed., pp. 81–101. Chicago: Rand McNally College.

(2001). *Classroom Discourse: The Language of Teaching and Learning*. 2nd edition. Portsmouth: Heinemann.

Cazden, C., John, V., and Hymes, D. (1972/85). *Functions of Language in the Classroom*. New York: Teachers College Press.

Chafe, W. (1972). Discourse Structure and Human Knowledges. In *Language Comprehension and the Acquisition of Knowledge*. In J. B. Carrol and R. O. Freedle eds. Washington, DC: V. H. Winston.

(1979). The Flow of Thought and the flow of Language. In *Discourse and Syntax*. T. Givon, ed. New York: Academic Press.

(1980). The Deployment of Consciousness in the Production of Narrative. In *The Pear Stories: Cognitive and Linguistic Aspects of Narrative Production*. W. Chafe, ed., pp. 9–50. Norwood, NJ: Ablex.
(1988). Punctuation and the Prosody of Written Language. *Written Communication*. 5: 395–426.
Chafe, W., and Danielewicz, J. (1987). Properties of Spoken and Written Language. In *Comprehending Oral and Written Language*. R. Horowitz and S. J. Samuels eds., pp. 83–113. San Fransisco: Academic Press.
Cherry-Wilkinson, L. (1982). *Communicating in the Classroom*. New York: Academic Press.
Cherry-Wilkinson, L. ed. (1981). A Sociolinguistic Approach to the Study of Teacher Expectations. *Discourse Processes*. 1: 373–394.
Cicourel, A. V. (1973). *Cognitive Sociology*. Harmondsworth, Middlesex: Penguin.
Cicourel, A. V., and Kitsuse, J. (1963). *The Educational Decision Makers*. New York: Bobbs-Merrill.
Cicourel, A. V., and Mehan, H. (1984). Universal Development, Stratifying Practices and Status Attainment. *Research and Social Stratification Mobility*. 4.
Cipolla, C. (1969). *Literacy and Development in the West*. Harmondsworth, Middlesex: Penguin.
Clark, H. H., and Haviland, S. E. (1974a). What's New? Acquiring New Information as a Process of Comprehension. *Journal of Verbal Learning and Verbal Behavior*. 13, 512–521.
(1974b). Psychological Processes as Linguistic Explanation. In *Explaining Linguistic Phenomena*. D. Cohen, ed. pp. 91– 124. Washington: V. H. Winston
Clay, M., and Imlach, C. (1971). Puncture, Pitch, and Stress as Reading Behavior Variables. *Journal of Verbal Learning and Verbal Behavior*. 10: 33–39.
Cochran-Smith, M. (1984). *The Making of a Reader*. Norwood, NJ: Ablex.
Cole, M., Gay, J., Glick, J., and Sharp, D. (1971). *The Cultural Context of Learning and Thinking*. New York: Basic Books.
Cole P., and Morgan, J. P. eds. (1975). *Syntax and Semantics* Vol. III, *Speech Acts*. New York: Academic Press.
Coles, G. (2000). *Misreading Reading: The Bad Science that Hurts Children*. Portsmouth, NH: Heinemann.
Collins, J. (1982). Discourse Style, Differential Treatment, and Social Inequality. *Journal of Reading Behavior*.
(1995). Literacy and Literacies. *Annual review of Anthropology*. 24: 75–93.
(1996). Socialization to text. In *Natural histories of discourse*. M. Silverstein and G. Urban, eds., pp. 203–228. Chicago: University of Chicago Press.
(2003). The Reading Wars in situ. *Pragmatics*. 13(1): 85–100.

Collins, J. and Blot, R. K. (2003). *Literacy and Literacies: Texts, Power and Identities*. Cambridge and New York: Cambridge University Press.

Cook-Gumperz, J. (1978/82). Instructional Talk. In the School-Home Ethnography Project (SHEP) Final Report to the National Institute of Education.

(2005). The Pragmatics of Literacy. In *The Handbook of Pragmatics*. J. Verschuren, ed., pp. 1–19. Amsterdam and Philadelphia: John Benjamins.

Cook-Gumperz, J., and Green J. (1984). A Sense of Story. In *Coherence in Written and Spoken Discourse*. Vol. XII. *Advances in Discourse Processes*. D. Tannen, ed., pp. 201– 218. Norwood, NJ: Ablex.

Cook-Gumperz, J., and Gumperz, J. J. (1978). Context in Children's Speech. In *The Development of Communication*. N. Waterson and C. Snow, eds. New York: John Wiley.

(1981). From Oral to Written Culture: The Transition to Literacy. In *Writing: The Nature, Development, and Teaching of Written Communication*. Vol. 1. *Variation in Writing: Functional and Linguistic–Cultural Differences*. M. F. Whiteman ed., pp., 89–136. Hillsdale, NJ: Lawrence Erlbaum Associates.

(1982). Communicative Competence in Educational Perspectives. In *Communicating in the Classroom*. L. Cherry-Wilkinson, ed. New York: Academic Press.

Cook-Gumperz, J., Gumperz J.J., and Simons, H. A. (1981). *Language and School and Home*. Final Report to the National Institute of Education. Washington DC.

Corpuz, P. (1970). *Education for National Development: New Directions, New Patterns*. Makati, Rizal, Philippines: Presidential Commission to Survey Philippine Education.

Cox, B. E., Shanahan, T., and Sulzby, E. (1990). Good and Poor Elementary Readers' use of Cohesion in Writing. *Reading Research Quarterly*. 25(1), 47–64.

Cremin, L. (1962). *The Transformation of the School*. New York: Random House.

(1989). *Public Education and its Discontents*. New York: Random House.

Cruickshank, D. R. (1976). Syntheses of Selected Recent Research on Teacher Effects. *Journal of Teacher Education*. 27(1): 57–60.

Dalton, S. S., and Tharp, R. G. (2002). Standards for pedagogy: Research, Theory and Practice. In *Learning for Life in the 21st century: Sociocultural Perspectives on the Future of Education*. C. G. Wells and G. Claxton, eds. Oxford: Blackwell.

Deutsch, M., ed. (1967). *The Disadvantaged Child*. New York: Basic Books.

Dickinson, D. ed. (1994). *Bridges to Literacy*. Oxford: Basil Blackwell.

Dore, J., Gearhart, M., and Newman, D. (1978). The Structure of Nursery School Conversation. In *Children's Language*. Vol. I. K. Nelson, ed. New York: Gardner Press.

Douglas, J. D., ed. (1970). *Understanding Everyday Life: Toward the Reconstruction of Sociological Knowledge*. Chicago: Aldine.

Downing J., and Ollila, F. (1975). Cultural Differences in Children's Concepts of Reading and Writing. *British Journal of Educational Psychology*. 54: 312–316.

Dreeben, R. (1968). *On What is Learned in School*. Reading MA: Addison-Wesley.

Dunkin, M. J., and Biddle, B. J. (1974). *The Study of Teaching*. New York: Holt, Rinehart and Winston.

Duranti, A. and Goodwin, C. (1992). *Rethinking Context: Language as an Interactive Phenomenon*. Cambridge and New York: Cambridge University Press.

Durrell, D. (1940). *Improvement on Basic Reading Abilities*. New York: World Book Company.

Eckert, P. (2000) *Linguistic Variation as Social Practice*. Oxford and Malden: Blackwell.

Eder, D. (1979). Stratification Within the Classroom: The Formation and Maintenance of Ability Groups. Unpublished Doctoral Dissertation, University of Wisconsin, Madison.

Edwards, D. (1958). Reading from the Child's Point of View. *Elementary English*. 35: 239–241.

Eerdmans, S. L., Prevignano, C. L., and Thibault P. J. (2003). *Language and Interaction: Discussions with John J Gumperz*. Amsterdam and Philadelphia: John Benjamins.

Ehri, L. (1979). Linguistic Insight. Threshold of Reading Acquisition. In *Reading Research: Advance in Theory and Practice*. Vol. I. New York: Academic Press.

Erickson, F. (1976). Gatekeeping Encounters: A Social Selection Process. In *Anthropology and the Public Interest*. P. Sanday, ed., pp. 111–145. New York: Academic Press.

(1977). Some Approaches to Inquiry in School/Community Ethnography. *Anthropology and Education Quarterly*. 8(2): 58–69.

(1982). Classroom Discourse as Improvisation: Relationship between Academic Task Structure and Social Participant Structure in Lessons. In *Communicating in the Classroom*. L. Cherry-Wilkinson, ed., pp. 153–181. New York: Academic Press.

(2004). *Talk and Social Theory*. Cambridge and Malden MA: Polity Press.

Erickson, F., and Mohatt, G. (1982). Cultural Organization of Participant Structures in Two Classrooms of Indian Students. In *Doing the Ethnography of Schooling: Educational Anthropology in Action*. G. Spindler, ed., pp. 132–174. New York: Holt, Rinehart and Winston.

Erickson, F. and Schultz, J. (1981). When is a Context? Some Issues and Methods in the Analysis of Social Competence. In *Ethnography and Language in Educational Settings*. J. Green and C. Wallat, eds., pp. 147–160. Norwood, NJ: Ablex.

Ervin-Tripp, S. (1980). Speech Acts, Social Meaning, and Social Learning. In *Language: Social and Psychological Perspectives*. H. Giles, W. P. Robinson, and P. M. Smith, eds. Oxford: Pergamon Press.

Fairclough, N. (1996). *The Technologisation of Discourse in Texts and Practices*. S. R. Caldas-Coulthard and M. Coulthard, eds., pp. 71– 83. London: Routledge.

Fass, P. (1989). *The Outside In: Minorities in American Education*. London and New York: Oxford University Press.

Feinberg, W. (1983). *Understanding Education. Towards a Reconsideration of Educational Enquiry*. Cambridge: Cambridge University Press.

Fillmore, C. J. (1975). Santa Cruz Lectures on Deixis. Lecture notes, Indiana Linguistics Club, Indiana University, Bloomington, IN.

(1982). Ideal Readers and Real Readers. In *Proceedings of the Georgetown Round Table of Language and Linguistics; Analyzing Discourse: Text and Talk*. D. Tannen ed. Norwood NJ: Ablex.

Finnegan, R. (1981). Literacy and Literature. In *Universals in Human Thought*. B. Lloyd and J. Gay, eds., pp. 234–255. Cambridge: Cambridge University Press.

Fischer C., Hout, M., Jankowski, M. S., Lucas, S. R., Swidler, A., and Voss, K. (1996). *Inequality by Design: Cracking the Bell Curve Myth*. Princeton, NJ: Princeton University Press.

Flanders, N. A. (1970). *Analyzing Teacher Behavior*. Reading, MA: Addison-Wesley.

Florio, S. (1978). Learning How to Go to School: An Ethnography of Interaction in a Kindergarten/First Grade Classroom. Unpublished doctoral dissertation, Graduate School of Education, Harvard University.

Fowler, R., Hodge, R., Kress, C. and Trew, T. (1979). *Language and Control*. Boston, MA: Routledge and Kegan Paul.

Freedle, R. (2002). Correcting the SAT's Ethnic and Social Bias: a Method for Estimating SAT Scores. *Harvard Educational Review*. 72(3): 1–43.

Furet, F. and Ozouf, J. (1983). *Reading and Writing: Literacy in France from Calvin to Jules Ferry*. Cambridge: Cambridge University Press.

Gage, N. L. (1978). *The Scientific Basis of the Art of Teaching*. New York: Teaching College Press.

Gall, M. D. (1970). The Use of Questions in Teaching. *Review of Educational Research*. 40(5): 707–720.

Gallas, K. (1994). *The Languages of Learning: How Children Talk, Write, Dance, Draw, and Sing their Understanding of the World*. New York: Teachers College Press.

(1995). *Talking their Way into Science: Hearing Children's Questions and Theories, Responding with Curricula*. New York: Teachers College Press.

Gamoran, A. (1987). Organization, Instruction, and the Effects of Ability Grouping. *Review of Educational Research*. 66(4): 341–345.

Garfinkel, H. (1967). *Studies in Ethnomethodology.* Engelwood Cliffs, NJ: Prentice-Hall.

Garfinkel, H., and Sacks, H. (1970). On Formal Structures of Practical Actions. In *Theoretical Sociology: Perspectives and Developments.* J. C. McKinney and E. A. Tiryakian, eds., pp. 337–366. New York: Appleton-Century-Crofts.

Gee, J. P. (1996). *Social Linguistics and Literacies: Ideology in Discourses.* London: Taylor and Francis.

Gentner, D. (1977). Children's Performance on a Spatial Analogies Task. *Child Development.* 48: 1034–1039.

Giddens, A. (1982). *Central Problems of Sociology Theory.* California: Campus Books.

Glass, G. (1968). Students' Misconceptions Concerning their Reading. *The Reading Teacher.* 21: 765–768.

Glazer, N. and Moynihan, D. (1963). *Beyond the Melting Pot.* Cambridge, MA: MIT Press.

Glucksberg, S., Krauss, R., and Weisberg, E. (1966). Referential Communication in Nursery School Children. *Journal of Exceptional Child Psychology.* 3: 333–342.

Goelman, H., Oberg, A., and Smith, F. eds. (1984). *Awakening to Literacy.* Exeter, NH: Heinemann.

Goldberg, M., Passow, H. and Justman, J. (1966). *The Effects of Ability Grouping.* New York: Teachers College Press.

Goldman, S. R. (1997). Learning from Text: Reflections on the Past and Suggestions for the Future. *Discourse Processes.* 23: 357–398.

Goldman, S. R. and Murray, J. D. (1992). Knowledge of Connectors as Cohesion Devices in Text: a Comparative Study of Native-English and English-as-a-Second-Language Speakers. *Journal of Educational Psychology.* 84: 504–515.

Goodwin, C. (1981). *Conversational Organization: Interaction Between Speakers and Hearers.* New York: Academic Press.

Goodwin, M. H. (1990). *He-Said-She-Said: Talk As Social Organization Among Black Children.* Bloomington: Indiana University Press.

(2001). Participation. In *Key Terms in Anthropology* A. Duranti ed., pp. 172–175. Oxford, Malden MA: Blackwell Publishers.

Goody, E. N. (1978). Towards a Theory of Questions. In *Questions and Politeness: Strategies in Social Interaction.* E. N. Goody, ed., pp. 17–43. New York: Cambridge University Press.

(1983). *From Craft to Industry.* New York: Cambridge University Press.

Goody, J. (1977). *The Domestication of the Savage Mind.* Cambridge: Cambridge University Press.

Goody, J. ed. (1968) *Literacy in Traditional Societies.* Cambridge: Cambridge University Press.

Goody, J., and Watt, I. (1968). The Consequences of Literacy. In *Literacy in Traditional Societies.* J. Goody, ed., pp. 27–58. Cambridge: Cambridge University Press.

Graff, H. (1979). *The Literacy Myth: Literacy and Social Structure in a Nineteenth Century City.* New York: Academic Press.

Graff, H. ed. (1981). *Literacy and Social Development in the West: A Reader.* Cambridge: Cambridge University Press.

Graham, P. (1980). Whither the Equality of Educational Opportunity? *Daedalus.* 109 (3): 115–132.

Green, G. M., and Morgan, J. L. (1981). Writing Ability as a Function of the Appreciation of Differences between Oral and Written Communication. In *Writing*, Vol. II. *Process, Development and Communication.* C. H. Fredericksen and J. F. Dominic, eds., pp. 177–187. Hillsdale, NJ: Lawrence Erlbaum.

Green J., and Wallat, C. (1981). *Ethnography and Language in Educational Settings.* Norwood, NJ: Ablex.

Greenfield, P. M. (1972). Oral and Written Language: The Consequences for Cognitive Development in Africa, the US, and England. In *Language and Speech.* 15: 169–177.

Grice, H. P. (1971). Utterer's Meaning, Sentence Meaning and Word Meanings. In *The Philosophy of Language.* J. R. Searle, ed. Oxford: Oxford University Press.

(1989). Utterer's Meaning, Sentence Meaning and Word Meanings. In *Studies. The Way of Words.* Cambridge, MA and London: Harvard University Press.

Griffin, P., and Humphrey, F. (1978). Talk and Task at Lesson Time. In *The Study of Children's Functional Language and Education in the Early Years.* Final Report to the Canergie Corporation of New York. R. Shuy and P. Griffin, eds. Arlington, VA: Center for Applied Linguistics.

Griffin, P. and Mehan, H. (1981). Sense and Ritual in Classroom Discourse. In *Conversational Routine: Exploration in Standardized Communication Situations and Prepatterned Speech.* F. Coulmas, ed. The Hague: Mouton.

Groff, P. J. (1962). A survey of Basic Reading Group Practices. *The Reading Teacher.* 15: 232–235.

Gumperz, J. J. (1968). The Speech Community. In *International Encyclopedia of the Social Sciences.* D. Sills, ed., pp. 381–386. New York: Macmillan.

(1981). Conversational Inference and Classroom Learning. In *Ethnography and Language in Educational Settings.* J. Green and C. Wallat, eds., pp. 3–23. Norwood, NJ: Ablex.

(1982a). *Discourse Strategies.* Cambridge: Cambridge University Press.

(1982b). The Linguistic Basis of Communicative Competence. In *Georgetown University Round Table on Language and Linguistics 1981.* D. Tannen ed., pp. 323–334. Washington, DC: Georgetown University Press.

(1990). Speech Community in Interactional Perspective. In *La Communaute en Parole: Communication, Consensus, Ruptures.* H. Parret, ed. Brussels: Mardarga Publishing House.

Gumperz, J. J., and Cook-Gumperz, J. (1979). Beyond Ethnography: Some Uses of Sociolinguistics for Understanding Classroom Environments. Paper Presented at the Annual Meeting of the American Educational Research Association, San Francisco.

(2005). Language Standardization and the Complexities of Communicative Practice. In *Complexities: Beyond Nature and Nurture*. S. Mackinnon and S. Silverman. eds., pp. 268–288. Chicago: University of Chicago Press.

(in press). Style and Identity in Interactional sociolinguistics. In *Social Identity and Communicative Style: an alternative approach to linguistic variability*. P. Auer and W. Kallmeyer eds. Berlin: Mouton de Gruyter.

Gumperz, J. J. and Herasimchuk, E. (1975). A Conversational Analysis of Social Meaning: a Study of Classroom Interaction. In *Sociocultural Dimensions of Language Use*. M. Sanches and B. Blount, eds., pp. 81–115. New York: Academic Press.

Gumperz, J. J., and Hymes, D. H. (1972/86). *Directions in Sociolinguistics*. Oxford and New Malden, MA: Blackwell.

Gumperz, J. J., Kaltman, H. and O'Connor, M. C. (1984). Thematic Cohesion in Spoken and Written Discourse. In *Coherence in Spoken and Written Discourse*. D. Tannen, ed., pp. 3–20. Norwood, NJ: Ablex.

Gumperz, J. J. and Levinson, S. C. (1996). *Re-thinking Linguistic Relativity*. Cambridge: Cambridge University Press.

Gumperz, J. J., and Tannen, D. (1979). Individual and Social Differences in Language Use. In *Individual Differences in Language Ability and Language Behavior*. C. Fillmore, D. Kempler, and W. Wang, eds., pp. 305–325. New York: Academic Press.

Gundlach, R., McLane, J., Stott, F., and McNamee, G. (1985). Social Foundations of Children's Writing Development. In *Children's Early Writing Development*. M. Farr ed. Norwood, NJ: Ablex.

Guthrie, G. M., and Azores, F. (1968). Philippine Interpersonal Behavior Patterns. In *Modernization: Its Impact in the Philippines*. Vol. III. W. Bello and A. de Guzman, eds., pp. 3–63. Quezon City, Philippines: Ateneo de Manila University Press.

Hacking, I. (1999). *The Social Construction of What?* Cambridge, MA: Harvard University Press.

Halliday, M. A. K.(1967). Notes on Transitivity and Theme in English: Part 2. *Journal of Linguistics* 3: 177–274.

(1968). Notes on Transitivity and Theme in English: Part 3. *Journal of Linguistics* 4: 179–215.

(1975). *Learning How to Mean*. London: Arnold.

(1989). *Spoken and Written English*. Oxford: Oxford University Press.

Halliday, M. A. K., and Hasan, R. (1976). *Cohesion in English*. London: Longman.

Halsey, A. H. (1975). Sociology and the Equality Debate. *Oxford Review of Education*. 1(1): 9–73.

Handel, W. (1982). *Ethnomethodology: How People Make Sense*. Englewood Cliffs, NJ: Prentice-Hall.

Hanks, W. F. (1996). *Language and Communicative Practice*. Boulder, CO: Westview Press.

Hauser, R. M., Sewell, W. H., and Alwin, D. F. (1976). High School Effects on Achievement. In *Schooling and Achievement in American Society*. W. H. Sewell, R. M. Hauser, and D. L. Featherman, eds., pp. 309–341. New York: Academic Press.

Hawkins, M. L. (1966). Mobility of Students in Reading Groups. *The Reading Teacher*. 20: 136–140.

Heath, A. (1981). *Social Mobility*. London: Fontana.

Heath, S. B. (1981). Toward an Ethnohistory of Writing in American Education. In *Variation in Writing: Functional and Linguistic Cultural Differences*. M. Whiteman, ed., pp. 25–46. Baltimore MD: Lawrence Erlbaum.

(1982a). Questioning at Home and at School: A Comparative Study. In *Doing the Ethnography of Schooling: Educational Anthropology in Action*. G. Spindler, ed., pp. 102–131. New York: Holt, Rinehart and Winston.

(1982b). What No Bedtime Story Means: Narrative Skills at Home and at School. *Language in Society*. 11: 49–76.

(1983). *Ways with Words*. Cambridge: Cambridge University Press.

Heider, E., and Cazden, C. (1971). Style and Accuracy of Verbal Communication Within and Between Social Classes. *Journal of Personality and Social Psychology*. 18(1): 33–47.

Hernstein, R. and Murray, C. (1994). *The Bell Curve: Intelligence and Class Structure in the United States*. New York: Free Press.

Hess, R. D., and Shipman, V. (1966). Early Experience and the Socialization of Cognitive Modes in Children. *Child Development*. 36: 869–886.

Hewitt, R. (1986). *Black Talk, White Talk* Cambridge: Cambridge University Press.

Heyns, B. (1974). Social Selection and Stratification Within School. *American Journal of Sociology*. 6: 1434–1451.

Hill, C. and Larsen, E. (2000). *Children and Reading Tests*. Stanford, CT: Ablex.

Himmelfarb, G. (1984). *The Idea of Poverty*. New York: Alfred Knopf.

Hoggart, R. (1958). *The Uses of Literacy*. Harmondsworth Middlesex: Penguin.

Holt, J. C. (1967). *Children Fail*. New York: Dell.

Hymes, D. (1971). On Linguistic Theory, Communicative Competence, and the Education of Disadvantaged Children. In *Anthropological Perspectives on Education*. M. Wax, S. Diamond, and F. Gearing, eds., pp. 51–66. New York: Basic Books.

(1972). Introduction. In *Functions of Language in the Classroom*. C. Cazden, V. John, and D. Hymes, eds., pp. xii–xvii. New York: Teachers College Press.

(1974). *Foundations in Sociolinguistics: An ethnographic Approach*. Philadelphia: University of Pennsylvania Press.

(1980). *Language in Education: Ethnolinguistic Essays*. Washington DC: Center for Applied Linguistics.

(1982). *In Vain I Tried to Tell You*. Philadelphia: University of Pennsylvania Press.

(1996). *Ethnography, Linguistics Narrative Inequality: Toward an Understanding of Voice*. London and Bristol: Taylor and Francis.

Illich, I. (1972). *Deschooling Society*. New York: Arrow Books.

Ivanic, R. (1997). *Writing and Identity*. Amsterdam: John Benjamins.

Jackson, B. (1964). *Streaming: An Educational System in Miniature*. London: Routledge and Kegan Paul.

Jencks, C. et al. (1998). The Black-White Test Score Gap. *The American Prospect*. 9: 41–43.

Jewson, J., Sachs, J., and Rohner, R. (1981). The effect of a Narrative Context on the Verbal Style of Middle-Class and Lower-Class Children. *Language in Society*. 10: 201–215.

Jocano, F. L. (1975). *Slum as a Way of Life: A Study of Coping Behavior in an Urban Environment*. Quezon City, Philippines: University of the Philippines Press.

Johns, J. M. C. (1974). Concepts of Reading in Good and Poor Readers. *Education*. 95: 58–60.

Johnson, M. C. (1979). *Discussion Dynamics: An Analysis of Classroom Teaching*. Rowley, MA: Newbury House.

Karabel J., and Halsey, A. H. (1977). *Power and Ideology in Education*. London: Oxford University Press.

Katz, M. (1971). *Class, Bureaucracy and Schools*. New York: Praeger Books.

Kay, P. (1977). Language Evolution and Speech Style. In *Sociocultural Dimensions of Language Change*. B. G. Blount and M. Sanches, eds., pp. 21–34. New York: Academic Press.

King, R. (1978). *All Things Bright and Beautiful? A Sociological Study of Infant Classrooms*. Chichester: John Wiley.

Kintsch, W., and van Dijk, T. A. (1978). Toward a model of text comprehension and production. *Psychological Review*. 85: 363–394.

Kleinman, G., Winograd, P., and Humphey, M. (1979). Prosody and Children's Phrasing of Sentences. Technical Report 123, Center for the Study of Reading, Champaign, Illinois.

Kohl, H. (1967). *Thirty-Six Children*. New York: New American Library.

Kozol, J. (1967). *Death at an Early Age*. Boston: Houghton Mifflin.

(1985). *Illiteracy in America*. Boston: Houghton Mifflin.

Krauss, R., and Glucksberg, S. (1969). The Development of Communication: Competence as a Function of Age. *Child Development*. 40: 255–261.

Krauss, R., Glucksberg, S., and Rotter, G. (1968). Communication Abilities as a Function of Age and Status. *Merrill-Palmer Quarterly*. 14: 161–173.

Kress, G. (1993). *Learning to Write*. London: Routledge.

Labov, W. (1972a). *Sociolinguistic Patterns*. Philadelphia: University of Pennsylvania Press.

(1972b). The Logic of Nonstandard English. In *Language in the Inner City: Studies in the Black English Vernacular*, pp. 201–240. Philadelphia: University of Pennsylvania Press.

(1982). Objectivity and Commitment in Linguistic Science: The Case of the Black English Trial in Ann Arbor. *Language and Society*. 11 (2): 165–201.

(1995). Can Reading Failure be Reversed? In *Literacy and African-American youth*. V. Gadsden and D. Wagner, eds., p. 39–68. Cresskill, NJ: Hampton Press.

Labov, W. and Fanshel, D. (1977). *Therapeutic Discourse: Psychotherapy as Conversation*. New York: Academic Press.

Labov, W. and Robins, C. (1969). A Note on the Relation of Reading Failure to Peer-Group Status in Urban Ghettos. *Florida FL Reporter*. 7(1): 544–547.

Langer, J. (1987). A Sociocognitive Perspective on Literacy. In *Language, Literacy and Culture: Issues of Society and Schooling*. J. Langer ed. Norwood, NJ: Ablex.

Laqueur, T. (1976a). The Cultural Origins of Popular Literacy in England: 1500–1850. *Oxford Review of Education*. 2: 255–275.

(1976b). *Religion and Respectability. Sunday Schools and English Working Class Culture 1780–1850*. New Haven: Yale University Press.

Lardiere, D. (1992). On the linguistic shaping of thought: Another response to Alfred Bloom. *Language in Society*. 21: 231–251.

Lareau, A. (2003). *Unequal Childhoods: Class, Race, and Family Life*. Berkeley: University of California Press.

Lave, J., and Wegner E. (1991). *Situated Learning: Legitimate Peripheral Participation*. Cambridge and New York: Cambridge University Press.

Lawless, R. (1969). *An Evaluation of Philippine Culture–Personality Research*. Monograph Series No. 3, Asian Center, University of the Philippines. Quezon City, Philippines: University of the Philippines Press.

Leacock, E. B. (1969). *Teaching and Learning in City Schools: A Comprehensive Study*. New York: Basic Books.

(1972). Abstract Versus Concrete Speech: A False Dichotomy. In *Functions of Language in the Classroom*. C. Cazden, V. John, and D. Hymes, eds., pp. 111–135. New York: Teachers College Press.

Leiter, K. (1980). *A Primer on Ethnomethodology*. New York: Oxford University Press.

Lemann, N. (1997). The Reading Wars. *The Atlantic Monthly*. 282: 128–134.

Levin, P. (1978). Questioning and Answering: A Cultural Analysis of Classroom Interrogative Encounters. Paper presented at the Annual Meeting of the American Anthropological Association, Los Angeles, November 1978.

Levine, K. (1982). Functional Literacy: Fond Illusions and False Economies. *Harvard Educational Review*. 52: 249–259.

Levinson, S. (1983). *Pragmatics*. Cambridge: Cambridge University Press.

Lewis, O. (1960). *Five Families: a Mexican Case Study in the Culture of Poverty*. New York: Basic Books.

Lockridge, K. (1981). Literacy in the West. In *Literacy and Social Development in the West*. H. Graff ed., pp. 183– 200. Cambridge and New York: Cambridge University Press.

Long, M. (2003). Ebonics, Language, and Power. In *Language and social identity*. R. Blot, ed. Westport, CT: Greenwood.

Lorch, R. F., Jr (1989). Text Signaling Devices and their Effects on Reading and Memory Processes. *Educational Psychology Review*. 1: 209–234.

Lou, Y., Abrami, P., Spence, J., Poulson, C., Chambers, B. and d'Appolonia, S. (1996). Within class grouping: A meta-analysis. *Review of Educational Research* 66(4): 423–458.

Luria, A. V. (1976). *Cognitive Development: Its Social and Cultural Foundations*. Cambridge, MA: Harvard University Press.

Lutz, F. W., and Ramsey, M. A. (1974). The Use of Anthropological Field Methods in Education. *Educational Researcher*. 3(10): 5–9.

Lynch, F. (1964). Lowland Philippine Values: Social Acceptance. In *Four Readings in Philippine Values*. F. Lynch, ed., pp. 1–21. Quezon City, Philippines: Ateneo de Manila University Press.

Lyons, J. (1977). *Semantics*. Vol. II. Cambridge: Cambridge University Press.

MacClendon, S. (1977). Cultural Presuppositions and Discourse Analysis: Patterns of Presupposition and Assertion of Information in Eastern Pomo and Russian. In *Anthropology and Linguistics, G. U. R. T. on Languages and Linguistics*. M. Saville-Troike, ed. Washington, DC: Georgetown University Press.

Macmillan. (1975). *Basic Reader*.

Manuel, J. L. (1974). Implementing Guidelines for the Policy on Bilingual Education. Department Order No. 25, Series 1974. Office of the Secretary, Department of Education and Culture, Republic of the Philippines.

Mason, G. (1967). Preschoolers' Concepts of Reading. *The Reading Teacher*. 21(2): 130–132.

Mattingly, I. G. (1972). Reading, the Linguistic Process, and Linguistic Awareness. In *Language by Ear and by Eye: The Relationship between Speech and Reading*. J. F. Kavanagh and I. G. Mattingly, eds. Cambridge, MA: MIT Press.

McDermott, R. P. (1974). Achieving School Failure: An Anthropological Approach to Illiteracy and Social Stratification. In *Education and Cultural Processes: Toward an Anthropology of Education*. G. Spindler, ed., pp. 82–118. New York: Holt, Rinehart and Winston.

(1976). Kids Make Sense: an Ethnographic Account of Interactional Management of Success and Failure in One First-Grade Classroom. Unpublished Doctoral Dissertation, Department of Anthropology, Stanford University.

(1978). Relating and Learning: an Analysis of Two Classroom Reading Groups. In *Linguistics and Reading*. R. Shuy, ed., pp. 253–276. Rowley, MA: Newbury House.

McDermott, R. P., Gospodinoff, K., and Aron, J. (1978). Criteria for an Ethnographically Adequate Description of Concerted Activities and Their Contexts. *Semiotica*. 244(3/4): 245–275.

McGraw Hill. (1973). *Comprehensive Test of Basic Skills*.

McNamee, C. D. (1979). The Social Interaction Origins of Narrative Skills. *The Quarterly Newsletter of the Laboratory of Comparative Human Cognition*. 1(4): 63–68.

Mehan, H., (1974a). Accomplishing Classroom Lessons. In *Language Use and School Performance*. A. Cicourel, Jennings, K., Jennings, S., Leiter, K., Mehan, H., Macay, R., and Roth, D. pp. 76–148. New York: Academic Press.

(1974b). Ethnomethodology and Education. In *Sociology of the School and Schooling*. Proceedings of the Second Annual Conference of the Sociology of Education Association. D. O'Shea, ed., pp. 141–198. Washington DC: National Institute of Education.

(1977). Viewpoint: Ethnography. In *Bilingual Education: Current Perspectives*. Vol. I: *Social Science*. Arlington, VA: Center for Applied Linguistics.

(1978). Structuring School Structure. *Harvard Educational Review*. 48 (1), 32–64.

(1979). *Learning Lessons: Social Organization in the Classroom*. Cambridge, MA: Harvard University Press.

(1996). The Construction of an LD Student: a Case Study of the Politics of Representation. In *Natural Histories of Discourse*. M. Silverstein and G. Urban eds., pp. 253–276. Chicago and London: University of Chicago Press.

Mehan, H., Hertweck, A., and Meihls, J. L. (1983). *Handicapping the Handicapped: Decision-Making in Students' Educational Careers*. Palo Alto CA: Stanford University Press.

Mehan, H. and Wood, H. (1975). *The Reality of Ethnomethodology*. New York: John Wiley.

Mercer, N. (1995). *The Guided Construction of Knowledge*. Clevedon UK: Multilingual Matters.

Merritt, M. (1982). Repeats and Reformulations in Primary Classrooms as Windows of the Nature of Talk Engagement. *Discourse Processes*. 5 (2): 127–145.

Michaels, S., and Cazden, C. (1986). Teacher-Child Collaboration as Oral Preparation for Literacy. *Acquisition of Literacy: Ethnographic Perspective*. B. Schieffen, ed. Norwood, NJ: Ablex.

Michaels, S. and Cook-Gumperz, J. (1979). A Study of Sharing Time with First Grade Students: Discourse Narratives in the Classroom. In *Proceedings of the Fifth Annual Meeting of the Berkeley Linguistic Society.* C. Chiarello, ed., pp. 647–660. Berkeley CA: Berkeley Linguistics Society.

Michaels, S., O'Connor, M. C., and Richards, J. (1994). Literacy as Reasoning within Multiple Discourses: Implications for Policy and Educational Reform. In *Proceedings of the Council of Chief State School Officers 1990 Summer Institute on 'Restructuring Learning'*, pp. 107–121. Washington, DC: Council of Chief State School Officers.

Mishler, E. (1975). Studies in Dialogue and Discourse: An Exponential Law of Successive Questioning. *Language in Society.* 4: 31–51.

Moffett, J. (1968). *Teaching the Universe of Discourse.* Boston: Houghton Mifflin.

Morgan, M. (2001). The African-American Speech Community. In *Linguistic Anthropology: A Reader.* A. Duranti, ed., pp. 74–94. Oxford: Blackwell.

(2002). *Language, Discourse and Power in African American Culture.* Cambridge and New York: Cambridge University Press.

Mosenthal, P., and Jin-Ma, T. (1980). Quality of Text Recall as a Function of Children's Classroom Competence. *Journal of Experimental Child Psychology.* 30: 1–21.

Murphy, S. (1986). Children's Comprehension of Deictic Categories in Oral and Written Language. *Reading Research Quarterly.* 21(2): 118–131.

Nassaji, H., and Wells, G. (2000). What's the Use of Triadic Dialogue? An Investigation of Teacher–Student Interaction. *Applied Linguistics.* 21 (3): 333–363.

Neisser, U., Boodoo, G., Bouchard, T. J., Boykin, A. W., Brody, N., Ceci, S., Halpern, D., Loehlin, J., Perloff, R., Sternberg, R. J., and Urbina, S. (1996). Intelligence: Knowns and Unknowns. *American Psychologist.* 51(2): 77–101.

Nunberg, G. (1995). Transfers of Meaning. *Journal of Semantics.* 12: 109–132.

Nystrand, M., Gamoran, A., Kachur, R., and Prendergast, C. (1997). *Opening Dialogue: Understanding the Dynamics of Language and Learning in the English Classroom.* New York: Teachers College Press.

Oakes, J. (1985). *Keeping Track: How Schools Structure Inequality.* New York: Longmans.

O'Connor, M. C. (1989). Aspects of Differential Performance by Minorities on Standardized Tests. In *Testing and the Allocation of Opportunities.* B. R. Gifford ed., pp. 129–181. Boston, MA: Kluwer Academic Publishers.

(1992). Rethinking Aptitude, Achievement and Instruction: Cognitive Science Research and the Framing of Assessment Policy. In *Changing Assessments: Alternative Views of Aptitude, Achievement, and*

Instruction. B. R. Gifford and M. C. O'Connor, eds., pp. 9–35. Boston, MA: Kluwer Academic Publishers.

Ochs, E. (1995). The Impact of Language Socialization on Grammatical Development. In *The Handbook of Child Language*. P. Fletcher and B. MacWhinney eds., pp. 73–94. Oxford: Blackwell.

(1996). Linguistic Resources for Socializing Humanity. In *Rethinking Linguistic Relativity*. J. Gumperz and S. Levinson, eds., pp. 407–437. New York: Cambridge University Press.

Ochs, E. and Schieffelin, B. (1983). *Acquiring Conversational Competence*. Boston: Routledge and Kegan Paul.

Ogbu, J. and Matute-Bianchi, M. E. (1986). Understanding Sociocultural Factors: Knowledge, Identity and School Adjustment. In *Beyond Language: Social and Cultural Factors in Schooling Language Minority Students*. pp. 73–142. Bilingual Education Office. Evaluation, Dissemination and Assessment Center, California State University, Los Angeles.

Olsen, D. R. (1977). From Utterance to Text: The Bias of Language in Speech and Writing. *Harvard Educational Review*. 47: 257–281.

(1994). *The World On Paper: the Conceptual and Cognitive Implications of Writing and Reading*. Cambridge and New York: Cambridge University Press.

Olsen, D. R. and Torrence, N. (1981). Learning to Meet the Requirements of Written Text: Language Development in the School Years. In *Writing: The Nature, Development, and Teaching of Written Communication*. C. H. Frederiksen and J. F. Dominic eds. Hillsdale, NJ: Lawrence Erlbaum.

Olson, D. (1977). From Utterance to Text: The Bias of Language in Speech and Writing. *Harvard Educational Review*. 47(3): 257–81.

O'Neill, W. (1970). A Proper Literacy. *Harvard Educational Review*. 40: 260–244.

Ong, W. (1982). *Orality and Literacy: Technologizing the world*. New York: Methuen.

Overholt, G. E., and Stallings, W. M. (1976). Ethnographic and Experimental Hypotheses in Educational Research. *Educational Researcher*. 5(8): 12–14.

Oxenham, J. (1980). *Literacy: Writing, Reading and Social Organization*. London: Routledge and Kegan Paul.

Pallas, A., Entwisle, D., Alexander, K., and Stulka, M. F. (1994). Ability-group Effects: Instructional, Social or Institutional? *Sociology of Education*. 67: pp. 27–46.

Parsons, T. (1959). The School as a Social System. *Harvard Educational Review* 29: 297–318.

Pascasio, E., ed. (1977). *The Filipino Bilingual: Studies on Philippine Bilingualism and Bilingual Education*. Quezon City, Philippines: Ateneo de Manila University Press.

Perry, T. and Delpit, L. eds. (1998). *The Real Ebonics Debate*. Boston: Beacon.

Philips, S. (1972). Participant Structures and Communicative Competence. Warm Springs Children in Community and Classroom. In *Functions of Language in the Classroom*. C. Cazden, V. John, and D. Hymes, eds., pp. 370–394. New York: Teachers College Press.

Piestrup, A. (1973). Black Dialect Interference and Accommodation of Instruction in First Grade. Monograph #4, Language Behavior Research Laboratory, University of California Berkeley.

Pontecorvo, C., and Sterponi, L. (2002). Learning to Argue and Reason through Discourse in Educational Settings. In *Learning for Life in the 21st Century: Sociocultural Perspectives on the Future of Education*. C. G. Wells and G. Claxton eds., pp. 127–140. Oxford: Blackwell.

Rampton, B. (1996). *Crossings*. London and Boston: Routledge.

(2006). *Language in Late Modernity: Interaction in an Urban School*. Cambridge: Cambridge University Press.

Resnick, D., and Resnick, L. (1977). The Nature of Literacy: An Historical Explanation. *Harvard Educational Review*. 47: 370–385.

Rickford, J. (1999). *African American Vernacular English*. Oxford and Malden MA: Blackwell.

Rist, R. C. (1970). Student Social Class and Teacher Expectations: The Self-Fulfilling Prophecy in Ghetto Education. *Harvard Educational Review*. 40(3): 411–451.

Robinson E. J., and Robinson, W. P. (1982). The Advancement of Children's Verbal Referential Skills: The Role of Metacognitive Guidance. *International Journal of Behaviour Development*. 5: 329–355.

Rosen, H. (1971). Towards a Language Policy Across the Curriculum. In *Language, the Learner, and the School*. D. Barnes, J. Britton and H. Rosen, eds., p. 141. Revised edition. London: Penguin.

Rosenbaum, J. (1976). *Making Inequality: The Hidden Curriculum of High School Tracking*. New York: John Wiley.

(1980). The Social Implications of Educational Grouping. In *Review of Research in Education*. Vol. VIII. D. Berliner, ed. Washington: American Education Research Association.

Rosenshine, B. (1976). Resent Research on Teaching Behaviors and Student Achievement. *Journal of Teacher Education*. 27: 61–64.

Rosenthal, R. and Jacobson, L. (1968). *Pygmalion in the Classroom: Teacher Expectation and Pupils' Intellectual Development*. New York: Holt, Rinehart and Winston.

Rozin, P. S., and Gleitman, L. (1977). The Structure and Acquisition of Reading II: The Reading Process and the Alphabetic Principle. In *Toward a Psychology of Reading*. S. Reder and D. Scarborough, eds. Baltimore, MD: Lawrence Erlbaum.

Rubin, A. (1978). *A Theoretical Taxonomy of the Differences between Oral and Written Language. Report #3731*. Cambridge, MA: Bolt, Beranek and Newman.

Rumelhart, D. (1982). Schemata: The Building Blocks of Cognition. In *Theoretical Issues in Reading Comprehension*. R. I. Spiro, B. Bruce, W. Brewer eds. Hillsdale, NJ: Lawrence Erlbaum.

Rymes, B. (2001). Relating Word to World. In *Linguistic Anthropology of Education*. S. Wortham and B. Rymes, eds., pp. 122–150. Westport, CT: Praeger.

Sacks, H. (1972). Notes on Police Assessment of Moral Character. In *Studies in Social Interaction*. D. Sudnow, ed., pp. 280–293. New York: Free Press.

Sacks, H., Schegloff, E., and Jefferson, G. (1974). A Simplest Systematics for the Organization of Turn Taking for Conversation. *Language*. 50: 696–735.

Salaman, G. (1981). Class and Corporation. *Fontana New Sociology Series*. London: Fontana.

Savin, H. B. (1972). What the Child Knows about Speech when He Starts to Learn to Read. In *Language by Hear and by Eye: The Relationship between Speech and Reading*. J. F. Kavanaugh and I. G. Mattingly, eds. Cambridge, MA: MIT Press.

Schallert, D., Kleiman, G., and Rubin, A. (1977). *Analyses of Differences between Written and Oral Language. Report #29*. Cambridge MA: Bolt, Beranek and Newman.

Schenkein, J. ed. (1978). *Studies in the Organization of Conversational Communication*. New York: Academic Press.

Scollon, R., and Scollon, S. (1982). *Narrative Literacy and Face in Interethnic Communication*. Norwood, NJ: Ablex.

Scribner, S. (1984). Literacy in three metaphors. *American Journal of Education*. 93: 6–21.

Scribner, S., and Cole, M. (1981). *The Psychology of Literacy*. Cambridge MA: Harvard University Press.

Searle, J. (1975). Indirect Speech Acts. In *Syntax and Semantics*. Vol. III, *Speech Acts*. P. Cole and J. Morgan, eds., pp. 59–82. New York: Academic Press.

(1977). A Classification of Illocutionary Acts. *Language in Society*. 5: 1–23.

Sennett, R., and Cobb, J. (1973). *The Hidden Injuries of Class*. New York: Random House.

Silverstein, M. (1981). The Limits of Awareness. Unpublished Manuscript, Department of Anthropology, University of Chicago.

(1993). Metapragmatic Discourse and Metapragmatic Function. In *Reflexive Language*. J. A. Lucy ed., pp. 33–58. Cambridge and New York: Cambridge University Press.

Silverstein, M. and Urban, G. (1996). *Natural Histories of Discourse*. Chicago: University of Chicago Press.

Simmel, G. (1971). *Individuality and Social Forms*. Chicago: University of Chicago Press.

Simons, H., and Gumperz, J. J. (1980). *Language at School: Its Influence on School Performance*. Paper presented at the Annual Meeting of the American Educational Research Association, Boston, MA, April 1980.

Sinclair, J. McH., and Coulthard, R. M. (1975). *Towards an Analysis of Discourse: The English Used by Teachers and Pupils*. London: Oxford University Press.

Slavin, R. (1987). Ability Grouping and Student Achievement in Elementary Schools. *Review of Educational Research*. 66(4): 293–336.

Smith, S. S. (1997). A longitudinal study: The Literacy Development of 57 Children. In *Inquiries in Literacy Theory and Practice, Forty-sixth Yearbook of the National Reading Conference*. C. Kinzer, K. Hinchman and D. Leu, eds., pp. 250–264. Hillsdale, NJ: Lawrence Erlbaum.

Smitherman, G. (1977). *Talkin and Testifyin: The Language of Black America*. Boston: Houghton Mifflin.

Snow, C. (1983). Literacy and Language: Relationships during the Preschool Years. *Harvard Educational Review*. 53(2), 165–185.

Snow, C., and Ferguson, C., eds. (1977). *Talking to Children*. Cambridge: Cambridge University Press.

Soltow, L., and Stevens, E. (1981). *The Rise of Literacy and the Common School: A Socioeconomic Analysis to 1870*. Chicago: University of Chicago Press.

Soriano, L. B. (1969). Science Education in the Philippines. *Bulletin of the UNESCO Regional Office for Education in Asia*. 4(1): 95–101.

Steele, C. M. and Aronson, J. (1995). Stereotype Threat and the Intellectual Test Performance of African American Students. *Journal of Personality and Social Psychology*. 69: 797–811.

Sternberg, R. (1992). CAT: a Program of Comprehensive Abilities Testing. In *Changing Assessments: Alternative Views of Aptitude, Achievement, and Instruction*. B. R. Gifford and M. C. O'Connor, eds., pp. 9–35. Boston, MA: Kluwer Academic Publishers.

Stone, L. (1967). Literacy and Education in England, 1640–1900. *Past and Present*. 42: 69–193.

Street, B. (1984). *Literacy in Theory and Practice*. Cambridge and New York: Cambridge University Press.

Street, B. ed. (1993). *Cross-Cultural Perspectives on Literacy*. Cambridge and New York: Cambridge University Press.

Stubbs, M. (1976). *Language, School and Classrooms: Contemporary Sociology of the School*. London: Methuen.

Sudnow, D. (1978). *Ways of the Hand: The Organization of Improvised Conduct*. Cambridge MA: Harvard University Press.

Sudnow, D. ed. (1972). *Studies in Social Interaction*. New York: The Free Press.

Szwed, J. (1981). The Ethnography of Literacy. In *Writing* Vol. I, *Variations in Writing: Functional, Linguistic and Cultural Differences*.

M. Farr-Whiteman, ed., pp. 13–23: Hillsdale, NJ: Lawrence Erlbaum.

Tannen, D. (1982). Oral and Written Strategies in Spoken and Written Narratives. *Language*. 58(1): 1–21.

Tharp, R., and Gallimore, R. (1988). *Rousing Minds to Life*. New York: Cambridge University Press.

Thompson, E. P. (1963). *The Making of the English Working Class*. New York: Pantheon Books.

Thurrow, L. (1972). Education and Economic Equality. *The Public Interest*. 28: 66–81.

Tizard, B., and Hughes, M. (1984). *Young Children Learning: Talking and Thinking at Home and at School*. London: Fontana.

Tucker, G. R., and D'Anglejan, A. (1976). New Directions in Language Teaching. In *English as a Second Language in Bilingual Education: Selected TESOL Papers*. J. Alatis and K. Twaddell, eds., pp. 205–211. Washington, DC: Georgetown University Press.

Turner, Ralph (1960). Sponsored and Contest Mobility and the School System. *American Sociological Review*. 25: 855–867.

Turner, Roy ed. (1974). *Ethnomethodology: Selected Readings*. Baltimore: Penguin.

Tyack, D. (1977). City Schools: Centralization of Control at the Turn of the Century. In *Power and Ideology in Education*. J. Karabel and A. H. Hasley, eds., 397–411. Oxford: Oxford University Press.

Umiker Sebeok, J. (1979). Preschool Children's Intra-Conversational Narratives. *Journal of Child Language*. 6: 91–109.

UNESCO (1976). Experimental World Literacy Programme: A Critical Assessment. Paris: UNESCO Report.

Vande Kopple, W. J. (1985). Some Exploratory Discourse on Metadiscourse. *College Composition and Communication*. 36: 82–93.

(1986). Given and New Information and Some Aspects of the Structures, Semantics, and Pragmatics of Written Texts. In *Studying Writing*. C. Cooper and S. Greenbaum eds., pp. 72–111. Beverly Hills: Sage.

Varenne, H., McDermott, R., Goldman, S., Naddeo, M. and Rizzo-Tolk, R. (1998). *Successful Failure: The School America Builds*. Boulder, CO: Westview.

Vincent, D. (2000). *Mass Literacy: Reading and Writing in Modern Europe*. Cambridge and Malden MA: Polity Press.

Vygotsky, L. S. (1978). *Mind in Society The Development of Higher Psychological Processes*, M. Cole et al. trans. Cambridge, MA: Harvard University Press.

Walkerdine, V. (1982). From Context to Text. A Psycho-Semiotic Approach to Abstract Thought. In *Children Thinking Through Language*. M. Beveridge, ed. London: Arnold.

Weber, E. (1983). The Refinement of the Brute: Review of 'Histoire Générale de l'enseignement et de l'éducation en France'. Vols. I–IV. *Times Literary Supplement,* 13 May, pp. 219–220.

Weinstein, R. (1976). Reading Group Membership in First Grade: Teacher Behavior and Pupil Experience Over Time. *Journal of Educational Psychology.* 68: 103–116

Weintraub, S. and Denny, T. (1963). Exploring the First Graders' Concepts of Reading. *The Reading Teacher.* 16: 363–365.

Wells, C. G. (1981a). *Learning through Interaction: The Study of Language Development.* Cambridge: Cambridge University Press.

(1981b). Some Antecedents of Early Educational Attainment. *British Journal of Sociology of Education.* 2: 181–200.

(1985). *Language Development in the Pre-School Years.* Cambridge: Cambridge University Press.

(1986a). Pre-School Literacy Related Activities and Success in School. In *The Nature and Consequences of Literacy.* D. Olson, A. Hildyard and N. Torrance, eds., Cambridge: Cambridge University Press.

(1986b). *The Meaning Makers: Children Learning Language and using Language to Learn.* Portsmouth, NH: Heinemann.

(1999). *Dialogic Inquiry: Towards a Sociocultural Practice and Theory of Education.* Cambridge: Cambridge University Press.

Wells, C. G. ed. (2001). *Action, Talk, and Text: Learning and Teaching through Inquiry.* New York: Teachers College Press.

Wells, C. G., MacLure, M., and Montgomery, M. M. (1981). Some Strategies for Sustaining Conversation. In *Conversation, Speech, and Discourse.* P. Worth ed., London: Croom Helm.

Wells, C. G., and Mejía-Arauz, R. (2006). *Toward Dialogue in the Classroom: Learning and Teaching through Inquiry.*

Wells, C. G., and Montgomery, M. M. (1981). Adult Child Discourse at Home and at School. In *Adult Child Conversation: Studies in Structure and Process.* P. French and M. MacLure, eds. London: Croom Helm.

Wells, C. G., Montgomery, M. M., and MacLure, M. (1979). Adult-Child Discourse: Outline of a Model of Analysis. *Journal of Pragmatics.* 3: 337–380.

Wertsch, J. (1978). Adult–Child Interaction and the Roots of Metacognition. *The Quarterly Newsletter of the Institute for Comparative Human Cognition.* 1(1): 15–18.

Wertsch, J., and Stone, C. A. (1978). Microgenesis as a Tool for Developmental Analysis. *The Quarterly Newsletter of the Laboratory of Comparative Human Cognition.* 1(1): 8–10.

Wheelock, A. (1992). *Crossing the Tracks: How Untracking can Save America's Schools.* New York: New Press.

(1994). *Alternatives to Tracking and Ability Grouping.* Arlington VA: American University Press.

Williams, R. (1961). *The Long Revolution.* Harmondsworth Middlesex: Penguin.

Wilson, B. and Schmits, D. (1978). What's New in Ability Grouping? *Phi Delta Kappa*. 59: 535–536.

Wood, D., McMahon, L., and Cranstoun, Y. (1980). *Working with Under Fives*. London: Grant McIntyre.

Zwick, R. (2002). *Fair Game? The Use of Standardized Admissions Tests in Higher Education*. New York: Routledge Falmer.

Author index

Subject index